NIGHT+DAY
NEW YORK

Brian Niemietz

PULSE GUIDES

Distributed in the United States and Canada by National Book Network (NBN).
First Edition. Printed in the United States. 30% postconsumer content.
Copyright © 2006 ASDavis Media Group, Inc. All rights reserved.
ISBN-10:0-9766013-1-1; ISBN-13:978-0-9766013-1-9

Credits

Executive Editor	Alan S. Davis
Editor	Diane Weipert
Contributing Editor	Wil Klass
Author	Brian Niemietz
Contributors	Erin Wylie, Annelise Sorenson
Copy Editors	Gail Nelson-Bonebrake, Elizabeth Stroud
Maps	Chris Gillis
Production	Jo Farrell, Samia Afra
Cover Design	Wil Klass, Clara Teufel

Photo Credits: (Front cover, left to right) Les Byerley, Barca 18, MoMA-Timothy Hursley; (Back cover, left to right) Bryant Park-Karen Chang, Hiro Lounge, Lever House-Roberto D'Adonna, Hotel Gansevoort; (Inside cover, top to bottom) Michael Klineberg, Laura Reseni, 6s and 8s, Empire State Building; (p.6) Mary Lou D'Auray (p.8) Brian Niemietz.

Special Sales

For information about bulk purchases of Pulse Guides (ten copies or more), email us at bookorders@pulseguides.com. Special bulk rates are available for charities, corporations, institutions, and online and mail-order catalogs, and our books can be customized to suit your company's needs.

NIGHT+DAY
The *Cool Cities* Series from **PULSE**GUIDES

P.O. Box 590780, San Francisco, CA 94159
pulseguides.com

Pulse Guides is an imprint of ASDavis Media Group, Inc.

The Night+Day Difference

Pulse of the City

Our job is to point you to all of the city's peak experiences: amazing museums, unique spas, and spectacular views. But the complete *urbanista* experience is more than just impressions—it is grownup fun, the kind that thrives by night as well as by day. Urban fun is a hip nightclub or a trendy restaurant. It is people-watching and people-meeting. Lonely planet? We don't think so. Night+Day celebrates our lively planet.

The Right Place. The Right Time. It Matters.

A Night+Day city must have exemplary restaurants, a vibrant nightlife scene, and enough attractions to keep a visitor busy for six days without having to do the same thing twice. In selecting restaurants, food is important, but so is the scene. Our hotels, most of which are 4- and 5-star properties, are rated for the quality of the concierge staff (can they get you into a hot restaurant?) as well as the rooms. You won't find kids with fake IDs at our nightlife choices. And the attractions must be truly worthy of your time. But experienced travelers know that timing is almost everything. Going to a restaurant at 7pm can be a very different experience (and probably less fun) than at 9pm; a champagne boat cruise might be ordinary in the morning but spectacular at sunset. We believe providing the reader with this level of detail makes the difference between a good experience and a great one.

The Bottom Line

Your time is precious. Our guide must be easy to use and dead-on accurate. That is why our executive editor, editors, and writers (locals who are in touch with what is great—and what is not) spend hundreds of hours researching, writing, and debating selections for each guide. The results are presented in four unique ways: The *99 Best* with our top three choices in 33 categories that highlight what is great about the city; the *Experience* chapters, in which our selections are organized by distinct themes or personalities (Hot, Cool, Original, and Classic); a *Perfect Plan* (Three Days and Nights) for each theme, showing how to get the most out of the city in a short period of time; and the *New York Black Book,* listing all the hotels, restaurants, nightlife, and attractions, with key details, contact information, and page references.

Our bottom line is this: If you find our guide easy to use and enjoyable to read, and with our help you have an extraordinary time, we have succeeded. We review and value all feedback from our readers, so please contact us at **feedback@pulseguides.com.**

From the Publisher

I live in San Francisco, but I'm a New Yorker. I was born in New York (well, specifically, the Bronx), grew up within frequent-visiting distance of the city, and I returned from college to go to law school and live in Greenwich Village. I'm so New York that I know *Annie Hall*, not *Manhattan*, is the best movie written about New Yorkers. And from the other side of the continent, I can still see that New York is the center of the universe. I'm thrilled to have the opportunity to prove it to you with this book.

The success of my first book, *The Fun Also Rises* (named after Ernest Hemingway's *The Sun Also Rises,* which helped popularize what has become perhaps the most thrilling party on earth, Pamplona's Fiesta de San Fermín, also known as the Running of the Bulls), persuaded me that there were others who shared my interest in a different approach to travel. Guidebooks were neither exciting nor informative enough to capture peak experiences—whether for world-class events or just a night on the town.

Night+Day, the first series from Pulse Guides, is for Gen-Xers to Zoomers (Boomers with a zest for life), who know that if one wants to truly experience a city, the night is as important as the day. **Night+Day** guides present the best that a city has to offer—hotels, restaurants, nightlife, and attractions that are exciting without being stuffy—in a totally new format.

Pulse Guides was created with one abiding principle: *Never settle for the ordinary.* I hope that a willingness to explore new approaches to guidebooks, combined with meticulous research, provides you with unique and significant experiences.

Wishing you extraordinary times,

Alan S. Davis, Publisher and Executive Editor
Pulse Guides

P.S. To contact me, or for updated information on all of our **Night+Day** guides, please visit our website at **pulseguides.com**.

TOC

About the Author

A Chicago native who moved to New York City in the summer of 1999, Brian Niemietz has been a nightlife writer for six years, including a one-year stint as the senior editor for *New York's Shecky's Bar, Club and Lounge Guide,* a comprehensive collection of reviews and listings that became the best-selling nightlife guide in the city under his direction. (He was also a major contributor to *Shecky's Los Angeles* and *Chicago* guides.) Currently working as a  freelancer, Niemietz routinely writes nightlife and entertainment coverage for the *New York Post,* and his "Best of New York" feature in May 2005's *Playboy* magazine confirms his standing as one of New York City's foremost authorities on the Big Apple's social circuit. Drawing from his unparalleled access to New York City's hottest venues and events, the author is excited about sharing his insider knowledge with an entirely new audience through Pulse Guides' *Night+Day New York.*

About the Contributors

Annelise Sorenson has travel-written (and wine-tasted) her way across four continents, covering the United States, Spain, Scandinavia, and India for guidebooks, magazines and websites. She splits her time between New York City—a metropolis that continually rewards her wanderlust—and Europe.

Erin Wylie is a fashion forecaster at *The Committee for Colour & Trends* and editor of *fashionFACTSfolio*. She has written for *Nylon* and *The Fader.*

Acknowledgments

My successes are owed to too many family members, friends, mentors, professional associates, and bartenders to name, but especially warm regards go to dear friends Marc Dufour, Laura Buchwald, and Josh Orth—all of whom have picked up more than their share of tabs while I learned my way around this great city and practiced my trade. I would also like to thank Alan Davis for hiring me to author this book, thus making *Night+Day New York* possible, and both Diane Weipert and Wil Klass, whose editing, personal skills, and patience seemingly have no bounds. I sincerely hope that all who use this book while visiting New York City enjoy their time here as much as I've enjoyed every moment I've been lucky enough to live and learn in this incomparably stimulating place.

Brian Niemietz

Introduction

New York: What It Was

Biggest, best, fastest, toughest ... New York City is a place that's generally described in superlatives, and the 8 million–plus people who live in its five boroughs wouldn't have it any other way. You gotta problem with that? As America's most populous city, New York exists in a vacuum. It is oblivious to what's going on in the rest of the country, and it couldn't care less. This is a "live and let live" society, where everybody's seen it all, and still no one is impressed. What could be more American? You want to worship an obscure god? Go ahead. You want to date someone half your age? Knock yourself out. You want to marry someone of the same gender? Go nuts. You want a quarter from someone who's minding his own business? Get outta here, ya bum.

So how did this Darwinian microcosm of the country come to be? Fittingly, New York City started with a real estate ripoff. In 1624, the Dutch settled in lower Manhattan after purchasing the land from the Lenape natives and naming it New Amsterdam. The price? Roughly $24, plus a few beads and trinkets. If that wasn't cheeky enough, the English arrived in 1664 and simply took over the island, renaming it New York. But as we know, what goes around comes around, and in 1781 the New World's colonists laid claim to New York and forced the English out. Eight years later, the Big Apple enjoyed a one-year stint as the nation's capital.

Though Brooklyn was settled in 1636, it didn't become part of New York City until 1898. At the time of its annexation, Brooklyn was the third largest city in America. The remaining boroughs saw scarce population growth throughout the 17th and 18th centuries, but in the 19th and 20th centuries, Manhattan's industrial boom invited an influx of immigrants. Surrounded by water, New York City was a necessary stop between Europe and the colonies, and its commercial success came quickly.

But the wealth wasn't shared by all. The Five Points area in Lower Manhattan, portrayed in Martin Scorsese's *Gangs of New York*, became the world's most famous ghetto. Immigrants from around the globe came here, only to fight off starvation, pestilence, and, more often than not, each other. When the Irish arrived during the potato famine of the 1840s, they began competing with the Italian immigrants for

> **"No one in New York knows north from south, as that would suggest a world outside the city."**

Night+Day's New York Urbie

Night+Day cities are chosen because they have a vibrant nightlife scene, standard-setting and innovative restaurants, cutting-edge hotels, and enough attractions to keep one busy for six days without doing the same thing twice. In short, they are fun. They represent the quintessential *urbanista* experience. This wouldn't exist but for the creativity and talents of many people and organizations. In honor of all who have played a role in making New York one of the world's greatest cities, Night+Day is pleased to give special recognition, and our Urbie Award, to an individual or organization whose contribution is exemplary.

THE URBIE AWARD: Steve Hanson

There are some great restaurateurs in New York City, but when it comes to well-conceived, service-oriented eateries that appeal equally to foodies and scenesters, few compare to Urbie recipient Steve Hanson.

To have a successful restaurant in the Big Apple is quite an achievement. To have opened 15 restaurants, a thriving nightclub, and a successful health club in New York City alone over the past 18 years is awesome. Hanson and his BR Guest group never seem to run out of energy or ideas. (Hanson's empire outside of the city includes, among others, Las Vegas's Fiamma and the Blue Water Grill in Chicago.)

What's most impressive about Hanson's endeavors is that they exemplify the importance of teaming ambition with adventure. Whether it be Barca 18's Spanish cuisine, Vento's Italian entrees, the fresh fish of Blue Fin, Ruby Foo's inventive take on Chinese dining, or the Dos Caminos Mexican eateries, no two of his ventures are alike.

Another remarkable characteristic of New York's Urbie winner is his continuing drive to give back to the community that's been so good to him. Hanson is a board member for both City Harvest and the Exploring Program, two non-profit groups that connect high school students with professional role models in the businesses that interest them most.

"While New York City is the most exciting restaurant scene in the world, it is also the most competitive," says the New York University graduate. His mantra: "Remember to always go that extra mile for your guests." It works.

scarce and low-paying jobs. The Italians had already been fighting with African-Americans for available work, and so the Downtown melting pot became a simmering stew of violence and desperation.

Of course, struggle often provides fertile ground for the imagination, and these same areas thrived with creativity. "Skid Row" became as known for storytelling as it was for its poverty and violence. Through the transmission of song, dance, theater, and literature, tales of the extreme wealth and gut-wrenching poverty of mythical New York reached the rest of the world, and the immigrants' experiences were felt thousands of miles away.

Key Dates

1624 The Dutch pay the Lenape Indians $24 for lower Manhattan.

1664 The English take over the island and name it New York.

1789 For one year, New York is the nation's capital.

1898 Brooklyn becomes a part of New York.

1840s Ireland's potato famine increases overseas immigration to the city.

1930s FDR's "New Deal" inspires the construction of the New York City skyscrapers.

1970s Rap music is born in the boroughs.

1971 John Lennon moves to New York.

2001 Terrorists attack the World Trade Center on September 11.

Eventually, many of the immigrants began to thrive, inspiring fresh migratory waves from China, Russia, the Middle East, the Caribbean, Greece, and other nations, to capitalize on the new prosperity. The 20th century's wars were also a boon to the economy, as banking, manufacturing, and shipping industries sprang up on the shores of the Hudson and East Rivers. In the 1930s, FDR's "New Deal" created many jobs by supporting construction projects like the Empire State Building, the Chrysler Building, and Rockefeller Center. Growth continued in the decades that followed, with the building of new landmark locations like the UN Headquarters, the Guggenheim Museum, Lincoln Center, and the World Trade Center.

Rap music, which was born in either Harlem, the Bronx, Queens, or Brooklyn, depending on whom you ask, has been boasting borough pride since its birth in the late '70s. LL Cool J and Run-DMC were the golden boys of Queens in the early '80s, and they often "battled" Brooklyn rappers like KRS-One and the Beastie Boys. Before that, New York bands like Blondie, the Ramones, the New York Dolls, and the Velvet Underground were busy inventing punk rock music. Though it quickly became popular in London, Los Angeles, and eventually everywhere else, you can bet your safety pin–pierced leather jacket that the genre traces its roots back to the seedy old Bowery, where these seminal bands practically learned to play their instruments onstage.

Like most of the country, New York enjoyed a period of peace and prosperity in the 1990s. Under the watch of President (and now New York resident) Bill Clinton and widely popular mayor Rudolph Giuliani, the 20th century ended in grand fashion.

The 21st century, however, opened with New York City's darkest moment. On September 11, 2001, Islamic extremists hijacked two airliners and crashed them into the World Trade Center towers, killing 2,746 civilians and rescue workers. The city responded with resilience by cleaning up the debris, burying its dead, and starting anew. Each day hundreds of banner-wielding supporters showed up to cheer the workers who hauled out the debris at Ground Zero. Flags waved, truck drivers honked, and for months, firemen couldn't pay for a drink or a meal out. It was only in 2004, when the Republican National Convention came to Madison Square Garden, stirring up a daily onslaught of spirited protests, that New York appeared to be back in the game, and as rabble-rousing and opinionated as ever.

New York: What It Is

This international metropolis is still close to its Ellis Island roots, and the seeds sown by a million forefathers still bear fruit, from the Lower East Side's Jewish delis and the espresso shops of Little Italy, to the glorious Midtown towers of (in)famous developers like Donald Trump and Leona Helmsley. There's a strong civic pride in the Big Apple, and since so many of its inhabitants have migrated from other places, being a "New Yorker" is really just a state of mind.

Though the styles and the mediums have changed, New York continues to inspire artists today. Filmmakers like Martin Scorsese and Woody Allen bring the city's grit and glamour to life. The hip-hop music scene, which comes straight from the New York ghettos, could be compared to the vaudevillian tales of gangland grandeur told in the Five Point days.

Today, no one in New York knows north from south, as that would suggest a world outside the city. Here, there's simply Uptown, Downtown, and across town. In spite of their camaraderie, New Yorkers are a competitive bunch. The 212-area-code-owning Manhattanites often refer to the 718 outer boroughs as "Bridge and Tunnel," a derogatory reference to how those New Yorkers must travel to reach the city. Though "The City" itself consists of all five boroughs, and though Manhattan contains less than 20% of the city's residential population, its denizens consider the other islands to be little more than glorified suburbs. Of course, if you want to see a Manhattanite and a Brooklynite bond, throw a poor sap from New Jersey into the mix and let the alienation begin.

Because of this fierce individualism, NYC has a reputation for rudeness. People are not good about standing in line (or "on line," as they say), and cashiers consistently skip niceties like "Hello," "Can I help you?," and "Thank you." Here, small talk goes unsaid, and once you stop taking it personally, "rude" begins to feel relative.

> Because ambitions are so lofty, and because there aren't enough hours in the day for all the work and fun to be had, few people here sweat the small stuff.

As you walk through this city, it's hard not to marvel at its grand buildings, bustling sidewalks, and unparalleled diversity. So maybe its streets are noisy and a little bit dirty. Because ambitions are so lofty, and because there aren't enough hours in the day for all the work and fun to be had, few people here sweat the small stuff. There is simply no place like it in the world.

Welcome to fabulous New York ...

Party Conversation—A Few Surprising Facts

- There are a lot of stories about where the name "The Big Apple" was coined, but most historians believe it came from the jazz world, when booking a show at "The Big Apple" was a reference to getting work in the world's prime jazz town.

- The New York City administrative code still requires hitching posts be located in front of City Hall so that reporters can tie their horses.

- There are 17,312 restaurants in the city, and the average cost per person including a drink, tax, and tip is $36.95. There are 9,796 liquor licenses in the city as well.

- In 1827, the country's first local bus route began operating in New York City, running along Broadway between Houston and Wall Streets.

- Manhattan's Fashion Institute of Technology (FIT) is the only school in the world that offers a bachelor of science degree with a major in Cosmetics and Fragrance Marketing.

- Gennaro Lombardi opened the first U.S. pizzeria in 1897 in New York City. In 1905 he moved the pizzeria across the road to 32 Spring Street, where his pizza is sold to this day.

- New York City occupies 310 square miles, and has 722 miles of subway track and 6,400 miles of streets.

- The Statue of Liberty's index finger is eight feet long.

- 25% of Manhattan's area is landfill.

- New York City has 570 miles of shoreline.

- While digging the Harlem Canal in 1983, workmen discovered the tusk of a prehistoric mastodon near where Broadway and 14th Street intersect today.

- The Bronx is the only New York City borough that is connected to the mainland.

- The five boroughs produce 26.4 million pounds of garbage per day.

- New York is America's most visited city, drawing slightly fewer than 40 million visitors a year (34 million domestic), and collecting close to $21 billion annually on tourism. (Thank you!)

THE 99 BEST of NEW YORK

What does it mean to be the "best" in New York City? It probably means you're the best at what you do—period. Modeling, banking, panhandling, collecting garbage—you name it. This is where the publishing houses are located; where financial institutions are based; where fashion magazines shoot; where TV, radio, and movies are, if not made, financed; and it's where every international corporation has either a headquarters or an office of extreme significance. When the Yankees don't win the World Series, it's a losing season. Yes, it's a tough place to live, but what a place to visit!

All-Night Restaurants

#1–3: In a city that never sleeps, good round-the-clock eateries are essential. Otherwise, where will the hungry actors, bartenders, and weary clubbers find quality meals before heading home?

Cafeteria

119 7th Ave., Chelsea, 212-414-1717 • Cool

The Draw: Bar-hoppers who aren't ready to end the fun at closing time flock to this 24-hour eatery. The traditional American cuisine will cure any late-night craving for comfort food.

The Scene: For years this place had a huge gay following, and as Chelsea diversified, so did Cafeteria's crowd. The futuristic, washed-out interior has a timeless quality that works as well at 6am as it does at 6pm. The host doubles as a doorman, barring entry to the loud and stupid. *24/7.* $ F≡

Hot Tip: Cafeteria does every meal, but breakfast is its strength. Since Chelsea is always entertaining, the best seats are by the window.

Diner 24

102 8th Ave., Chelsea, 212-242-7773 • Original

The Draw: Night owls with sophisticated palates will find this welcoming, window-lined diner a refreshingly upscale take on the greasy spoon.

The Scene: During the day, Diner 24 gets the local Chelsea blue boys along with blue-collar grunts who keep strange hours. The walls are covered in cut stones and pleather furnishings, à la Brady Bunch house. Late nights here attract models and clubbers who love the food and get the gimmick. *24/7.* $ F≡

Hot Tip: The meat loaf is trustworthy, and the gravy-soaked "Disco Fries" should not be missed. This is the kind of drunken 4am food you won't regret in the morning.

French Roast

78 W. 11th St., Greenwich Village, 212-533-2233 • Hot

The Draw: A 24/7 brasserie? Try finding that in Paris. How about a duck mousse pâté at 3am?

The Scene: Those mounds of coffee beans behind the bar can't last long with the *très* chic late-nighters that head to French Roast for a kick-start. When summer comes and the outdoor seating is set up, this authentic-feeling bistro is just the place to air out your club clothes and refuel. *24/7.* $$ F≡

Hot Tip: While sitting outside is nice in the summer, being anywhere near the front door is murder in the winter.

Best

Always-Trendy Restaurants

#4–6: Though it's easier for a cup of coffee to stay hot in the Antarctica than for a restaurant to stay hot in Manhattan, these places never cool off.

Balthazar*
80 Spring St., Soho, 212-965-1785 • Cool

The Draw: Faux Franco-American hotspot Balthazar is a link in Keith McNally's chain of hits, such as Pastis and Schiller's Liquor Bar, and its location in the always-trendy Soho neighborhood all but guarantees a "happening" night, any day of the week.

The Scene: This fashionable crowd is often a mix of those who make art and those who buy it—a combination that works nicely. On weekends, unshaven de-suited Wall Streeters in jeans and sweaters are tough to distinguish from their artsy brethren. *Mon-Thu 7:30am-1am, Fri 7:30am-2am, Sat 8am-4pm and 5:45pm-2am, Sun 8am-4pm and 5:30pm-midnight.* $$ ⓎⒻ≡

Hot Tip: The crowded bar is a popular after-work stop, but those who plan ahead will enjoy the rich Parisian-style cuisine in dark wood booths.

Cipriani Downtown*
376 W. Broadway, Soho, 212-343-0999 • Cool

The Draw: The Cipriani restaurants around town (not to mention the one in Venice) are known for being as blue-blooded as they are hot-blooded. Cipriani Downtown is more energetic and fashionable than its culinary contemporaries, and that includes its siblings.

The Scene: Cipriani Downtown skews a bit younger than Harry Cipriani in Midtown, thanks largely to a sidewalk terrace and a back-room club space, which is where the Hilton Sisters sometimes party with the parents after dinner. *Daily noon-11pm.* $$ ⓎⒻ≡

Hot Tip: With Cipriani Downtown's demanding crowd, the waitstaff runs hot and cold. Asking for recommendations can lighten their mood.

Public*
210 Elizabeth St., Soho, 212-343-7011 • Cool

The Draw: A beautiful place for beautiful people, Public has a decor as refreshingly inventive as its cuisine. If combining youth and taste is a crime, Public had better have a good lawyer.

The Scene: Concrete floors, exposed beams, and a thoughtfully raw design provide ample room for the super-trendy crowd. *Mon-Thu 6-11:30pm, Fri-Sat 6pm-12:30am, Sun 6-10:30pm, Fri-Sat the bar stays open until 3am.* $$ ⓍⒷ≡

Hot Tip: Limited seating is available between the wine shelves up front, and that's where you want to be. Save room for a cocktail by the fireplace in the tiny lounge in back.

Asian Dining

#7–9: Nowhere is New York's nonpareil diversity more evident than in its restaurants. When famously malleable Asian cuisine meets the Big Apple, the fusion can be magical.

Indochine*

430 Lafayette St., Greenwich Village, 212-505-5111 • Cool

The Draw: As old as Asia itself (if you consider the speed of a New York minute), the 20-plus-year-old Indochine could be considered a New York classic. But because of its hip downtown locale, its look, and its crowd, this glam spot remains young at heart.

The Scene: Hipster, foodie, and long-time patrons alike converge on this French-Indonesian hybrid. The palm-leaf decor is matched by ubiquitous plants as alive as the socialite atmosphere. Soups in coconut milk and filet mignon in peanut sauce are prepared to perfection. *Sun-Mon 5:30-11:30pm, Tue-Sat 5:30pm-2am.* $$ ☒☐≡

Hot Tip: The bar gets very busy—opt for one of the slightly weathered crescent-shaped booths in the middle of the room. Weekdays are slower and more relaxed, but this place is an event—do it on a Saturday night.

Kittichai

60 Thompson Hotel, 60 Thompson St., Soho, 212-219-2000 • Hot

The Draw: Is it the beautifully appointed room surrounding the underlit fountain or Chef Ian Chalermkittichai's excellent Thai cooking that brings people here in droves? The answer is yes.

The Scene: The crowd is both young and old, and dressed on the classic side of hip. With tall orchids shielding quiet tables, the large room pulls off an intimate feel. This makes Kittichai as good a date spot for first-timers as it is for celebrating a 25th anniversary. *Sun-Thu 7-11am, noon-2:30pm, 6-11pm, Fri-Sat 7-11am, noon-2pm, 6pm-midnight.* $$ ≡

Hot Tip: Diners tend to stroll around the lovely fountain area, making the surrounding tables good for socializing, but less private. The eastmost seats provide a good view, and are not on the way to the kitchen.

Megu*

62 Thomas St., Tribeca, 212-964-7777 • Hot

The Draw: This huge space is sumptuously designed and impossibly beautiful. Who expects modesty from a favorite of "The Donald?"

The Scene: The gorgeous Kimono Lounge upstairs overlooks the uplit Buddha ice sculpture in the dining room. Models and celebs abound. *Sun-Wed 5:30-10:30pm, Thu-Sat 5:30-11:30pm.* $$$$ ☒☐≡

Hot Tip: If you have the time, try one of the tasting menus, which take two-and-a-half to three hours to conquer.

Best

Bagels

#10–12: When it comes to bagels, is there a better place on earth than New York? *Oy vay*, why would anyone even suggest such a thing?

Ess-a-Bagel

359 1st Ave., Murray Hill, 212-260-2252 • Cool
831 3rd Ave., Midtown, 212-980-1010

> **The Draw:** Open since 1976, these bagels-on-the-go are often said to be the city's best. Both locations get a big morning crowd and do steady business throughout the day.

> **The Scene:** Can you have much of a bagel "scene"? Apparently so, according to the patrons who eat these meaty breads in-house while reading the morning paper. The service is efficient. *1st Ave.: Mon-Sat 6:30am-9pm, Sun 6:30am-5pm; 3rd Ave.: Mon-Fri 6am-9pm, Sat-Sun 7am-5pm.* $- ▣

> **Hot Tip:** Bagels aren't just for breakfast—come by for lunch and get a bagel with lox, along with a side of potato salad.

H&H Bagels

2239 Broadway, Upper West Side, 212-595-8003
639 W. 46th St., Midtown, 212-595-8000

> **The Draw:** What's so good about H&H? Ask one of its fans, like Woody Allen, Barbra Streisand, Dustin Hoffman, Jerry Stiller, or Bill Clinton, to name a few.

> **The Scene:** This busy bagelry is a buy-on-the-fly joint. H&H bagels are so popular they're shipped all over the world, counting annually into the millions. Try these bagels sans toppings—they're that good. *24/7.* $- ▣

> **Hot Tip:** For the most "New Yorkie" experience possible, grab a *New York Times,* get a plain bagel, and devour them both while waiting for the bus.

Murray's Bagels

500 6th Ave., Greenwich Village, 212-462-2830 • Classic
242 8th Ave., Chelsea, 646-638-1334

> **The Draw:** This beloved mom-and-pop shop rolls its light and fluffy bagels by hand so they look, taste, and feel fresh. Weekend mornings are a good time to catch them hot out of the oven.

> **The Scene:** There are a few popular and oft-occupied tables inside this small place, where brick walls and soda pop bottles call to mind a Jewish *Happy Days* set. In warm weather, the wood benches outside are a great place to people-watch while scarfing down a quick breakfast. *Mon-Fri 6am-9pm, Sat 6am-7pm.* $- ▣

> **Hot Tip:** Unless you want to look like a tourist, don't ask Murray's to toast your bagel. It's unlikely they have a toaster, and if they do, they're hiding it. Get there early and try the poppy seed bagel.

Chic Restaurants

#13–15: With all due respect to our friends on the Left Coast, New York is arguably the best restaurant city in the country, and its eye for design and style-conscious crowds make for some of the chicest restaurants in the world.

Harry Cipriani

781 5th Ave., Midtown, 212-753-5566 • Cool

> **The Draw:** There are several Cipriani restaurants around town, but this locale sets the Midtown standard for chic dining.
>
> **The Scene:** Lofty and rich in every way, this window-lined room is dimly lit and opulent. The Italian cuisine is as exquisite as the posh crowd, and reservations are as hard to land as they come. *Call for hours.* $$$$ ⬚
>
> **Hot Tip:** This place claims to have invented the Bellini. That we can't confirm, but we do know they've perfected it.

Lever House

390 Park Ave., Midtown, 212-888-2700 • Hot

> **The Draw:** Futuristic Aussie designer and chef Dan Silverman combines form and function in this excellent restaurant, where brilliance is the only predictable item on the menu and in the sci-fi design.
>
> **The Scene:** Afternoons bustle with the biggest power lunches known to Manhattan's high-rolling martini crowd. By night, ties loosen and pearls and diamonds come out as an attractive clientele turns to the business of socializing. *Mon-Thu 11:45am-2:30pm and 5:30-11pm, Fri 11:45am-2:30pm and 5:30-11:30pm, Sat 5:30-11:30pm, Sun 5-10pm.* $$$ ▣≡
>
> **Hot Tip:** Special event tables can be reserved in the elevated VIP room. Ask for a booth to get a panoramic view of the attractive surroundings.

Mr. Chow

324 E. 57th St., Midtown, 212-751-9030 • Hot

> **The Draw:** Though its decor was once enjoyed by Andy Warhol and his shabby chic crowd, Mr. Chow has effortlessly maintained its of-the-moment cachet.
>
> **The Scene:** Celebrity visits are commonplace, yet go unheralded in the gossip pages. Old and young alike come to these glam confines, where formal wear is a suggestion, but fun is a rule. Throw a few things into a wok and wear whatever comes out. *Mon-Sun 6-11:45pm.* $$$ ≡
>
> **Hot Tip:** Still a favorite haunt of the pop art crowd, Mr. Chow is lively following big events at the nearby Museum of Modern Art. Book a table after museum hours end, particularly when a big exhibit is opening.

Best   City Tours

#16–18: Sure, tours are inherently touristy, but they also give visitors the opportunity to cover a lot of ground in a short amount of time. The trick is to find the ones that are fun, and steer clear of the fanny packs and Bermuda shorts.

Circle Line Cruise

W. 42nd St., Pier 83, Midtown, 212-563-3200 • Classic

The Draw: Sail the Manhattan shores; get an outside look at the island and a peek at the Statue of Liberty.

The Scene: Circle Line offers Magellan-esque all-island tours that circle Manhattan (3 hours), and Columbus-like mini trips around the Statue of Liberty (2 hours). Both trips run year-round, with Tuesdays and Wednesdays off in January and February, and Tuesdays off in March. *Tours run daily, every half hour 9:30am-4:30pm.* $$

Hot Tip: These waters are choppy, so be sure to buy Dramamine or an equilibrium bracelet at a drugstore in advance.

The LimoTour

1636 3rd Ave., Upper East Side, 212-423-0101

The Draw: Driving in NYC is anything but relaxing, since drivers regard yellow lines as suggestions, yellow lights as dares, and Yellow Cabs as the enemy. The anything-but-yellow pedestrians routinely stand in the street while waiting to cross. Let an expert fight it out while you enjoy the ride.

The Scene: Providing door-to-door service, LimoTours offers everything from one-hour evening "Champagne Tours" to eight-hour, customized day tours. The chauffeurs are all licensed guides, so you might want to lower the divider. *Tours are made by appointment and most times can be accommodated.* $$$$

Hot Tip: Be aware of events in town. If something big's happening at the Garden, your one-hour tour might be from 34th to 35th Streets.

Sex and the City Tours

Pulitzer Fountain, 5th Ave., Midtown, 212-209-3370 • Cool

The Draw: Starting just outside Central Park, the *Sex and the City* Tour packs would-be fashionistas onto a bus and shows them locations where memorable episodes of the HBO program were shot.

The Scene: Buses may be a bit gauche for the *Sex and the City* girls, but it works fine for touring women who live for shopping and cosmos. *Tours are Mon-Fri 11am and 3pm, Sat-Sun 10am, 11am, and 3pm.* $$$

Hot Tip: Since *Sex and the City* was all about NYC's coolest "scenes," bring a notepad and write down the names and addresses of the places you might want to revisit later (then check this book for details).

Clubs for Celebrity Sighting

#19–21: Celebrities have to go somewhere, and these are among their most oft-visited places. If you see someone in these clubs who looks like "that guy from ..." whatever, odds are good it *is* that guy.

Bungalow 8

515 W. 27th St., Chelsea, 212-279-3215 • Hot

The Draw: Among the sea of palms, you're likely to spot Sean Penn, Quentin Tarantino, the Olsen twins, and/or other tabloid mainstays who come here in part because photographs are not allowed.

The Scene: Club queen Amy Sacco's little lounge behind the big bouncer just may be the hottest VIP spot in town, with guests so glam they can arrange helicopter exits. Don't take it personally if you can't get in. *Daily 11pm-4am.* B≡

Hot Tip: This club is at its best on Wednesdays and Sundays. Though 3am is the peak time, you're more likely to get past the doorman at 10pm.

Cain

544 W. 27th St., Chelsea, 212-947-8000 • Hot

The Draw: It's always a wild time at this South African–themed boîte, where live drummers pound along with a DJ who actually works from behind a chiseled two-ton boulder.

The Scene: Jamie Mulholland, of Lotus and PM fame, is the driving force behind this hotspot. Sweet cocktails of Cape Town sugars and fruits routinely draw Owen and Luke Wilson, Mariah Carey, and international models who make this a "must" stop between fashion shoots. Since Cain holds about 400 people, it's a tougher entry than Marquee, and easier than Bungalow 8. *Mon-Sat 10:30pm-4am.* ≡

Hot Tip: Reservations, with its commitment to bottle service (approximately $250 per person, all told), greatly increases your chance of admittance. If you can, book a table in the back of the room where the promoters and celebs hold court.

Marquee

289 10th Ave., Chelsea, 646-473-0202 • Hot

The Draw: Expect to see the likes of Paris Hilton, Tara Reid, Vincent Gallo, P. Diddy, and other A-listers whose entrances tend to be less than subtle.

The Scene: Famed architect Philip Johnson designed the arching staircase dividing the two smaller lounges from the high-ceilinged main space, where a huge crystal chandelier twinkles with the light of the disco ball. *Daily 10pm-4am.* C≡

Hot Tip: Calling to reserve a table is a good idea, but it doesn't guarantee entry, especially for large groups that skew male. Try arriving when the doors open around 11pm.

Best ## Cocktail Mixologists

#22–24: Drink designers have chef-like cachet in the modern cocktail era, where nothing sells like the right elixir. Despite their best efforts, bars can still end up with "mixed" results. These shake, stir, and chill their offerings just right.

Bemelmans Bar

35 E. 76th St., Upper East Side, 212-744-1600 • Classic

The Draw: Drink experts Dale Degroff and Audrey Saunders put together this cocktail menu, which goes down well with the place's old-school vibe, complete with a mood-setting piano player.

The Scene: The nightlife scene ranges from old to older, but in this city, that just means no velvet rope and angry bouncer. The classic cocktails are good, but new drinks, like the cognac and citrus Bemelmans Barter, really hit the spot. *Mon-Sat noon-12:30am, Sun noon-11:30pm.* B_

Inside Tip: Avoid the cover by coming Tuesday to Saturday around 9pm. Pianists start around 9:30pm.

The Dove

228 Thompson St., Greenwich Village, 212-254-1435 • Cool

The Draw: The place looks like a Victorian-era parlor; the staff is hip, yet girl-next-door charming; and the excellent cocktails are served on chic pewter trays.

The Scene: Jazz plays from 3pm to 8pm while a hip but mature crowd chooses between classic cocktails and creative infusions. At night, the alt-rock music draws a younger crowd. *Daily 3pm-4am.* =

Hot Tip: Call and reserve a table by the bay window (table five).

Verlaine

110 Rivington St., Lower East Side, 212-614-2494 • Original

The Draw: High ceilings, colorful cocktails, and a sexy orange hue attract Lower East Side gallery types who've recently graduated from dive bars to lounges.

The Scene: Enter from under the high DJ booth, where jazzy-electronica and Brazilian beats play softly for a 30-and-up crowd in horn-rimmed and cat-eye glasses. The cocktails are individually patented, so don't get any bright ideas. Asian (primarily Vietnamese)–inspired drinks are a good match for the mini-rolls and appetizers. The lychee martinis are fantastic. *Mon-Wed 5pm-1am, Thu 5pm-2am, Fri 5pm-4am, Sat 6pm-4am, Sun 6pm-1am.* B=

Hot Tip: This place gets crowded between 5pm and 10pm, when many of the cocktails are half-price. Get there before 5pm, grab one of the sofas to the left of the entrance, and watch as the envious crowds pile in.

Dance Clubs

#25–27: It's sad how many New York nightclubs have replaced spacious dance floors with pricey bottle-service tables. For those who like to get down and get funky, there's still hope at these venues.

Cielo
18 Little W. 12th St., Meatpacking District, 212-645-5700 • Hot

The Draw: Unlike most clubs in the city, this Miami-esque space has managed to stay fresh since its 2002 opening. How do they do it? They have an actual dance floor, and the top-notch DJs know their stuff. European and Latin visitors love this place, and you don't need to "know somebody" to get in.

The Scene: A welcome departure from bottle service and VIP-only admissions, Cielo offers a roomy bar, a backyard space with heat lamps, and a big dance floor, complete with disco ball. While Cielo isn't exclusive, it's not necessarily friendly either. *Wed-Sat 10pm-4am.* C≡

Hot Tip: Friday night's Turntables on the Hudson party brings in some of the world's best house music DJs and a loyal following of 20-to-30-something singles.

Pink Elephant
527 W. 27th St., Chelsea, 212-463-0000 • Hot

The Draw: There are seven clubs on 27th Street (really, seven)—with this being the new kid on the block.

The Scene: A long carpeted hallway with a palatial feel leads to this unique room, where rather than having a dance floor, there are podiums behind each booth, making the party seem as though it's everywhere. Electronic and house music pleases both tail shakers and money makers. *Tue-Sat 11pm-4am.* C≡

Hot Tip: The action starts a little earlier here than in most clubs. Show up at 11:30pm and entry will be faster. Thursday nights are the hippest.

Quo
511 W. 28th St., Chelsea, 212-268-5105 • Hot

The Draw: There are big dance clubs in West Chelsea, and there are stylish nightclubs. Quo manages to be a bit of both.

The Scene: Stefan Dupont, a designer known for his work on Miami clubs, gave this place its white, tan, and neon look. There's also something Miami about the crowd—they're fit and tightly clad, and they absolutely love to dance. *Wed-Sun 10pm-4am.* C≡

Hot Tip: Thursday nights are best. Splurge for table service, as those elevated seats provide a nice view of the place.

Best

Delis

#28–30: Whether the deli was invented in New York City is debatable, but it was certainly perfected here. Each deli has a very distinct flavor, and while everyone has a favorite, only a few are accepted as landmarks.

Carnegie Deli

854 7th Ave., Midtown, 212-757-2245 • Classic

The Draw: Perhaps you're familiar with Carnegie Deli from watching the countless TV shows that have taped here. At this New York favorite, sandwiches are named after the stars that inspired their creation.

The Scene: Autographed photos of Broadway and silver screen greats line the walls, announcing the caliber of the clientele. This is old-school New York, and while Times Square has changed dramatically over the years, this old classic has stayed the same. Who can resist career waiters in tux vests and bow ties? *Daily 6:30am-4am.* $$ ⬚≡

Hot Tip: The portions here are big, so try a little variety and pass the plates around. The corned beef seems to be at its best around lunchtime.

E.A.T.

1064 Madison Ave., Upper East Side, 212-772-0022 • Hot

The Draw: Imported gourmet goodies, the aptly named "Tower of Bagel," and the choicest bakery this side of the Atlantic lure the crowds.

The Scene: It's a bustling, very Upper East Side aromatic shrine to upscale eats with prices to match. Twelve dollars may seem like an awful lot to pay for a chopped liver sandwich, but what with the gargantuan portions, you won't have to eat again for the rest of the day. *Daily 7am-10pm.* $ ≡

Hot Tip: The best deal on the menu is the fragrant bread, and for a buck-fifty you can get a warm baguette to enjoy in nearby Central Park.

Katz's Delicatessen

205 E. Houston St., Lower East Side, 212-254-2246 • Original

The Draw: Katz's has been a Lower East Side staple for over a century, and it's likely to see 100 more years. This is also where Meg Ryan delivered mainstream film's most memorable faked orgasm in *When Harry Met Sally*.

The Scene: Upon entering this deep cafeteria, visitors are given a ticket that they're required to take to each station, where they purchase their food. Servers then use a wax pencil to write a total that a cashier reads at the exit. For god's sake, don't lose your ticket. *Mon-Tue 8am-10pm, Wed, Thu, and Sun 8am-11pm, Fri-Sat 8am-3am.* $- ⬚≡

Hot Tip: Slip a buck into the cafeteria workers' tip cups and watch your portions get bigger. It's not fair, but it's how things work.

Easy Local Vibe

#31–33: There are places that "become one" with their neighborhoods by understanding the natives and giving them what they want. Past the flash and fury of Manhattan's tourist draws, these local haunts tell an area's story.

Living Room
154 Ludlow St., Lower East Side, 212-533-7235 • Original

The Draw: Live music performances in back are cheap or free. The up-and-comers this place attracts would be most cities' superstars.

The Scene: The crowd is a little bit country and a little bit rock 'n' roll, but not at all scene-y. The original (and much smaller) Living Room, right around the corner, was best known for having launched Norah Jones. *Sun-Thu 6pm-2am, Fri-Sat 3pm-4am.* =

Hot Tip: Pick up local papers like the *Village Voice* and *New York Press* for show listings and reviews. Tables are first come, first serve, so arrive about a half hour before the music starts (generally around 8pm).

Pianos
158 Ludlow St., Lower East Side, 212-505-3733 • Original

The Draw: Lower East Side hipsters love this spacious and versatile venue, which used to be an actual piano store.

The Scene: There's plenty of denim and retro tees on the slender rockers at Pianos. A 30-and-up crowd piles in to see comedians like David Cross and the Stella show, as well as drop-in musical acts, like Wilco (who did a surprise set for 20-plus people in early '05). *Daily 3pm-4am. Upstairs lounge opens at 7pm.* CF≡

Hot Tip: Occasionally smaller bands will be joined by big-shot friends. If you see a band that looks interesting in the listings, check website for mention of special guests.

Session 73
1359 1st Ave., Upper East Side, 212-517-4445 • Cool

The Draw: The Upper East Side is far from hip, so the places that draw the fun crowd draw it en masse. Live classic-rock cover bands play here for free, and it's not uncommon to see the Upper East Side financiers and well-toned socialites singing along.

The Scene: While the restaurant does OK, the stage is the main draw. Barely post-collegiate revelers mingle with middle-aged singles, all agreeably singing along with Black Crow and Blues Traveler covers. The lounge and screening room in back work for those who want to sit. *Sun-Wed 5pm-2am, Thu-Sat 5pm-4am.* F≡

Hot Tip: Grab one of the tables by the stage and dance the night away with your jacket on your seat.

Best | French Bistros

#34–36: OK, this might be one of those times when the Big Apple has to settle for a close second, but *c'est la vie*. The bistros here are the real deal—minus cigarette smoke, unleashed dogs, and rude waiters.

Félix
340 W. Broadway, Soho, 212-431-0021 • Cool

The Draw: For over a decade, this Downtown staple and its cozy outdoor space have been sucking in every passerby who wants to be seen among the beautiful clientele.

The Scene: Brazilian jazz and other world music plays to a stylish crowd. The dining room is an informal affair, but less so than the patio. Despite the bar room's foozeball table, the vibe is very grown-up, perhaps because of the martini-and-specialty-cocktail–oriented menu and late-night hours. *Mon-Fri noon-midnight, Sat 11:30am-midnight, Sun 11:30am-10:30pm.* $$ B≡

Hot Tip: Brunch here is a welcome break from a busy day of Soho shopping. You can't go wrong with a sidewalk table and the spicy steak tartare.

Le Bilboquet
25 E. 63rd St., Upper East Side, 212-751-3036 • Hot

The Draw: An exquisite menu sates the well-heeled crowd of young socialites and veteran foodies. The place is unmarked, but those in the know could find it blindfolded.

The Scene: Uptown girls clad in expensively informal duds huddle around the bar looking for Uptown guys and European jet-setters. The dining experience is a social and culinary event. *Mon-Sun noon-11pm.* $$ ≡

Hot Tip: Request a table by the big front windows to enjoy the view inside and out. This place gets ridiculously crowded, so those looking to try the food without the scene should come during the less chaotic lunch hour.

Pastis
9 9th Ave., Meatpacking District, 212-929-4844 • Hot

The Draw: Restaurant crowds in the hopping Meatpacking District are inevitable, but for food this good, the scenesters come in droves.

The Scene: Though Pastis was one of the first bistros in this über-trendy neighborhood, the A-list keeps on coming for reliable steak tartare, mahi mahi, pâtés, and more. The crowd takes a casual approach to high fashion; the waitstaff has French indifference down pat. S*un-Thu 9am-2am, Sat-Sun 9am-2:30am.* $$ ⓎFⒹ≡

Hot Tip: The host may try to seat you by the busy door, but the rear dining room is where you want to be.

Galleries

#37–39: Simply stated, making it in New York City is a mark of excellence. The art found in this city's galleries is a representation of the finest work from all over the world.

Marcoart

181 Orchard St., Lower East Side, 646-479-2263 • Cool

The Draw: Marco is one of the city's rapidly rising stars, doing pop art in the neighborhood where Warhol, Basquiat, and Haring invented it.

The Scene: Brightly colored postmodern work fills this high-ceilinged room, where street art has hit the big time. Cartoonish and fun, this best-selling artist designed Swatch watch's beloved "The Alien Baby," which, if you can't afford the paintings, is sometimes carried at the nearby Swatch store on Broadway and Bleecker St. *By appointment, though on weekends the doors tend to be open.*

Hot Tip: Marco started selling his art on the corner of Green and Prince Streets in Soho. While he's since given up the corner in lieu of a fancy gallery, inspired followers now sell their art in his place.

Momenta Art

72 Berry St., Williamsburg, 718-218-8058 • Original

The Draw: Williamsburg is arguably the city's most actively artistic neighborhood, and Momenta Art is one of its more experimental venues.

The Scene: Curiosity-seeking Uptowners, art-crazed Downtowners, and Williamsburg artists come here to look at installations and watch performance pieces. Every medium imaginable is put on display here. *Thu-Mon noon-6pm.*

Hot Tip: Modern art collectors may want to stock up—pieces are less expensive than in Manhattan, and lots of Momenta works have found their way into famous museums.

Zito Studio Gallery

122 Ludlow St., Lower East Side, 646-602-2338 • Original

The Draw: Downtown eccentric and self-proclaimed "Underground Celebrity" Anthony Zito paints everything from city landscapes to celebrity portraits on "urban artifacts," like doors from abandoned buildings, car hoods, and smaller, more portable items.

The Scene: The junk shop atmosphere is a little "adventurous" for many high-earning collectors, and the artist and his peers sometimes hang around the shop looking slightly menacing. Don't be afraid. They're highly approachable. *Sat-Sun noon-5pm, Mon-Fri by appointment.*

Hot Tip: Check out Zito's art on the outside walls of some downtown locales, like Lombardi's Pizza, Mars Bar, and the Apocalypse Lounge.

Best Gay/Lesbian Bars

#40–42: What do Harvey Fierstein, Barry Manilow, Rosie O'Donnell, and David Gest have in common? They're all wonderful New Yorkers. Now, on a completely unrelated note, here's a list of the city's most popular gay bars.

Dick's Bar
192 2nd Ave., East Village, 212-475-2071 • Original

The Draw: Dick's is the most laid-back of neighborhood watering holes, where guys sit around downing pints and chatting about everything from Broadway to Buicks.

The Scene: With the ball game on TV and friendly guys hunkered over their beers, straight men sometimes spend an afternoon here without ever feeling the gay vibe. The first clue comes after dark, when the sports are switched off to make way for *Dick at Night* porn. *Daily 4pm-4am.* ▤

Hot Tip: The bartenders are quick to provide the occasional free shot for those who keep things lively.

Henrietta Hudson
438 Hudson St., West Village, 212-924-3347 • Cool

The Draw: For such a narrow space, this club holds wide appeal. The pool table, dance floor, and pick-up scene are always in full swing, but just drinking at the bar is also fun, and better for getting to know your neighbor.

The Scene: Late nights often require a $10 cover, and while these disco and techno DJs earn their keep, the scene is unassuming and full of possibilities. Whether things get crazy or run mellow all night really depends on the chemistry of the crowd. This dark room is long and narrow, and gets packed beyond belief. *Mon-Fri 4pm-4am; Sat-Sun 1pm-4am.* ⒸⒺ

Hot Tip: Arrive before 11pm or you'll have no chance of sitting down.

Stonewall
53 Christopher St., West Village, 212-463-0950 • Classic

The Draw: This landmark bar is the site of the 1969 gay rights riots, where New York's harassed gay clientele fought back for the first time, forging the way to equal rights for all! (Well, in the West Village, at least.) Stonewall's crowd blends modern with old fashion, and young with young-at-heart.

The Scene: The main level is your run-of-the-mill pub, which fills with locals and tourists who come to bask in the history. Upstairs is a slightly more bumpin' club area, which concerns itself with the here and now. *Daily 3pm-4am.* ▤

Hot Tip: If you're feeling lucky, come by on Tuesday for bingo night. Of course, if you want to get lucky, Friday night is a better bet.

Hotel Lounges

#43–45: There's a difference between tourists and travelers. While map-toting "tourists" who complain about the city are a drag, a nightcap among carpe diem–type "travelers" is fun, and hip lounges are where they come together.

Grand Bar and Lounge*

Soho Grand Hotel, 310 W. Broadway, 2nd Fl., Soho, 212-519-6500 • Hot

The Draw: Expertly mixed cocktails and small appetizers are delivered by runway model–like servers, as polished as the jet-setter clientele.

The Scene: The room is bathed in diffused light, with chocolate-y earth tones, leather bar stools, and low sofas. DJs spin ambient lounge music. In confines this hot, it's hard to tell the New Yorkers from the globe-trotting guests of the hotel. *Mon-Thu 7am-2am, Fri-Sat 7am-4am, Sun 7am-midnight.* B –

Hot Tip: Book a table—few people realize that can be done.

Hudson Bar

Hudson Hotel, 356 W. 58th St., Midtown, 212-554-6500 • Cool

The Draw: Designed in part by Studio 54 impresario Ian Schrager, this lounge isn't without its glitz. The floor is lit from below, the bar is lit from inside, and the clientele are lit from the colorful cocktails.

The Scene: Let's just say nothing here is understated; that's the fun of Hudson Bar. Drinks are adorned with flowers, and the people are dressed to the nines. DJs spin rock tunes and hip-hop classics that are designed to keep everyone grooving, though without dancing on the tables. *Daily 4pm-4am.* –

Hot Tip: If there are long lines or the velvet rope is out, head upstairs to the Library Bar, which is a good place to wait out the chaos.

Oak Room

Algonquin Hotel, 59 W. 44th St., Midtown, 212-840-6800 • Classic

The Draw: The centerpiece of the legendary Oak Room is a grand piano that's been played by the likes of Diana Krall, Michael Feinstein, and Harry Connick, Jr.

The Scene: The Algonquin's lobby is timeless and gorgeous, with high ceilings, solid pillars, and a mature, semiformal crowd. As Oak Room regular Dorothy Parker once said: "Take care of the luxuries and the necessities will take care of themselves." *Tue-Sat 7-11:30pm. Shows are at 9pm, 2nd show at 11:30pm Fri-Sat.* F –

Hot Tip: Dressing well may get you better tables and stronger drinks.

Best

Informal Upscale Restaurants

#46–48: Sometimes it's nice to eat well without having to dress the part. After all, your credit card is just as gold, regardless of the texture of your trousers.

The Biltmore Room*
290 8th Ave., Chelsea, 212-807-0111 • Cool

The Draw: Not only is this one of the city's best restaurants, it's also one of the finest places to dine while wearing jeans. The food is heavily Asian influenced, but chef Gary Robbins isn't afraid to mix it up.

The Scene: The Biltmore Room's decor consists largely of items rescued from the landmark Biltmore Hotel when it was lost in a fire. The staff is young and attractive; the crowd is a blend of young couples on dates and food connoisseurs out on the town. *Mon-Thu 5:30-10:30pm, Fri-Sat 5:30-11:30pm, Sun 5:30-10pm. The lounge stays open until 4am daily.* $$$ ⓎⒻ▭

Hot Tip: Request a banquette in back rather than one of the tables in the middle of the room, and enjoy the view.

Bread Bar @ Tabla*
11 Madison Ave., Gramercy, 212-889-0667 • Hot

The Draw: The fine modern Indian menu draws a white-collar, trend-seeking crowd. If you you prefer to mingle, dinner is also served in the bar downstairs.

The Scene: Bread Bar @ Tabla is a lavishly decorated room that meets the lofty demands of its high-earning, 20-to-30-something crowd. Specialty cocktails and a small outdoor space make for an easy-to-meet atmosphere. *Mon-Sat noon-11pm, Sun 5:30-10:30pm.* $ ⓎⒻ▭

Hot Tip: Located at the base of the Metlife building connected to Grand Central, Bread Bar is at its busiest when the after-work crowd comes in to unwind.

Five Points
31 Great Jones St., Greenwich Village, 212-253-5700 • Original

The Draw: The grill and outdoor seating draw folks down this sleepy street on warm summer nights. In the winter, the wood-burning oven makes it the perfect cozy escape.

The Scene: Five Points is a bit of a secret, and its regulars will not be happy to see it in our guidebook. White tablecloths belie the casualness of the crowd, kicking around in jeans and sneakers, with the occasional blazer over a tee shirt. *Mon-Fri noon-3pm and 6pm-midnight, Sat 11:30am-3pm and 6pm-midnight, Sun 11:30am-3pm and 6-10pm.* $$ Ⓕ▭

Hot Tip: The understated classic American menu adds lots of fresh fruits and veggies to meaty and fishy evening entrees, and the Sunday brunch is incredible. Arrive early for outdoor seating.

Jazz Clubs

#49–51: Names like Charlie Parker, Thelonious Monk, Duke Ellington, and John Coltrane have topped the billing in New York clubs of the past. Fortunately, the crème de la crème still riff away in the West Village and Harlem.

Blue Note

131 W. 3rd St., West Village, 212-475-8592 • Classic

The Draw: Though it's only been open about 20 years, the Blue Note is a jazz venue of historic proportions. The lines are long, the cover can be steep, and the food is mediocre, but, hey, this joint is always jumping.

The Scene: The sound system is good and the bookings top-notch. Ticket prices for bigger acts go up to $45 for table seating and $30 to stand at the bar. The Sunday brunch is a good deal, but don't expect to see household names playing at midday. *Sun-Thu 7pm-2am, Fri-Sat 7pm-4am.* C F ≡

Hot Tip: There are many superior restaurants in this area, but if you want the good seats, dinner at the Blue Note may be a necessary evil.

Iridium Jazz Club

1650 Broadway, Midtown, 212-582-2121 • Cool

The Draw: With its neon lights and flashy Times Square location, Iridium combines the refined comfort of polished, modern, tourist-friendly Times Square with the spirit of old-school New York jazz.

The Scene: In 1994, Iridium and its state-of-the-art sound system resurrected the historic jazz scene in this neighborhood, which teemed with clubs in the '50s and '60s. *Fri-Sat 6:30pm-1am, Sun-Thu 6:30pm-midnight.* C F ≡

Hot Tip: When Les Paul says, "That guitar has my name all over it," he's not kidding. The legendary inventor and strummer plays here every Monday night.

Village Vanguard

178 7th Ave. S., West Village, 212-255-4037 • Classic

The Draw: Opened in 1935, this legendary room is small and rich with history. When jazz musicians of the past bragged of playing big gigs in the City, they generally meant the Village Vanguard.

The Scene: You can almost hear the ghosts of Sonny Rollins, Bill Evans, John Coltrane, and the other giants who recorded here. The crowd sometimes dresses the part, but a fedora count wouldn't take long. *Daily 8pm-2am.* C ≡

Hot Tip: The Vanguard fills up in a hurry. If you want to see Roy Hargrove and Wynton Marsalis, buy your tickets in advance.

Best

Live Tapings

#52–54: Schmaltz doesn't fly in Gotham, where "good television" isn't an oxymoron. Tickets to worthwhile live tapings aren't easy to come by, but planning in advance can net prime-time results.

The Daily Show with Jon Stewart
733 11th Ave., Midtown, 212-586-2477 • Hot

The Draw: In case you haven't heard, Jon Stewart's "fake news" program is all the rage among the liberal intelligentsia. In fact, Tucker Carlson aside, *The Daily Show* sometimes reaches politicos from "across the aisle" as well.

The Scene: The crowd outside could easily be mistaken for that of the Ivy League debates tournament. *Tapes Mon-Thu; doors open at 5:45pm. Tapings generally air the same night.*

Hot Tip: The show generally books one month before tapings, so plan in advance. Write in for tickets and hope for the best: *Daily Show* Tickets, 1775 Broadway, 9th Fl., New York, NY 10019.

The Late Show with David Letterman
1697 Broadway, Midtown, 212-975-6644 • Classic

The Draw: Living legend David Letterman holds court in the historic Ed Sullivan Theater, which is also where the Beatles first met America.

The Scene: No longer limited to the college crowd that filled the chairs 20 years ago, this collection of tourists ranges from Columbia undergrads to Hoosiers from Dave's home state of Indiana. No one under 18 is admitted. *Tapes Mon-Fri afternoons. Tapings air that night at 11:30pm.*

Hot Tip: Tickets can be reserved online, in person, or by phone. Call at 11am on the day of the show, and be prepared to answer a trivia question. If that doesn't work, train your dog to play guitar and contact a producer.

Saturday Night Live
NBC Studios, 30 Rockefeller Plz., Midtown, 212-664-3056 • Original

The Draw: Live from New York, it's Saturday night!

The Scene: *SNL* forever changed television when it debuted in 1975. Now, 18 Grammys later, it's still going strong. The crowd is largely comprised of those who "know somebody," but hard work can sometimes turn up tickets. This is the kind of thing people plan their trips around. *Dress rehearsal Sat 8pm, live taping 11:30pm.*

Hot Tip: Every August, *SNL* holds a ticket lottery that can be entered with a submission to snltickets@nbc.com. Or, if you've led a virtuous life and all of your stars are aligned, show up outside the studio on Saturday at 7am, and you just might claim a stand-by ticket.

Of-the-Moment Dining

#55–57: In New York, everyone wants a restaurant with an angle, but they're quick to lambaste a gimmick. Tough crowd, huh? These places have managed to find the middle ground.

B.E.D. NY*

530 W. 27th St., Chelsea, 212-594-4109 • Hot

The Draw: Rows of big futons wrap around a circular group table, giving trendy patrons the option of dining like prim and proper adults, or literally eating dinner in bed.

The Scene: B.E.D. Miami was an instant sensation, and it's a hit in New York as well. (Many imitators have opened, including the unremarkably named Duvet.) The cocktail menu was arranged by famed mixologist Dale DeGroff, prompting several patrons to indulge in before-, during-, and after-dinner drinks. *Tue-Thu 7pm-midnight, Fri-Sat 7pm-1am, Sun 2-7pm, Tue-Sat bar until 4am.* $$$ 🍸🍴🚭☰

Hot Tip: It's hard to cut food in bed, so go with tender meats and fish over the tougher stuff. Also, be sure to wear clean socks, because you will have to remove your shoes.

Lure Fishbar*

142 Mercer St., Soho, 212-431-7676 • Cool

The Draw: A strong surf-and-turf menu, a prime Soho location, and lots of good press have sold foodies on Lure Fishbar ... hook, line, and sinker.

The Scene: Designed to look like the inside of a luxury ocean liner, this spot caters to a crowd familiar with boat parties, showy fashion, and entertainment industry events. The sunken dining area is more conducive to conversation than the bar, so feel free to discuss quantum physics with the model across the table. *Mon-Fri noon-11pm, Sat-Sun noon-3pm and 5:30-11pm.* $$$ 🍸🚭☰

Hot Tip: The best place to sit is in the main room's corner booths. Portions are small, so consider an appetizer.

Spice Market*

403 W. 13th St., Meatpacking District, 212-675-2322 • Hot

The Draw: This is the hip sibling of the Jean-Georges Vongerichten family, and its dramatic Asian-influenced stage seems set for an *Indiana Jones* movie.

The Scene: The "in" crowd is everywhere, and they're all on their cell phones. Group tables force the clique-inclined to be a bit more social. Unlike in other Vongerichten restaurants, the scene is the thing here, and it's tough to get a table. *Daily noon-3pm and 5:30pm-midnight, Fri-Sun until 1am.* $$ 🍸🍴☰

Hot Tip: Be sure to have a nightcap in the downstairs lounge.

Best

Off-Broadway Theaters

#58–60: What is an off-Broadway theater? Besides the obvious geographical clue, it's often just as professional as the Great White Way, but tends to have fewer seats, less-commercial performances, and a not-for-profit bent.

Cherry Lane Theater

38 Commerce St., West Village, 212-989-2020 • Classic

The Draw: As New York's oldest continuously running off-Broadway theater, Cherry Lane attracts plenty of professional talent for its purist pieces, like *The Crucible* and *American Buffalo,* as opposed to long-running works about, say, singing felines.

The Scene: Located in the heart of historic bohemian stomping grounds (once home to Alan Ginsberg, Jack Kerouac, Bob Dylan, and Lou Reed, to name a few), this former barn silo had a major facelift in the 1950s, when it received many an ornamental donation from Radio City Music Hall. *Shows generally run Tue-Sat 7-10pm, with Sat 3pm matinee.* C⎯

Hot Tip: The aged and charming Blue Mill restaurant, located on the same sleepy street, is perfect for a postshow dinner.

Playwrights Horizon

416 W. 42nd St., Midtown, 212-564-1235

The Draw: Playwrights Horizon is a writer-driven theater that has produced four Tony winners since opening in 1971. Wendy Wasserstein's *The Heidi Chronicles* is one of this theater's best-known originals.

The Scene: In this smallish theater, it's scripts first, special effects ... never. Though it isn't about stars, per se, it's not uncommon to see big-screen names like Mia Farrow, Morgan Freeman, and Kevin Spacey gracing the Playwrights' stage. *Showtimes generally Tue-Sun at 8pm, matinees on Sat and Sun.* C⎯

Hot Tip: Even if you can pay top dollar for tickets, the egalitarian energy on "pay what you can" nights makes for a great audience.

The Public Theater

425 Lafayette St., Greenwich Village, 212-539-8500

The Draw: The Public features a wide range of classic and original works, from Shakespeare to today's up-and-comers. Since opening in 1967, the Public has brought home 40 Tonys, 135 Obies, and 4 Pulitzers.

The Scene: Edgier than Broadway and more mainstream than Soho, the Public draws an eclectic crowd. Suits and ties are welcome here, but as with most things Downtown, an evening at the Public is an informal affair. *Shows generally run Tue-Sun 8pm-midnight.* C≡

Hot Tip: Joe's Pub is a fantastic music venue connected to the Public Theater. For one-stop entertainment, pick a good night for both places.

Best Outdoor People-Watching

#61–63: Outdoor people-watching in Manhattan is an inexpensive way to see the latest fashions, and, for all of you celeb gawkers, it's one of the most sure-fire ways to spot models and movie stars sans makeup and entourage.

Bryant Park
500 5th Ave., Midtown, 212-768-4242 • Cool

The Draw: Located smack dab in the middle of Midtown, this oasis of greenery is a popular spot for tourists, Midtown workers, dog walkers, and the occasional summer concert series.

The Scene: Some people come here to tan, some to enjoy a long lunch break, and others simply to people-watch. The crowd is a perfect example of New York's everyday folks, minus the crackheads and beggars that can make some parks less than relaxing.

Hot Tip: During the summer Bryant Park hosts a Monday night film series featuring classic flicks. Bring a blanket, stake out a spot, and wait for the sun to set.

Central Park
Between 58th and 110th Sts., and 5th and 8th Aves. • Classic

The Draw: With 25 million visitors each year and 9,000 benches for prime perching, Central Park is a people-watching paradise.

The Scene: Every kind of person imaginable comes through this park. During the day it's perfectly safe to find a private spot on the lawn to watch joggers, stroller pushers, and the occasional pigeon-feeder in a chicken suit. Street performers abound, but with the park's 843 acres, they're as easy to avoid as they are to find.

Hot Tip: Stay toward the lower end of the park for more "polished" people-watching (60th–80th Streets), where you'll find a cross-section of Fifth Avenue shoppers, upwardly mobile residents, and Eastside-Westsiders. Maps can be purchased for $4 at the Arsenal (64th St. and 5th Ave.).

Washington Square Park
5th Ave. and Thompson St., Greenwich Village • Classic

The Draw: This lovely, tree-lined oasis, with its sprawling lawns and central fountain, provides hours of entertainment for gazers, complete with musicians, magicians, and uninhibited NYU students.

The Scene: Washington Square Park may be the city's liveliest. Night or day, folksy Villagers sit around the commons playing guitars, banjos, drums, and whatever else they can cart down the street (pianos have been seen!). Despite the omnipresent cameras and cops, loiterers hang about trying to sell fake pot to unsuspecting tourists and students.

Hot Tip: Teams of gymnasts make Saturday afternoons particularly fun.

Best   # Piano Bars

#64–66: Whether it be great has-beens of yore, future stars waiting for their big break, or actual working performers looking to pass the time, Manhattan's piano bars offer more than many big stages around the world.

Brandy's Piano Bar

235 E. 84th St., Upper East Side, 212-744-4949 • Classic

The Draw: This gay-owned and gay-operated lounge has been going strong for over 20 years. With a total capacity of 75, this intimate space leaves no room for sour notes, which, happily, is not Brandy's style.

The Scene: Unlike the drunken jock-rock singalongs commonly found in this neighborhood, Brandy's leans more toward Broadway and disco diva standards. While the occasional visitor is invited to strut his or her stuff, the waitstaff and pianists do most of the singing, which keeps the place from becoming a karaoke mess. *Daily 4pm-4am.*

Hot Tip: In the late-night hours, the tables closest to the small stage are best.

Don't Tell Mama

343 W. 46th St., Midtown, 212-757-0788 • Classic

The Draw: Beyond the spirited bar, two cabaret rooms host a combination of Broadway talent and drag queen performances, like the ever-popular "Judy Garland Live."

The Scene: International tourists, local performers, and after-workers come here to watch uneven renditions of the Broadway musicals onstage just steps away. Admission is charged for the back rooms, and a two-drink minimum holds tables up front. *Daily 5pm-4am.*

Hot Tip: The best days to catch the real talent sipping martinis and giving performances are Mondays, when the big Broadway shows are dark.

Duplex

61 Christopher St., West Village, 212-255-5438 • Original

The Draw: It's sing-and-be-seen at this lively piano bar in the historic heart of the West Village, where joke-cracking MCs roam the room, lowering inhibitions and setting the stage for fun.

The Scene: A fabulous, flamboyant staff tends to the informal mix of tourists and locals in an anything-goes environment. Wear whatever's comfortable, and feel free to sing outside of your range. Sure they'll rib you a bit, but they'll also give you another shot—of opportunity and libation. *Daily 4pm-4am.*

Hot Tip: Those looking for a little action might roam upstairs, where there are often small cabaret shows. The scene up there is a bit more cruise-y.

Pizza

#67–69: Downtown Manhattan was once among the most Italian places on earth. Pizza here is thin with limited crust, and "Lemmegetaslice" is understood to be an order for one slice of plain cheese pizza.

John's of Bleecker Street

278 Bleecker St., West Village, 212-243-1680 • Original

The Draw: Many New Yorkers believe that John's is the best pizza in town. There are no individual slices here, but who can stop at just one?

The Scene: Since 1929, John's has served up their 12-inch and 14-inch brick oven pizzas to the likes of Mickey Mantle, Frank Sinatra, and even Vanilla Ice, whose pictures are all on the wall. (Let us never mention those three names in the same sentence again.) Nothing fancy here, just wood-planked walls, tiled floors, and the sweet smell of red sauce and cheese. *Daily noon-11:30pm.* $$ ▣

Hot Tip: Your best bet is to come during the week at off-peak hours. The meaty toppings are fresh, but purists do it plain.

Lombardi's

32 Spring St., Soho, 212-941-7994 • Classic

The Draw: Opened in 1905, Lombardi's is said to be the oldest pizzeria in the country. There's always a debate to be had about who has the best pizza in town, but it inevitably goes, "Lombardi's or _____?"

The Scene: Cola ovens bake up great pies for the noisy crowd, which generally packs the place to capacity. The staff aren't arrogant—they're proud. *Mon-Thu 11:30am-11pm, Fri-Sat 11:30am-midnight, Sun 11:30am-10pm.* $ ▣▣

Hot Tip: Lombardi's pays the price of popularity, aka: screaming kids and tourists. Come on the late side if you can.

Otto*

1 5th Ave., Greenwich Village, 212-995-9559 • Cool

The Draw: This is master chef Mario Batali's most accessible restaurant, with small, minimalist pies reminiscent of the motherland.

The Scene: By day, the place is filled with mothers and kids on their way home from Washington Square Park. By night, scenesters and foodies pack the labyrinthine dining area and the tables up front. The wine list is extensive, and the pizza menu complicated. You may want to ask for help, and listen closely. *Daily 11:30am-midnight.* $ ▣▣▣

Hot Tip: They don't take reservations, but request a table in the back of the room overlooking the Washington Mews—a private alleyway of Old European–style houses.

Best

Power Lunches

#70–72: Some of the biggest financial and entertainment deals ever made have gone down in this city, where restaurants are also playing fields for high-rollers looking to shock and awe clients.

Delmonico's

56 Beaver St., Wall Street, 212-509-1144 • Classic

> **The Draw:** Said to be "the oldest restaurant in the United States," this place exudes history. The building itself is an 1837 landmark.

> **The Scene:** Delmonico's is wall-to-wall with Wall Street sharks, and ready to feed their high expectations. After all, this classic steak house has hosted events for Abraham Lincoln, Mark Twain, Charles Dickens, and Andrew Jackson. Coat and tie are required. *Mon-Fri 11:30am-10pm, Sat 5:30-10pm.* $$$ ☲☰

> **Hot Tip:** These guys have a full menu, but stick with the surf and turf that made them famous—the lobster is excellent, as are all of the steaks. After all, you wouldn't get egg rolls in Rome.

The Four Seasons*

99 E. 52nd St., Midtown, 212-754-9494 • Classic

> **The Draw:** This landmark restaurant boasts a Philip Johnson design, four-star American cuisine, and an aura of power emanating from the well-heeled, beautiful clientele.

> **The Scene:** Steaks, wild boar, sausage soup—this is a place for the top of the food chain. The brass-lined Grill Room sits under cathedral ceilings, while the more romantic Pool Room surrounds a big marble fountain. *Mon-Fri noon-2pm and 5-9:30pm, Sat 5-11pm.* $$$$ ☲☰

> **Hot Tip:** The tables by the Pool Room's fountain are fantastic, and therefore the first to fill up. Call first and give it a whirl.

The Palm

837 2nd Ave., Midtown, 212-687-2953 • Classic

> **The Draw:** In D.C., the Palm is where lobbyists take senators. In LA, it's where producers seduce starlets. The Palm in NYC is where financiers and realtors buy and sell the most expensive properties on earth.

> **The Scene:** The original Palm is a vintage steak house that has scarcely changed since opening in 1926. The walls are lined with sketches from such artists as Mort Walker (*Beetle Bailey*), Matt Weilman (*Popeye*), and Carmine Infantino (*Batman*). Caricatures portray past diners like Hugh Hefner, J. Edgar Hoover, and Jackie Gleason. *Mon-Fri noon-11:30pm, Sat 5-11:30pm.* $$$ ☰

> **Hot Tip:** In-house caricature artist Bronwyn Bird can draw your likeness while you wait for your steak.

Restaurant Lounges

#73–75: Whether New York started this trend, who knows? But combining a restaurant environment with a nightlife scene results in a whole greater than the sum of its parts.

BondSt*
6 Bond St., Greenwich Village, 212-777-2500 • Cool

> The Draw: This is the only place abuzz on an otherwise desolate street, and the heavily seasoned fish is as good as the cocktails are fruity. BondSt is always a weekend "scene," but it never overshadows the food ... not on the top floor, at least.
>
> The Scene: Though celebrity sightings aren't what they were in 2003, they aren't uncommon. White-collar weekenders and couples fill the spacious upstairs, while investment bankers and *Sex and the City* types energize the scene from the white-washed lounge downstairs. *Mon-Sat 5pm-2am (kitchen closes at midnight), Sun 6pm-1am.* $$ XB≡
>
> Hot Tip: Those looking to chat and chew will want to go straight for the lower level before the place crowds with those enjoying cocktails à la carte.

Lotus*
409 W. 14th St., Meatpacking District, 212-243-4420 • Cool

> The Draw: There aren't many nightlife institutions in town, but this Asian-inspired double-decker has been going since the turn of the century. The club-by vibe downstairs spices up the restaurant scene, where the crowd enjoys Asian fusion cuisine.
>
> The Scene: The crowd upstairs is earlier to bed, but they enjoy the bird's-eye vantage point of the flirtatious young energy below. *Tue-Sat 7pm-4am, Sun 10pm-4am (kitchen closes at 11:30pm).* CF≡
>
> Hot Tip: Asking a hotel concierge for tips will be helpful at Lotus, possibly netting a contact name at the door that could minimize your waiting time.

Odea*
389 Broome St., Soho, 212-941-9222 • Cool

> The Draw: An elegant decor of dark wood, exposed brick, and sultry light creates a sexy, laid-back vibe at this first-rate tapas bar.
>
> The Scene: Beautiful people worthy of the velvet-rope test opt for Odea's egalitarian principles and maximum hipness. The underlit onyx bar serves fresh cocktails to singles up front, while groups gather in the curtained-off, elevated enclaves in back. *Tue-Wed 6pm-2am, Thu-Sat 6pm-4am.* F≡
>
> Hot Tip: Groups should reserve a table and hog the space all night long. Those looking for company should hang around the bar.

Best   Rock Clubs

#76–78: The clothes are tight, the crowd fashionably disheveled, and the evenings late—there's nothing like rock 'n' roll. And because so many rock stars come through NYC, you never know who will stop by for a drink.

Hiro Lounge
371 W. 16th St., Chelsea, 212-727-0212 • Hot

The Draw: Hiro's Japanese-themed cocktails are generally poured by Asian beauties. This low-roofed lounge is fun, and on some nights, the stage of the adjacent ballroom rocks out.

The Scene: Located in a hotel basement, Hiro's stylish Japanese decor may not say rock 'n' roll, but it sure is stunning. The music is a crap shoot, but the crowd is always throbbing, especially after midnight. Keep an eye out for big celebs like Mick Jagger, who's been known to grace the place with his presence. *Thu-Sat 10pm-4am.* ≣

Hot Tip: The best night is Monday, when owner Nur Khan drops by with his modelicious friends. As with most New York City clubs, calling for a reservation is a good idea.

6's & 8's
205 Chrystie St., Lower East Side, 212-477-6688 • Original

The Draw: Don't let first impressions fool you. The semisleazy downtown locale and windowless black exterior belie the posh interior.

The Scene: In Vegas-speak, 6's & 8's is code for T&A. If you don't know what *that* means, this isn't the club for you. Red walls, leather banquettes, concrete floors, and dim chandeliers give the place a postapocalyptic *Blade Runner* appeal. The Vegas-themed downstairs lounge packs in a deceptively shabby-chic Uptown crowd. *Mon-Sat 6pm-4am.* ≣

Hot Tip: 6's & 8's "turns it up to 11" after 2am. Stop in early and ask the bartender about the late-night guest list.

Snitch
59 W. 21st St., Flatiron, 212-727-7775 • Hot

The Draw: Owned in part by Guns N' Roses founder Duff McKagan, Stone Temple Pilots former frontman Scott Weiland, and Fuel singer Brett Scallions, Snitch is an all-access backstage pass. While there are legendary stories about these rockers stopping in for an impromptu late-night set, the no-name bands that play Snitch can also hold their own.

The Scene: Sassy waitresses too young for their customized '70s and '80s concert tees deliver buckets of bottled beer to the sounds of AC/DC and the Stones. *Mon-Thu 5pm-4am, Fri-Sun 24 hours.* C B ≣

Hot Tip: Stop by when the owners' new band, Velvet Revolver, is in town, and you might be treated to an unexpected show.

Singles Scene

#79–81: There's no point raising a family in Manhattan's cramped, over-priced apartments. Though baby strollers abound near Central Park, the city is truly a playground for singles who insist on access to the world's greatest nightlife.

Level V

675 Hudson St., West Village, 212-699-2410 • Hot

The Draw: These subterranean confines, which once housed a popular S&M dungeon, have traded whip-wielding dominatrices for a more conventional, if eager, singles scene.

The Scene: White collars may have replaced black leather, but this cavernous club still has enough of an edge. Stone walls and iron bars hold back a large-ly single crowd that's otherwise unrestrained. Expect to hear hip-hop and soul, with more than a sprinkling of rock. *Tue-Sat 8pm-4am.* B≣

Hot Tip: The door is tight. Getting dinner reservations at Vento upstairs, where the club's manager subtly recruits guests, could provide an inside track to Level V.

Libation*

137 Ludlow St., Lower East Side, 212-529-2153 • Original

The Draw: Once a haven for rock 'n' roll dive bars, Ludlow Street is making the leap from grungy hipness to scenester sybaritism. The prime example—Libation.

The Scene: Velvet ropes mark the entrance to this trilevel restaurant-lounge-club hybrid, where weekenders flock in from Uptown and out of town. An "American tapas" menu invites fashionably dressed singles to share in dishes like mini filet mignon and a three-cheese fondue. The table service–driven second floor, which is where the DJ spins jazzy electronic lounge music, is laid out like a terrace, allowing singles to scout out the bar scene below. *Daily noon-4am.* F≣

Hot Tip: Book an upstairs table for a late dinner, and keep it when the crowd pours in around 11pm.

Whiskey Blue

541 Lexington Ave., Midtown, 212-407-2947 • Cool

The Draw: Young-at-heart professionals and guests of the W Hotel make up this singles scene, which goes strong from after-work to after-hours.

The Scene: It's dark in Whiskey Blue, which is suggestively designed around two big beds in the center of the room. The bar area crowds with mingling sin-gles who, though lacking that cutting edge, have trendy and hard-working wardrobes. *Daily 4pm-4am.* ≣

Hot Tip: Get in for the after-work scene and hang out before the doormen arrive around 10pm. Call ahead to reserve one of the beds.

Best Spas

#82–84: Everyone in this town could use a massage and a bit of pampering. Considering Manhattan's collective and oh-so-contagious stress, nothing less than the best will do.

Bliss Soho

568 Broadway, 2nd Fl., Soho, 212-219-8970 • Hot

The Draw: Facialist and utopic visionary Marcia Kilgore has a hit with Bliss Soho, which just may have the highest posh factor of all the city's spas.

The Scene: The crowd can be intimidating, and so can the staff, but such is the price of vanity. At Bliss, there are 11,000 square feet of peels, wraps, facials, massages, manicures, pedicures, and anything-that-ails-you cures. *Mon-Fri 9:30am-8:30pm, alternate Wed 12:30-8:30pm, Sat 9:30am-6:30pm.* $$$$

Hot Tip: If you fall in love with your fuzzy robe and comfy slippers, there's no need to try and smuggle them out. Brand-spanking new ones are available for sale in the Bliss shop up front.

Metamorphosis Day Spa

127 E. 56th St., 5th Fl., Midtown, 212-751-6051 • Cool

The Draw: A very tranquil spa with a subtle New Age vibe, Metamorphosis is all about serenity.

The Scene: Upscale and quiet as a pin-drop, Metamorphosis has all the amenities one expects from a top-notch spa, including specialized "services for him." A Metrosexual Male Makeover is $225. Being just off Park Avenue, Metamorphosis is a mecca for the ladies-who-lunch clique. *Mon-Fri 10am-9pm, Sat 10am-6pm.* $$$$

Hot Tips: Endermologie treatments are popular with those looking to reduce the appearance of cellulite, and now that the FDA has approved the LPG machine, the 30-minute treatment is more accessible than ever.

Oasis Day Spa

108 E. 16th St., Gramercy, 212-254-7722 • Classic

The Draw: Luxurious accommodations at three Manhattan locations attract moderate-to-high rollers with everything from pedicures to Pilates.

The Scene: Pampered housewives, working women, and metrosexual males alike come to this modern spa, where its corporate nature actually holds some appeal. Should you not have time to visit while in town, book an appointment at their JFK Jet Blue facility. *Mon-Fri 10am-10:15pm, Sat-Sun 9am-9:15pm.* $$$$

Hot Tip: Those on a busy schedule should consider having an Oasis massage therapist come to their room for a 60-minute rubdown.

Steak Houses

#85–87: Great steaks are brought in from all over the world to sate the New York power brokers who buy and sell Fortune 500 companies. While steak houses tend to be boys' clubs for fat cats, the best ones also have a little panache.

Churrascaria Plataforma

316 W. 49th St., Midtown, 212-245-0505 • Cool
221 W. Broadway, Tribeca, 212-245-0505

The Draw: Churrascaria Plataforma has a fresh take on the traditional steak house—a carnivores' Carnaval. Samba and bossa nova bands shake it up Thursday through Saturday, and the staff's skillful presentation of meats could be mistaken for a choreographed dance number.

The Scene: If you've never eaten at a Brazilian steak house, you're in for a surprise. Servers buzz about with meat-piled trays and skewers for anyone who wants them, filling plates until they see the "stop" card on your table. You should know when to say when. *Daily noon-midnight.* $$ ≡

Hot Tip: Don't fill up on salads and appetizers. The $46.95 prix fixe is chock-full of exotically marinated meats you won't want to miss.

Dylan Prime*

62 Laight St., Tribeca, 212-334-4783 • Hot

The Draw: Beef is just the beginning at this candlelit chophouse, where the cuts are thoughtfully seasoned and extremely generous.

The Scene: The crowd is younger and sexier than you'd expect from a meatery, looking more fit for sushi than for steak. There's something about the fine smell of a porterhouse steak that gives the place an attractive air of primal seduction. *Mon-Wed noon-2:30pm and 5:30-11pm, Thu-Fri noon-2:30pm and 5:30pm-midnight, Sat 5:30pm-midnight, Sun 5:30-10pm.* $$$ ⓎⒻ≡

Hot Tip: Since this is near Wall Street, late afternoons and early evenings get a little stuffy. Come after 8pm to see Dylan Prime at its best.

Strip House

13 E. 12th St., Greenwich Village, 212-328-0000 • Hot

The Draw: Though Chef David Walzog is one of the best things to happen to strip steak, the cheeky bordello decor, complete with red velvet walls and "cheesecake" photographs, is what gives Strip House its character.

The Scene: The young power players who frequent Strip House are still 20 years and 20 pounds away from what you'll find at more traditional meateries. Unlike most steak houses, this one actually attracts women. *Mon-Thu 5-11:30pm (bar until 1am), Fri-Sat 5pm-midnight (bar until 2am), Sun 5-11pm (bar until 1am).* $$$ Ⓑ≡

Hot Tip: The further away from the bar you sit, the more privacy you'll get.

Best

Sushi

#88–90: In New York, sushi is regarded as a staple on the dating scene. In addition to being a suspected aphrodisiac, it also makes for a low-calorie meal that keeps people looking and feeling sexy for those A-list nightclubs.

Blue Ribbon Sushi

119 Sullivan St., Soho, 212-343-0404 • Hot

The Draw: Many true aficionados would give first prize in the best sushi competition to Blue Ribbon (whose sake selection is hard to beat as well).

The Scene: With daily shipments fresh from the Sea of Japan, Blue Ribbon keeps a full house, even well into the night. The scene here is as sexy and romantic as you'll find in a restaurant, and the hip daters aren't shy about hand-feeding one another. *Daily noon-2am.* $$$ B≣

Hot Tip: Book a table in the rear dining room if you've brought a date; order from the bar if you're looking to meet one.

Nobu

105 Hudson St., Tribeca, 212-219-0500 • Classic

The Draw: When Nobu opened in 1994, not only did it change the way New Yorkers saw sushi, it kick-started the trendiness of the Tribeca neighborhood. Since then, Nobu restaurants have opened in Los Angeles, Paris, Milan, Tokyo, Las Vegas, and London.

The Scene: The place is as fashionable as its shabby-chic crowd, with their ripped sneakers and $200 jeans. The miso-marinated sweet black cod is hot, and the sushi and sashimi are very, very cool. *Mon-Fri 11:45am-2:15pm and 5:45-10:15pm, Sat-Sun 5:45-10:15pm.* $$$ F−

Hot Tip: Tables by the windows facing Hudson Street are the best, with great outdoor people-watching on one side and a hopping bar on the other.

Sushi Samba 7*

87 7th Ave. S., West Village, 212-691-7885 • Cool

The Draw: Sushi Sambas have popped up in several U.S. cities, but wouldn't you know, it all started here. The pioneering Park Avenue locale has great food and a hip crowd, but the newer West Village spot has one of the coolest scenes in the cold fish world.

The Scene: This colorful, multilevel Samba has a rooftop lounge that's all the rage in the summer. The crowd of publicists and *Sex and the City* retreads sometimes gets a little too energetic, but to their credit, they know how to find the freshest places. *Mon-Wed 11:45am-1am, Thu-Sat 11:45am-2am, Sun 12:15pm-midnight.* $$ ⵝF≣

Hot Tip: Go with what's cold. The spicy tuna roll best exemplifies Samba's signature blend of Japanese fish and Latin spices.

Theme Bars

#91–93: In a city with nearly 10,000 liquor licenses, every bar struggles to stand out. Some hit on themes that stick in people's minds, while others ... what was I talking about? Oh, yeah. These bars have more shtick that sticks.

Barcade
388 Union Ave., Williamsburg, 718-302-6464 • Original

The Draw: Is Pac Man fever still driving you crazy? Barcade's 30-plus vintage video games will feed your addiction. These irresistibly retro sights and sounds will have even the most jaded mod cashing his dollars.

The Scene: Williamsburg's 30-something struggling artists flock to Barcade for a nostalgic spin down junior high memory lane. The "just rolled out of bed" look reigns. *Mon-Sat 5pm-4am, Sun 5pm-2am.* ▣

Hot Tip: Bring your own quarters to minimize waiting time at the bar. Expect to wait for high-demand games like Asteroids and Ms. Pac Man.

Happy Ending
302 Broome St., Soho, 212-334-9676 • Cool

The Draw: Once an illegal massage parlor (hence the name), Happy Ending is now a friendly lounge with a buzzing singles scene. It may not promise gratification, but it's a good place to start.

The Scene: Getting in is easy—just show up. The hip but informal crowd mingles to retro pop and modern rock, or lounges on the banquettes of former steam rooms. *Tue 10pm-4am, Wed-Sat 7pm-4am.* ▣

Hot Tip: The place has a sense of humor, and so should your outfit. Wear sneakers with a suit, if you want. Taking a cab is recommended—the neighborhood can be sketchy.

Red Rock West
457 W. 17th St., Chelsea, 212-366-5359 • Original

The Draw: A loud, Southern rock jukebox, raunchy bartenders dancing on the countertops, and a pool table to boot? Red Rock West is an urban honky-tonk where Dixie spirit meets Yankee attitude.

The Scene: Whether contractors or cops, the weekend crowd here likes to let loose. In the early evenings and on weeknights, Red Rock West sees more cowboys than fillies, if you get my drift. On weekends, swinging bachelorettes mob the bar, flirting free drinks out of the obliging blue-collar crowd. *Daily 11:30am-4pm.* ▣

Hot Tip: Buy the bartender a shot as soon as you walk in and she's more likely to remember you when things get crowded. Men—do not wear a tie. The bartender will cut it in half. Ladies, you can trade your bra for a shot.

Best

Unusual Museums

#94–96: A lot of people might feel more inclined to visit museums if they were sexier, grittier, and a little more like television. Wouldn't you know, this city has just what they're looking for.

Museum of Sex

233 5th Ave., Flatiron, 212-689-6337 • Cool

The Draw: Well, first off, it's the Museum of Sex! Though some of the displays are graphic, these galleries take a thoughtful look at the sexual revolution and how erotica affects our society.

The Scene: Visitors to the Museum of Sex are more about anthropology than pornography, but at times there's a pretty fine line. *Sun-Fri 11am-6:30pm, Sat 11am-8pm.* $

Hot Tip: Come on Saturday evening for fruity cocktails in the sex-themed Gallery Lounge next door, where the less-than-subtle floral decor puts an emphasis on the reproductive parts.

Museum of Television and Radio

25 W. 52nd St., Midtown, 212-621-6800 • Hot

The Draw: This wonderful museum pays homage to the legends of television and radio with tapes, photos, and fascinating memorabilia.

The Scene: Intellectuals and rarely mobilized couch potatoes alike come to celebrate the best thing to happen to audiovisual arts since the transistor. Two theaters show classic programs, so it's always a good idea to call ahead. *Tue, Wed, Fri, Sun noon-6pm, Thu noon-8pm.* $

Hot Tip: Go through the computer archives at the front desk to reserve a private booth, where tapes can be seen and/or heard.

Tenement Museum

108 Orchard St., Lower East Side, 212-431-0233 • Original

The Draw: Though the Lower East Side is now peppered with popular rock bars, it was once where Ellis Island immigrants first unpacked their bags. This tenement-cum-museum tells their story.

The Scene: The Tenement Museum is largely dedicated to the stories of Jews, who are most commonly associated with this neighborhood's beginnings. Still, these exhibits fairly depict the hopes and hardships of the "huddled masses" who arrived at this shore, to which many people can trace back their roots today. *Tours: Tue-Fri 1:20-4:45pm, Sat-Sun 11:15am-4:45pm; Store: Mon 11am-5:30pm, Tue-Fri 11am-6pm, Sat-Sun 10:45am-6pm.* $

Hot Tip: Bring comfortable walking shoes. Just like the building's one-time tenants, you'll have to ascend the 38 steps to reach the third floor, and no, there's no elevator. All tours are guided, so reservations are recommended.

Wine Bars

#97–99: There's whining and there's wining. One gets old fast, the other takes its time. While most of this book deals with New York's own, these wine bars show off some of the finest imports to come through Manhattan's many shores.

Bar Veloce

175 2nd Ave., East Village, 212-260-3200 • Cool

The Draw: Now that's Italian! The old vinos served in this very cozy, candlelit space, with clean lines and chrome countertops, have wine lovers singing songs of *amore*.

The Scene: Despite the mirrors on the wall, this room is so narrow that one couple too many shifts the mood from intimate to claustrophobic. The bar is beautiful, with long rows of bottles backlit with rosy light, and a muted television playing classic black-and-white films. *Daily 5pm-3am.* B≡

Hot Tip: Arrive early and sit at the bar, preferably in back where fewer people will run into you.

Morrell Wine Bar & Café*

1 Rockefeller Plz., Midtown, 212-262-7700 • Classic

The Draw: Great wine collection? *Oui.* The space between patrons? Wee. Despite there being two floors at Morrell's, outdoor seating around Rockefeller Center is all the rage.

The Scene: This modern, curvaceous wine bar fills up with weary Midtown shoppers. Tastings are available for the 2,000-plus wines on the vertiginous menu, and the staff is quite accommodating. *Mon-Sat 11:30am-midnight, Sun noon-6pm. (The kitchen closes an hour before the bar.)* F−

Hot Tip: In the winter, grab a window seat overlooking the Rockefeller Center ice-skating rink.

Rhone

63 Gansevoort St., Meatpacking District, 212-367-8440 • Hot

The Draw: Rhone is so well stocked, it's practically a wine club, with over 3,000 bottles (10% of which are on the menu at a given time) nestled in the 160-square-foot cellar.

The Scene: This stylish joint, set in an old Meatpacking warehouse, is designed around the oval zinc-and-walnut bar. A DJ spins ambient house music for the largely European crowd. While the tables are great for groups, the bar has an unassuming singles scene. *Daily 5pm-4am.* B≡

Hot Tip: Reserve a table in the back of the room to the west of the bar. There your sightlines are clear, and you won't have people crowding your table.

EXPERIENCE NEW YORK

Time flies when you're having fun, and a New York minute consists of about three seconds. That's why we've developed four unique itineraries that will allow you to maximize your experience in the Big Apple according to your tastes. If you want to hit the town with the glamorous "in" crowd and go where the Hilton sisters go to blow off steam, *Hot New York* (p.50) is just your style. If you're looking for the buzzing scene and beautiful people, but without the velvet-rope hassles, you'll want to check out *Cool New York* (p.80). *Original New York* (p.110) is a blend of all things that, as gossip columnist Cindy Adams might say, could be found "only in New York, kids." And finally, *Classic New York* (p.134) offers the storied world where Cary Grant and Deborah Kerr might have had an *Affair to Remember*.

Hot New York

In 1964, trend-spotting Supreme Court Justice Potter Stewart said of pornography, "I know it when I see it." Hot New York works that way too—minus the leather, chains, and random pool boys. (The less judicial can find what's "hot" by following the long lines of well-dressed people and flashing cameras). These spots change in a New York second, so while the Statue of Liberty might provide longer-lasting photo images of one's trip to the Big Apple, Hot New York leaves visitors with a feel for the pulse of this raging city. Hot venues may have fair-weather fans, but they're always in season. Bring your A-Game to these places, because they're in the big leagues, baby.

Note: Venues in bold are described in detail in the listings that follow the itinerary. Those with an asterisk are recommended for both drinks and dinner.

Hot New York:
The Perfect Plan (3 Days and Nights)

Highlights

Thursday

Mid-morning	Madison Avenue, Whitney Museum
Lunch	La Goulue, Fred's
Mid-afternoon	Museum of TV & Radio, Jon Stewart
Pre-dinner	Garden, Plunge
Dinner	Spice Market*, Ono
Nighttime	B.E.D. NY*
Late-night	Cain, Marqee, Quo, Bungalow 8

Friday

Breakfast	Hotel
Mid-morning	MoMA
Lunch	The Modern*, BiCE
Mid-afternoon	Spa at Mandarin
Pre-dinner	Fifty Seven Fifty Seven
Dinner	Mr. Chow, Le Bilboquet
Nighttime	Frederick's*, 58*
Late-night	G Spa, Level V, Cielo

Saturday

Breakfast	Pastis, French Roast
Mid-morning	United Nations
Lunch	Gotham Bar and Grill
Mid-afternoon	Meatpacking shopping
Pre-dinner	The Park*
Dinner	Kittichai, Lever House
Nighttime	MObar, Flatiron Lounge
Late-night	Hiro Lounge, Snitch

Morning After

Brunch	Bette

Hotel: Hotel Gansevoort

10am Stroll Madison Avenue, one of the prettiest and most exclusive shopping blocks in the world. Start on the east side of 60th Street walking north past Valentino, Donna Karan, Prada, and Ralph Lauren's flagship store. Don't worry about what you're missing on the other side of the street—you'll see it later.

11am It's three-quarters of a mile from 60th to 75th Street and the **Whitney Museum of American Art**, where urban landscape artist Edward Hopper held his first ever one-artist show in 1920 (before the Whitney was an actual museum). His work is a highlight of the permanent collection.

12:30pm Round out your window shopping by returning down the west side of Madison Avenue (go ahead, break in that credit card), with stores such as Armani, Clyde's Drug Store, Lalique, and Carolina Herrera.

1:30pm Lunch **La Goulue**, a Parisian-style bistro at its most air-kissingly chic, is en route. At the end of your Madison Avenue walk is another option, the often-frenetic

Fred's at Barneys New York atop the famous department store (a must-stop shop).

3:30pm A bit further south, check out the past and present of American entertainment chronicled at the **Museum of Television and Radio**. Lose yourself in the nostalgic displays, from Mr. Rogers' sweater to a rebuilt scene from *M*A*S*H*. If you'd rather see TV history in the making, plan in advance for tickets to a taping of *The Daily Show with Jon Stewart*.

7pm Midtown is lively by day, but hot New York nights happen downtown. There's no better place to start cocktailing than one of the Hotel Gansevoort's two outdoor options—either the aptly named **The Garden of Ono*** in back, or the rooftop deck, **Plunge** (hopefully a reference to its swimming pool).

8:30pm Dinner Follow the red brick road a block west through the Meatpacking District to Jean-George's Vongerichten and Gray Kunz's **Spice Market***, where Chinese "street food" meets an A-list clientele. If you can't get a table, try the more accessible but still über-fashionable scene at Jeffery Chodorow's **Ono**, serving pan-Asian cuisine to a loungey vibe. The **Strip House**, in Greenwich Village, will more than satisfy experienced meat lovers.

11pm West Chelsea is home to the hottest of New York hotspots. Starting with **B.E.D. NY***, also a trendy dining spot, sip mixologist Dale Degroff's legendary cocktails while lounging on a futon in your socks. Groovedeck, B.E.D.'s "top bunk," is a great outdoor lounge that provides a fashionable bird's-eye view over the neighborhood.

12:30am Within a mere 100 yards of B.E.D. are three of the hottest clubs on earth: opulent, South African–themed **Cain**; celebrity-filled **Marquee**; and slightly less scene-y, but still sizzling **Quo**.

2am Why go back to the hotel when you can hobnob with the celebrities at Amy Sacco's **Bungalow 8** across the street? This club hosts more high-profile glitterati than anywhere in the Big Apple, and though it stays open until 4am, know that the later it gets, the harder it is to get past the velvet rope.

Friday

9:30am Grab breakfast at **Ono** in the hotel, where you can contemplate which remedy works best—coffee or hair of the dog that bit you?

11am Take a cab to the **Museum of Modern Art**, more commonly known as MoMA, where the off-beat and sometimes interactive postmodern and avant-garde works will astound even the uninitiated (and the people-watching is fantastic).

1:30pm Lunch You don't have to travel far to enjoy one of New York's best lunches at the ultra-hip and aptly named **The Modern***. (There's also excellent lighter fare in the museum's **Cafe 2**.) For an Italian spin with a similar vibe, **BiCE Ristorante** is just around the corner.

3:30pm You could go back into the galleries, or just as easily head off to your spa appointment. If you're uptown, one of the best is **The Spa at Mandarin Oriental**; if downtown, try **Bliss Soho**.

6:30pm For an uptown drink in a tranquil setting, the bar at **Fifty Seven Fifty Seven,** inside the Four Seasons Hotel, ensures a classy start to your evening.

8pm Dinner Mr. Chow's chichi Chinese is where Warhol and the gang used to go to eat—and you too may have to sell a painting to cover the tab. For something *très français*, make your reservations at the stylish bistro **Le Bilboquet**. A chic newcomer nearby, **Frederick's Madison**, adds Spanish and Italian fare to its French-Mediterranean menu.

11pm Take advantage of Frederick's Madison's complimentary limo service to take you to the über-

chic, *après-dîner* lounge/night-club **Frederick's***. If this posh, sophisticated scene doesn't do it for you, walk a block west to the high-energy club **58***, where house DJs spin on weekends.

1am For late night, it's back to the Meatpacking District. You'll need to be in your hottest digs to get into the semiprivate nightclub **G Spa & Lounge**. You could also work those clothes at sexy, subterranean **Level V**. Should your dancing feet still have some life in them, visit **Cielo**, where Friday's Turntables on the Hudson party will be buzzing with a stylish European crowd.

Saturday

8am You brought golf clubs to New York?! About 40 minutes away is Farmingdale's **Bethpage State Park** golf course, a "black course" known for challenging even the best players, just as it did at the 2002 US Open. Of course, you'll miss out on ...

9:30am breakfast at **Pastis**, a fashionable bistro just a croissant's toss from the hotel, which is often filled with last night's flashy club crowd. If you're in need of fresh air and lots of coffee, stroll about half a mile east and grab an outdoor table at the brasserie **French Roast**.

11am World peace? We're not quite there yet, but a visit to the **United Nations** will give you a sense of who's on the case, and allow you to glimpse its Chagall stained-glass window.

1pm Lunch While golfers will have to settle for a hot dog at the cantina, it'll feel much more New York to eat at either the dramatic **Gotham Bar and Grill** or the upscale-rustic **Gramercy Tavern***.

3pm The Meatpacking District not only hosts some of the best restaurants and clubs, but has über chic stores as well. With shops like **Jeffrey New York**, Alexander McQueen, and **Stella McCartney**, you may feel like you're at the center of the shopping universe.

6:30pm Although primarily thought of as a restaurant, you can cool down your overheated credit card around the corner at **The Park***. Its charming, tree-lined patio is a dreamy spot for summer cocktail sipping, and the indoor fireplace is perfect for warming frozen toes in winter.

8:30pm Dinner Tonight's choices require a well-worth-it cab ride. When it comes to restaurant design, two of the city's most innovative are **Kittichai**, serving Thai food in Soho, and midtown's **Lever House**, with New American cuisine presented in a honeycombed setting. For a live-

lier scene, the French brasserie **Orsay** caters to fun-lovers of the Upper East Side.

11pm Uptowners might opt for a sophisticated drink with a view at the Mandarin Oriental's **MObar**. Back in the Flatiron District, the low-key, art deco **Flatiron Lounge** serves some of the city's best cocktails. Obsessed golfers can continue the gaming life at Jay Z's upscale sports lounge, **40/40 Club**.

1am New York loves its late nights, most of all on Saturdays. Located between the Flatiron and Meatpacking Districts, **Hiro Lounge** mixes rock and hip-hop for a model-and-rock-star–heavy crowd. At **Snitch**, co-owners Duff McKagan and Scott Weiland have been known to turn up spontaneously on the stage. If you're not up for rock, **Gypsy Tea**, which shares a wall with the restaurant Sapa, spins hip-hop, house, and '80s dance tunes.

The Morning After
Cap off your weekend with brunch at **Bette**, run by Amy Sacco (of Bungalow 8 fame), where the A-list nightlifers come to nurse their hangovers, and empirical evidence proves that models really do eat!

Hot New York:
The Key Neighborhoods

HOT

Chelsea This is the "it" neighborhood, with a cutting-edge art gallery scene and the most prestigious nightlife district on earth, particularly the West 27th Street strip. Weekends here are filled with those wishing to check out the newest clubs, but weekday evenings are often more fun, as that's when the VIPs come out to play.

Meatpacking District In terms of quality and quantity of nightclubs and singles, this was the West 27th Street of two years ago, but it still goes head to head with its northern neighbor. Because it's "old," the Meatpacking District doesn't get the celebrity visits and subsequent press it once did, but its cobblestone streets are always crowded, particularly on weekends. This area has also become home to some of the trendiest shops in New York.

Midtown With a few noteworthy exceptions, Midtown isn't as nightlife crazy as many downtown areas, but it is essentially the heart of the city, which means an awful lot of people are there looking for things to do. Not surprisingly, top-flight hotels, restaurants, and stores are there to help them.

Soho The best downtown shopping happens on and around Soho's Broadway stretch. It has lost the cutting-edge vibe it had in the '80s when scores of struggling artists lived and worked in illegal sublets, creating the works we now see in this area's many galleries, but scattered among the tourists, models and rock stars can still be spotted.

Upper East Side Central Park and a few of the world's finest museums are major attractions of this well-heeled part of town, which also offers some of the city's finest shopping and dining. There is no edge at all to the Upper East Side—it's (relatively) clean, refined, and moneyed, and its residents demand nothing less than the best.

Upper West Side · Central Park · Upper East Side · Midtown · Chelsea · Flatiron · Murray Hill · Meatpacking District · Gramercy · West Village · Greenwich Village · East Village · Soho · Tribeca · Little Italy · Chinatown · Lower East Side · Williamsburg · Wall Street · Brooklyn

Hot New York:
The Shopping Blocks

Madison Avenue (Upper East Side)

Welcome to designer row—the city's Rodeo Drive (or is it vice versa?). Donna, Calvin, and Ralph may all be quintessentially American, having worked their way from the bottom up, but they proudly stake their claim here, along with the top European houses.

Barneys New York Sophisticated but not stuffy, this designer department store manages to attract both the Upper East Side's old guard and downtown's fashion elite. 660 Madison Ave. (61st St.), 212-826-8900

Clyde's on Madison A rich emporium for the senses, this upscale pharmacy stocks European beauty products that you just can't find anywhere else. Even downtown girls come here to stock up—and enjoy great service. 926 Madison Ave. (74th St.), 212-744-5050

Ito En Hailed as the most beautiful teashop in the city, Ito En sells almost every imaginable type of tea from Asia in a lovely Zen atmosphere. 822 Madison Ave. (69th St.), 212-988-7111

Prada The store interior is as of-the-moment as the clothing and accessories. This trend-setting designer extraordinaire caters to both sexes, leaving a trail of knock-offs behind her. 841 Madison Ave. (70th St.), 212-327-4200

Ralph Lauren Set in a white mansion, the wood-paneled floors, oil paintings, hand-carved staircase, fully decorated rooms (everything is for sale), and familiar style of clothing offer a taste of the good life. 867 Madison Ave. (E. 72nd St.), 212-606-2100

Meatpacking District

Beef wholesalers (hence the area's name) are baffled by the sudden influx of well-heeled beauties dropping into the fashionable stores that line the western edge of Manhattan, particularly Washington Street.

An Earnest Cut & Sew The unisex ode to a trendy denim line offers off-the-rack and custom builds (in a few hours). 821 Washington St. (Gansevoort St.), 212-242-3414

Jeffrey New York In this upscale mini–department store, men and women will find plenty of designer clothing, shoes, and housewares to covet. (p.77) 449 W. 14th St. (9th Ave.), 212-206-1272

Scoop Something of a phenomenon, Scoop has disseminated its accessible, yet über-trendy, unisex wares. This location is more laid-back and not as mobbed. 430 W. 14th St. (Washington St.), 212-691-1905

Stella McCartney Airbrushed tees, tank tops, boots, and jewel-encrusted accessories make this designer's shop more than celeb-worthy. (p.78) 429 W. 14th St. (10th Ave.), 212-255-1556

Hot New York:
The Hotels

Chambers—A Hotel • Midtown • Modern (77 rms)
With its wall of glass and grand portal, the exterior of the Chambers Hotel looks like a posh nightclub. Inside, it's clearly an edgy, boutique hotel, with leather covered columns, high ceilings, and a two-story lobby fireplace. Fourteen floors, each designed by a different artist, accommodate a clientele of rambling celebrities and socialites. Displayed inside the hotel's 77 rooms are over 500 pieces of original art, including one by quirky film director John Waters. The rooms run from simply stunning to Deluxe, with luxuriant textures of silk, velvet, and mohair, and vibrant bursts of color. The Deluxe "04" line is on the corner, which means lighter rooms that at least feel bigger. Town, the New American restaurant within the hotel, is excellently scene-y, thanks largely to the glamorous guests of the Chambers, who seem to be in a perpetual state of transition to or from some fabulous affair. The hotel is pet friendly, which means you might see a few Gucci-clad lap dogs leading their people through the lobby. 24-hour desk. $$$ 15 W. 56th St. (5th Ave.), 212-974-5656 / 866-613-9330, chambershotel.com

Four Seasons Hotel New York • Midtown • Timeless (368 rms)
The 52-story limestone tower designed by I.M. Pei and overlooking Central Park looks like something you'd see in a movie; many of its guests, you have. This luxury hotel attracts celebrities of every kind. Its 1,500-square foot Presidential Suite, where Michael Jackson once spent three months, is among the best hotel rooms on earth. In a city where even the priciest hotel rooms are often small, the Four Seasons rises above the fray, with 370 rooms averaging 600 square feet apiece, including separate sitting areas and dressing rooms. The 120-square-foot marble bathrooms feature deep soaking tubs and separate showers. You can count on a Central Park view from the Park View Tower, though Deluxe rooms are slightly bigger, and likely to have great views as well. The Four Seasons attracts an older crowd, and is more about living it up than partying down. Should you want a ride anywhere in the Midtown area, request one of the hotel's private cars. $$$$$ 57 E. 57th St. (5th Ave.), 212-758-5700 / 800-819-5053, fourseasons.com

Hotel Gansevoort • Meatpacking District • Trendy (187 rms)
The location of this ultramodern, stylish hotel—the once sprawling industrial Meatpacking District and nearby West Chelsea—is almost too hot to sustain life. You won't find many business travelers or camera-toting tourists here. The upscale, social, good-looking clientele have come for the throbbing area nightlife, especially nearby hotspots like the Spice Market and Level V. LED light boxes change the color of the hotel's luminous exterior each night, and the lobby's über-hip mohair panels and eelskin columns foreshadow the chicness of the rooms. Plasma TVs, featherbeds, and closet and bathroom doors that glow with rosy or indigo light make these some of the most aesthetic digs in town. Hotel Gansevoort's duplex penthouse suite may be the height of hotel hot-dom, but you can't beat the Grande Deluxe River View rooms for window gazing. The higher you go, the better the view. $$$$ 18 9th Ave. (13th St.), 212-206-6700 / 877-426-7386, hotelgansevoort.com

Mandarin Oriental • Upper West Side • Modern (251 rms)
Occupying floors 35 to 54 of the Time Warner Building, the Mandarin Oriental is modern, polished, and popular. Between Lincoln Center and Midtown, over-looking Central Park, its towers stand out of the sleek cityscape like the best-looking person at a party. The rooms are modern, with chic, Asian-themed details, like sumptuous fabrics, sleek lines, and freshly cut flowers to match the furniture and linens. Fantastic views abound, with floor-to-ceiling windows in each room (some soaking tubs even have a view). People tend to pay more for the Central Park view rooms, but the corner Hudson River view is awesome. Below the hotel, the building houses several upscale shops, and four-star restaurants Gray's Café, V Steakhouse, Masa, and Per Se. Bilevel Asiate, on the lobby floor, offers a spectacular city vista, as does MObar, the sexy, lushly dec-orated cocktail lounge, where there's generally a wait for a seat. $$$$$ 80 Columbus Circle (W. 60th St.), 212-805-8800 / 866-801-8880, mandarinoriental.com

The Mercer Hotel • Soho • Trendy (75 rms)
The Mercer is the quintessential Soho hotel—posh, yet so understated it hides in plain sight. The Romanesque Revival building once held loft spaces for the artists who made this area hot before high rents drove them out. Now it's the place to be for ultrahip jet-setters and visiting celebrities drawn to the hotel's comfortable atmosphere, as well as its easy access to the trendy Soho scene. The best rooms are the Deluxe Studios, with the street side series getting the most light. The hotel hosts a Jean-George's restaurant, the Mercer Kitchen, which used to draw an A-list, New York crowd before the celebrity chef's newer eateries edged it out. Beneath the restaurant is the Submercer, which was the hottest after-hours club in town before it was cited for code violations. Since you never know whether an illegal club is still operating, staying at the Mercer is like knowing the city's secret handshake. $$$$ 147 Mercer St. (Prince St.), 212-966-6060, mercerhotel.com

60 Thompson • Soho • Trendy (98 rms)
Boutique hotels can be charming but soulless, leaving visitors to return home remembering only that their stay was forgettable. That's great in Omaha, but who comes to New York for an innocuous visit? At the Thompson Hotel, guest rooms are hip in a minimalist sense, with TVs and stereos tucked away and easy to miss. Sunlight shining in through big windows, specifically in westward-fac-ing units, compliments a light aesthetic of grays, tans, and off-whites. Of the King Deluxe rooms, those ending in "03" tend to be about 20 square feet larg-er, and are guaranteed to be remodeled. The location—a quiet block in the most convenient of areas, is ideal for jet-setters who've already seen all the tourist attractions. While it's a favorite of 20- and 30-somethings enjoying early suc-cess or a generous inheritance, those over 40 won't feel at all out of place here; the "hipness" is universal and unintrusive. The hotel's restaurant, Kittichai, and fun hotel lounges round out the incentives. $$$$ 60 Thompson St. (Broome St.), 212-431-0400 / 877-431-0400, 60thompson.com

Soho Grand • Soho • Trendy (363 rms)

Owned by the Hartz Mountain Group, the Soho Grand and its nearby sister, the Tribeca Grand Hotel, are faves of celebrities and fashion industry types, largely because they cater to human and mongrel alike. The entrance to the Soho Grand welcomes pooches and their credit card–toting leash holders with an antique marble dog trough. Inside, an illuminated glass staircase ascends from the lobby suspended from cast iron cables. The rooms may not be big, but hipsters love their uniqueness. Each interior is like an homage to the creativity of Soho artists, with furniture reminiscent of something you'd find in a sculptor's studio or an illustrator's office. Ask for a Deluxe Corner Room with two windows (generally the "04" line—the higher the better). Fido may not get much exercise in the room, but the hotel has dog walkers on staff, and pups are allowed in the lounges. Soho Grand's two hotel bars have a stylish industrial theme befitting Downtown. The Grand Bar is a good place to have a cocktail and appraise the scene. $$$$ 310 W. Broadway (Grand St.), 212-965-3000, sohogrand.com

Tribeca Grand Hotel • Tribeca • Trendy (203 rms)

Maybe it's the big iron-framed clock outside or the cosmopolitan crowd in the lobby, but there's something *très français* about this oh-so-hip hotel. The stunning lobby has walls of windows and a lofty, eight-story atrium culminating in a dramatic skylight. Each room features state-of-the-art technical amenities, including Bose CD players and iPods that have been programmed by one of the fantastic DJs who routinely work the hotel's lower level club and special events area. There's only one Executive King room per floor, and they have the best layout for space. Corner King rooms are slightly smaller, but have a better view. A diverse array of American cuisine is available until late in the Church Lounge, where people come to see and be seen (especially on weekends, when the velvet rope comes out). $$$ 2 6th Ave. (White St.), 212-519-6600 / 877-519-6600, tribecagrand.com

W New York—Union Square • Gramercy • Modern (270 rms)

Atop Todd English's fabulous Olives restaurant and Rande Gerber's Underbar stands the W New York—Union Square, a smoothly operated hotel, where old-world sophistication meets ultramodern panache. Inside the granite-and-limestone facade of the nearly century-old Beaux Arts building is a sumptuous, chic design. Sexy, arching windows overlook the vibrant bustle of Union Square, and lush plants climb the walls. The black-clad hotel staff look like fashion models, and the lobby buzzes with lookers who flock to the dimly lit bar for evening cocktails. Located between Midtown and Wall Street, and only steps from Union Square, the W New York is in the thick of it all. The rooms are luxurious, with 250-thread-count linens, Aveda bath products, and CD and video libraries selected to please an eclectic, if discerning, clientele. "Mega" rooms have a view of Union Square Park. $$$$ 201 Park Ave. S. (E. 17th St.), 212-253-9119 / 888-625-5144, whotels.com

Hot New York:
The Restaurants

B.E.D. NY* • Chelsea • New American
Best Of-the-Moment Dining The "bed" trend swept NYC's restaurants and clubs in late 2004, but this is where bed-heads now go to get three sheets to the wind. A respectable, but limited, menu is served to patrons who trade their shoes for new slipper-socks, and assume reclining positions on custom-made futons piled high with pillows. At the bar, cocktails from mixology king Dale DeGroff are served to a singles-y crowd lulled by trance music and slow-motion images projected onto a screen. The rooftop portion of this space, Groovedeck, is a runaway summer sensation. *Tue-Thu 7pm-midnight, Fri-Sat 7pm-1am, Sun 2-7pm, Tue-Sat bar open until 4am.* $$$ ⓎⒻⓘ≡ 530 W. 27th St. (9th Ave.), 212-594-4109, bedny.com

Babbo • Greenwich Village • Italian (G)
Celebrity chef Mario Batali's Babbo Cookbook was popular with the New Yorkers who already loved his restaurants Otto and Lupa. Nowhere else can you find an aggressive Italian menu like Babbo's, with items like lambs brain francobilli and goose liver ravioli. The restaurant is located in a charming, Euro-minimalist townhouse with warm, mustard-colored walls and natural wood seats. Those without a reservation at least a month in advance will be doomed to join the begging masses at the bar. *Mon-Sat 5:30-11:30pm, Sun 5-11pm.* $$ Ⓑ⎵ 110 Waverly Pl. (MacDougal St.), 212-777-0303, babbonyc.com

Bette • Chelsea • New American
If this homey, earth-toned restaurant's clientele looks more like the beautiful, velvet-rope crowd than your average diners, it's because the owner is Club Queen Amy Sacco, who also operates one of the city's hottest nightspots, Bungalow 8. Though the French/New American cuisine is prepared by a former Jean-Georges chef, this place is all about the scene. Bette is one of those places where you can dress up by dressing down, if you know how to pull off bourgeois-bohemian. Still, best to err on the side of fancy. *Daily noon-5pm and 6-11:30pm.* $$ Ⓑ≡ 461 W. 23rd St. (10th Ave.), 212-366-0404

BiCE Ristorante • Midtown • Italian
The light-wood, floral-accented decor may seem familiar to those who've dined in one of the 40-plus BiCE restaurants in this upscale franchise, stretching from Buenos Aries to Abu Dubai. Items like beef carpaccio don't get more complicated than a shake of parmesan, but dishes like duck with spinach and sunflower seeds will sate the more adventurous palate. The vibe can be a bit stuffy here, where the entertainment is mostly on your plate. *Mon-Fri 11:30am-midnight, Sat noon-midnight, Sun noon-11pm.* $$$ ≡ 7 E. 54th St. (5th Ave.), 212-688-1999, bicenewyork.com

Blue Ribbon Sushi • Soho • Sushi
Best Sushi This is where couples fall in love with tuna and eel, then make out with each other. The front dining area is pleasant, with distressed walls and a minimalist wood decor, but the scene is in the back room. During the day,

HOT

suit-clad clans of businessmen make deals at the group tables, but after 9pm, the crowd deals in a different kind of mergers and acquisitions. Even at 1am, late-night diners may find themselves waiting for a table. The hosts won't take reservations, but they will take a cell phone number and call when a table becomes available. *Mon-Sun noon-2am.* $$$ ᴮ≣ 119 Sullivan St. (Spring St.), 212-343-0404, blueribbonrestaurants.com

Bread Bar @ Tabla* • Gramercy • Indian Fusion
Best Informal Upscale Restaurants Bread Bar, known for its highly creative, Indian-influenced cocktails, is the informal half of the bilevel restaurant Tabla, which is among the city's most successful and inventive eateries. The Tablatini, a refreshing cocktail of citron vodka, fresh pineapple juice, and lemongrass, sets the stage for an excellent tandoori steak. Beyond the colorful, mosaic tile ceiling is the small, but busy, outdoor space, much coveted in summer's after-work hours. Get there before 5pm, and you're sure to be at the top of the caste system when the booze and schmooze begins. *Mon-Sat noon-11pm, Sun 5:30-10:30pm.* $ ⅩF≣ 11 Madison Ave. (25th St.), 212-889-0667, tablanyc.com

Café Boulud • Upper East Side • French
The younger—and less formal—sibling to Daniel Boulud's grande-dame restaurant, Daniel, Café Boulud offers exquisite French fare in an intimate dining room awash in earthy hues. Burnished mahogany-lined walls and cream curtains give way to rich brown banquettes, carved dark-wood chairs, and elegant lamps with rice-paper shades. The menu reveals Boulud's classical training, with such marvels as tender beef with black truffle, leeks, and poached foie gras. *Tue-Sat noon-2:30pm, daily 5:45-11pm.* $$$ ⊟ 20 E. 76th St. (Madison Ave.), 212-772-2600, danielnyc.com/cafeboulud

Cafe 2 (Museum of Modern Art) • Midtown • Italian
Of the three Danny Meyers restaurants in MoMa (The Modern, Café 2, and Terrace 5), Café 2 is the best bet for lunch. A community table lined with stylishly upholstered chairs could be an exhibit in the museum. The aesthetic style is modern meets Roman rosticceria, but the menu is purely Italian. Pastas, panini, and imported meats figure prominently. Of course, the vinos are Italiano, and the selection goes well beyond the expected museum options of either red or white. *Sat-Mon and Wed-Thu 11am-5pm, Fri 11am-7:30pm.* $ ≣ 11 W. 53rd St. (6th Ave.), 212-708-9400, moma.org/visit_moma/restaurants.html

Chow Bar* • West Village • Asian
With its seductive decor of Chinese calligraphy, paper lanterns, dark-wood veneer, and low red lighting, Chow Bar is as sexy as it is lively. Diners who don't like surprises will find comfort in menu items like the Szechuan steak-frîtes, but the noodle dishes, which combine lobster, caviar, and other fascinating fixings, are welcomingly complex. The Green Dragon Apple martini is also worth a try. Though the small dining area is comfortable, it offers no sanctuary from the noisy bar. And Chow Bar can get quite noisy. *Mon-Thu 5-11pm, Fri-Sat 5pm-midnight, Sun noon-4pm and 5-10pm.* $$ ⅩF≣ 230 W. 4th St. (W. 10th St.), 212-633-2212

Ciao Bella • Soho • Dessert
When we scream for ice cream, Ciao Bella hears our cry ... and offers us gelato. The exciting flavors of this New York favorite include espresso and pistachio,

hazelnut, and really fruity sorbets like mango, lemon, and coconut. These treats call out to the Soho area shoppers who need a break from sucking in their stomachs to pull on those designer jeans. There are also Ciao Bella locations in Chinatown and the Upper East Side, and it isn't uncommon to find it on the menus of finer restaurants. *Daily 11am-10pm.* $- ⊟ 285 Mott St. (Prince St.), 212-431-3591, ciaobellagelato.com

Cupping Room Café* • Soho • Cafe
Here's a piece of old New York, complete with pressed tin ceilings and a potbellied stove. An L-shaped restaurant and pub known for its sirloin burgers and broccoli omelets, the Cupping Room is said to be one of the city's oldest dining institutions (established 1877). Live bands play on Monday, Wednesday, and Friday, and there's never a cover charge to see them. All bands are a bit jazzy, with Monday's shows generally having a South American bent. *Sun-Thu 8am-midnight, Fri-Sat 8am-2am.* $$ ⒷⒷ⊟ 359 W. Broadway (Broome St.), 212-925-2898, cuppingroomcafe.com

davidburke & donatella • Upper East Side • New American
Despite the frenetic culinary offerings that range from Butterscotch Panna Cotta to an "angry lobster cocktail," this is no corny theme joint. The white-on-white decor is striking, and a limo is kept on the ready so that smokers can light up in comfort (which the big spenders appreciate, especially when toting armloads of shopping bags from nearby Bloomingdales). Unfortunately, the crowd isn't nearly as fun as the cuisine. Despite the huge mirrors on every wall, no one's here to people-watch. *Mon-Fri noon-2:30pm and 5-10:30pm, Sat 5-10:30pm, Sun 11am-2:30pm and 4:30-9pm.* $$$$ ⊟ 133 E. 61st St. (Park Ave.), 212-813-2121, dbdrestaurant.com

Dylan Prime* • Tribeca • Steak House
Best Steak Houses Steak houses often tend to be a bit cliché—bloated old business guys sipping bourbon and hitting on waitresses. Dylan Prime is not your grandfather's steak house. This trendy, upscale version has honeyed tones and a menu offering lighter options than the expected cartoonish brontoburgers. The stylishness of this chophouse sends the chicer side of Wall Street into the lounge next door, rather than home to bed. That said, ridiculously heavy steaks are certainly available, and they're among the city's best. *Mon-Wed noon-2:30pm and 5:30-11pm, Thu-Fri noon-2:30pm and 5:30pm-midnight, Sat 5:30pm-midnight, Sun 5:30-10pm.* $$$ ⒷⒷ⊟ 62 Laight St. (Greenwich St.), 212-334-4783, dylanprime.com

E.A.T. • Upper East Side • Deli
Best Delis For noshing on the East Side, there's no better spot than cheery E.A.T., where you can fill up on overstuffed sandwiches—from juicy roast lamb and chopped liver on raisin nut bread to the aptly named "Tower of Bagel"—and to-die-for blintzes and blinis. In a word, it's D.E.L.I.C.I.O.U.S. Owner Eli Zabar—youngest son of the creators of the famed Zabar's deli on the West Side—has followed in his family's footsteps—and then some. *Daily 7am-10pm.* $ ⊟ 1064 Madison Ave. (80th St.), 212-772-0022, elizabar.com

Fred's at Barneys New York • Upper East Side • American
It's hard to resist ordering a brontosaurus burger and pterodactyl omelet when eating in a place called Fred's at Barneys. Go ahead—this upscale joint has a sense of humor. Of course, any restaurant on the ninth floor of one of New York's

hippest department stores is going to be all about accessories, and the toppings on these big, juicy burgers are made from the freshest meats and veggies. Shopaholics abound, and this crowd always looks fabulous. *Mon-Fri 11:30am-9pm, Sat 11am-8pm, Sun 11am-6pm.* $$$ ▤ 660 Madison Ave., 9th Fl., (60th St.), 212-833-2200, barneys.com

Frederick's Madison • Upper East Side • French

Upper East Side precision meets Riviera Mediterranean chic in this hot bistro that opened in 2005. Tables are pushed tightly together in the gold-hued dining room; the French doors overlooking Madison Avenue are where you want to be. The menu takes its inspiration from various cuisines, most prominently French, Spanish, and Italian Mediterranean. Frederick's restaurant is owned by the LeSort Brothers, who also run the nearby Frederick's lounge. (Complimentary limousine rides between the venues are offered to patrons.) *Mon-Fri 8am-11pm, Sat 11:30am-11pm, Sun noon-11pm.* $$$ ▤ 768 Madison Ave. (66th St.), 212-737-7300, fredericksnyc.com

French Roast • Greenwich Village • French

Best All-Night Restaurants One could do worse than starting the day at this Franco-American bistro, where sidewalk seating is a summertime sensation and the rich wood interior is a termite's dream. While people do come here for romantic dinners, French Roast is at its best in the morning, when sipping the fantastic coffee to a soundtrack of vintage jazz could inspire the dimmest rube to write award-winning poetry. Breakfasts feature French toast and simple egg plates, and lunchtime satisfies with chicken salad sandwiches and mesclun salad. *24/7.* $$ ꓛ▤ 78 W. 11th St. (6th Ave.), 212-533-2233, tourdefrancenyc.com

Gotham Bar and Grill • Greenwich Village • New American (G)

Chef-cum-author Alfred Portali's Gotham Bar and Grill is an unflinchingly masculine place, where even the confident and bold American cuisine seems to work out at the gym. High ceilings, stately columns, latticed windows, and generously spaced tables keep the crowded room from feeling claustrophobic. The $25 lunch prix fixe and half-bottle wine options attract a buzzing lunchtime scene. There are cozy nooks and crannies in the back of the room, where couples enjoy privacy. However, the seats along the long wall opposite the bar work best for gazing at the handsome clientele. *Mon-Fri noon-2:15pm, Mon-Thu 5:30-10pm, Fri 5:30-11pm, Sat 5-11pm, Sun 5-10pm.* $$$ ꓐ▃ 12 E. 12th St. (5th Ave.), 212-620-4020, gothambarandgrill.com

Gramercy Tavern* • Gramercy • New American (G)

There are two insider secrets about this place. First, the dining room is nice, but the Tavern Room, with its draperies, dark wood, and wood-burning stove, is more real-deal New York (though they don't take reservations). Second, dinner here ranks among the city's top 50, but lunch is an easy top 5—that's when you want to go. The menu has an organic, if not obvious, logic to it. Cod with brussels sprouts, potato boulangère, and apple cider? Sure. Rabbit with roasted shallots, garlic sausage, olives, rosemary, and potato purée? But of course. *Dining room Mon-Thu noon-2pm and 5:30-10pm, Fri noon-2pm and 5:30-11pm, Sat 5:30-11pm, Sun 5:30-10pm. The Tavern Mon-Thu noon-11pm, Fri-Sat noon-midnight, Sun 5:30-10pm.* $$$$ ꓬꓞ▤ 42 E. 20th St. (Park Ave.), 212-477-0777, gramercytavern.com

Kittichai • Soho • Thai

Best Asian Dining There's no shortage of Thai food in the city, but there is a considerable quality deficiency. A stylish restaurant in the hip 60 Thompson Hotel, Kittichai hits the peak of panache without slipping over the top. Colorful orchids abound in this sleek room, which encircles a soothing meditation pool. Much to the liking of foodies, Kittichai's beauty isn't just decor-deep. Chef Ian Chalermkittichai's dishes are exciting and inventive, with highlights like sea bass in bean sauce and chocolate back ribs. *Call for hours.* $$ ☰ 60 Thompson Hotel, 60 Thompson St. (Spring St.), 212-219-2000, kittichairestaurant.com

Koi • Midtown • Japanese

The main room at this East Coast sister of LA's most stylish restaurant is very loud, very crowded, and very dark. Such is the way with fashionable dining, where of-the-moment scenesters collide with culinary purists who want to eat in peace. Koi's decor puts off a warm, sensual vibe, with bamboo, beige banquettes, and a giant mod fishnet covering ceilings and walls. If you can handle your heavily seasoned duck breast and hanger steaks with eye candy galore, it doesn't get much better than this. The sushi room is considerably more subdued. *Daily 7-11am. Mon-Fri noon-2:30pm, Mon-Wed 5:30-11pm, Thu-Sat 5:30-midnight, Sun 6-10pm.* $$$ B☰ 40 W. 40th St. (6th Ave.), 212-921-3330, koirestaurant.com

La Goulue • Upper East Side • French

With its brown leather banquettes and brass railings, Le Goulue feels like a typical neighborhood bistro—if your neighborhood is within walking distance of the Louvre. Named for the Moulin Rouge's most infamous dancer, immortalized by Lautrec's masterpiece "Moulin Rouge—La Goulue," this colorful fave is fit for an evening, burlesque-going crowd. Playboys like Giorgio Armani, Rod Stewart, and Jude Law have been seen at this scene, and locals Jackie O. and Catherine Deneuve used to be regulars. The steak au poivre has achieved legendary status over the past 30-plus years, and the homemade fries are *très bon.* *Mon-Sat noon-4pm and 6-11:30pm, Sun noon-4pm and 6-10:30pm.* $$$ ☰ 746 Madison Ave. (E. 64th St.), 212-988-8169, lagoulurestaurant.com

Le Bernardin • Upper East Side • Seafood (G)

Earning four out of four stars from the *New York Times,* being one of only four NYC restaurants to have received top honors from Europe's Michelin guide, honored as Zagat's top restaurant for the second year in a row (and now getting a confident nod from us), Le Bernardin had a good 2005. Eric Ripert's seafood-heavy French classic is a culinary masterwork. The seafood is swimming in butter, caviar, and rich seasonings, as ample sunlight floods through country windows. Jackets are required and advanced reservations are a very, very good idea. *Mon-Thu noon-2:30pm and 5-10:30pm, Fri noon-2:30pm and 5:30-11pm, Sat 5:30-11pm.* $$$$ ⚊ 155 W. 51st St. (6th Ave.), 212-554-1515, le-bernardin.com

Le Bilboquet • Upper East Side • French Bistro

Best French Bistros In France, *le bilboquet* is a kid's game played with a ball tethered to a stick. At this fine French restaurant, it's the excellent chef who's on the ball. The room is dimly lit and romantic, with colorful paintings accenting the formal white linen tablecloths. The waitstaff is sure to remind you of that fantastic, if slightly unfriendly, place near your hotel in the Latin Quarter. *Daily noon-11pm.* $$ ☰ 25 E. 63rd St. (Madison Ave.), 212-751-3036

HOT

Les Enfants Terribles • Tribeca • French-African

The colonial-inspired French-African Les Enfants Terribles is as exotic as the eponymous Cocteau film, with African masks, unique cocktails, and a DJ spinning worldly background tunes. A round bar reflects the global spirit of the menu, whose specialty is Korhogotefemougar, a steak frîtes dish with peppery African spices (yeah, I know. Just point at it on the menu). There's very little action in this part of town, with all of the fun concentrated in this warmly lit, palm-laden room. *Daily 9am-4pm and 5:30pm-midnight.* $ B≡ 37 Canal St. (Ludlow St.), 212-777-7518, lesenfantsterriblesnyc.com

Lever House • Midtown • New American

Best Chic Restaurants When the Four Seasons opened in 1959, it was considered "too modern." Now it's a cultural landmark and Power Lunch Central. Like the Four Seasons, Lever House is ahead of its time. With octagon-tiled walls, a 2010 tunnel of an entrance, and winning entrees like pan-roasted poussin topped with foie gras, and tuna with beet-ginger chutney, Lever House is forging the way to the future. The chic crowd dresses to impress in dark suits, little black dresses, and sparkling jewels. *Mon-Thu 11:45am-2:30pm and 5:30-11pm, Fri 11:45am-2:30pm and 5:30-11:30pm, Sat 5:30-11:30pm, Sun 5-10pm.* $$$ B≡ 390 Park Ave. (53rd St.), 212-888-2700, leverhouse.com

Megu* • Tribeca • Japanese

Best Asian Dining You don't want to miss out on Megu, a masterpiece in both design and culinary ambition, not to mention a favorite of The Donald. An iron temple bell and an uplit Buddha ice sculpture lord it over the attentive staff, who serve up tangy marinated Kobe beef and excellent uni sushi. Come early for a cocktail in the ultra-chic Kimono Lounge, which overlooks the main dining room's semicircular booths and symmetrical tables. The host warmly greets incoming patrons, and holds cabs for those departing. *Sun-Wed 5:30-10:30pm, Thu-Sat 5:30-11:30pm.* $$$$ ⓉB≡ 62 Thomas St. (Church St.), 212-964-7777, megunyc.com

The Modern* • Midtown • New American/French

Though housed in one of the world's most famous museums, the Modern has become a destination of its own. The airy main dining room, aptly designed with sleek lines and a minimalist decor, overlooks the museum's sculpture garden. Water-faring entrees reign supreme—try the duck, octopus, tuna tartare, or lobster soup. The chef uses olive oil not only to poach salmon, but to flavor ice cream (and it's surprisingly delicious). Beyond a wall of frosted glass, the lively bar offers cocktails and a lighter menu. When things get busy, snagging a table in the adjoining cafe without a lunch reservation is a possibility. *Mon-Thu noon-2:15pm and 5:30-10:30pm, Fri noon-2:15pm and 5:30-11pm, Sat 5:30-11pm.* $$$ ⓉF⎕ The Museum of Modern Art, 9 W. 53rd St. (5th Ave.), 212-333-1220, themodernnyc.com

Mr. Chow • Midtown • Chinese

Best Chic Restaurants It isn't easy staying hot for a quarter century, but somehow Mr. Chow, the most upscale of Chinese restaurants, has managed to do it. The sunken dining room is dramatic, with black lacquer and ubiquitous mirrors. Notorious customers Andy Warhol, Jean-Michel Basquiat, Keith Haring, and Julian Schnabel once painted portraits of the owner, and over the past decade these sauce-heavy wok dishes have become all the rage with hip-hop pioneers and their fussy entourages. (P. Diddy and Wyclef are regulars.) *Daily 6-11:45pm.* $$$ ▤ 324 E. 57th St. (2nd Ave.), 212-751-9030, mrchow.com

Ono • Meatpacking District • Asian Fusion
This Asian industrial hotspot is a visual feast, with vaulted ceilings, silk lanterns, and massive paintings of *yakuza* body art, all awash in a sexy low light. Spacious upstairs tables provide views of the mob scene at the lower-level bar and the Garden at Ono outdoor lounge. The menu offers everything from sushi foie gras to traditional beef and lobster entrees. Turnover is fast in order to accommodate the new waves of hipsters who line up at the reception desk, looking to see who's wearing the same Betsey Johnson dress. *Sun-Wed 7am-3pm and 5:30-11:30pm, Thu-Sat 7am-3pm and 5:30pm-12:30am.* $ ▣▤ Hotel Gansevoort, 18 9th Ave. (13th St.), 212-660-6766, hotelgansevoort.com

Orsay • Upper East Side • Brasserie
Mosaic floor tiles glisten, skillfully crafted arches bend overhead, and a zinc bartop bandies soft lighting about. Hmmm ... to eat or take pictures? Eat. This brasserie only looks like an extension of the Louvre, and the food is too good to miss. Tuna and steak tartare are both recommended at Orsay, where professionals young and old converge, though the younger Upper East Side crowd is fond of convening at the bar until closing time. *Mon-Fri noon-3pm and 5:30-11pm, Sat noon-3:30pm and 5:30-11pm, Sun 11am-3:30pm and 5:30-10pm.* $$$ ▣▤ 1057 Lexington Ave. (E. 75th St.), 212-517-6400, orsayrestaurant.com

The Park* • Chelsea • New American
It's hard to believe that this fashionable eatery, with multiple fireplaces, bearskin rugs, and regular celebrity sightings, was once a taxi garage. The featured New American cuisine ranges from basic seared tuna to heavy sausage gumbo. Outdoors, The Park boasts one of the city's finest alfresco scenes, with a shady patio that gets equal service. Unfortunately, the waitstaff is only slightly more interested in your needs than the bouncers manning the Japanese-themed nightclub upstairs, which makes The Park scene-y New York at its hottest and coldest. *Daily 10:30am-2am, bar until 4am.* $$ ▨▤ 118 10th Ave. (17th St.), 212-352-3313, theparknyc.com

Pastis • Meatpacking District • French Bistro
Best French Bistros Pastis was hot when the Meatpacking District wasn't. Now that this neighborhood has caught fire, Keith McNally's popular bistro has become legendary. On weekends, the no-frills furnished rooms with mosaic tiled floors and distressed mirrors on the walls throb with a pre-and-post–clubbing crowd. Servers are always searching for customers who've wandered to the packed bar to check out the scene. The skinny and very French french fries are a favorite, and the perfect complement to the hanger steak and roasted chicken. *Mon-Thu 6-11:30pm, Fri-Sat 6pm-12:30am, Sun 6-10:30pm, Fri-Sat the bar stays open until 3am.* $$ ▨▤ 9 9th Ave. (Little W. 12th St.), 212-929-4844, pastisny.com

Per Se • Upper West Side • French (G)
Thomas Keller, the man behind the Bay Area's wildly popular French Laundry is at it again, this time in the Upper West Side's Time Warner Building. The setting is exquisite, with pale leather walls and tables layered in white linen, and the French-New American menu includes uniquely prepared delicacies, like Keller's signature

oysters and pearls with tapioca and caviar, and rabbit in apple-smoked bacon. *Mon-Thu 5:30-10pm, Fri-Sun 11:30am-1:30pm, 5:30-10pm.* $$$$ ⊑ 10 Columbus Cir. (W. 60th St.), 212-823-9335, frenchlaundry.com/perse/

Restaurant Florent • Meatpacking District • French

Restaurant Florent is a semiseedy, yet hot, restaurant that's in the right place at the right time—namely, the Meatpacking District, 24/7. At first glance, this place looks like a spruced-up diner that could do with brighter bulbs. Upon further review, what comes to light is the trendy crowd that shows up before or after making the cut at the area's hottest nightclubs. Lunch and brunch here are popular with gallery hoppers. Restaurant Florent's evening menu has a bistro orientation of mussels, fries, and blood sausage. *24/7.* $$ 𝔽⊟ 69 Gansevoort St. (Greenwich St.), 212-989-5779, restaurantflorent.com

Sapa • Flatiron • French-Asian

Ornate hanging lamps and ubiquitous tea lights give this restaurant a clublike ambience to rival the three hot nightspots on the block. The onyx tables, fountains, and walnut floors are as stylish as the pre-clubbing clientele, and the emphasis on specialty cocktails primes them for the night. The ambitious menu is a French-Vietnamese hybrid, seasoning fish to the gills and barbecuing spareribs to the bone. The sweet pumpkin salad topped off with pumpkin seeds is an unexpected treat. *Mon-Fri 5:30-11:30pm, Sat 6pm-midnight, Sun 5:30-10:30pm.* $$ 𝔽⊟ 43 W. 24th St. (Broadway), 212-929-1800, sapanyc.com

Spice Market* • Meatpacking District • Asian Fusion

Best Of-the-Moment Dining All-star chefs Gray Kunz (Gray's Café) and Jean-Georges Vongeritchen (V, Vong, Jean-Georges) have co-created Spice Market's menu of "Asian street food," though it's hard to imagine a vending cart in Laos selling crisp squid with ginger, cashew, and papaya. Their venture into the Meatpacking District is perfect for the well-groomed, Ferrari-driving nightlifers who don't want to wear a tie to dinner. The capacious restaurant is lovely, with teak pagodas, but the downstairs lounge, which also requires a reservation, is also beautiful, with rough wood, velvety pillows, and padded banquettes. *Daily noon-3pm and 5:30pm-midnight, Fri-Sun until 1am.* $$ ⓧ𝔽⊟ 403 W. 13th St. (9th Ave.), 212-675-2322, jean-georges.com

The Spotted Pig* • West Village • British-American

If Dublin were full of superstar restaurateurs and celeb crowds, there'd be a place like the Spotted Pig on every corner. Just ask Bono, who's been spotted at this clever restaurant-cum-pub. Sure, there's shepherd's pie and well-poured pints of English and Irish ales, but one can feel the reach of well-manicured hands behind the scenes, especially when opening the menu. The Spotted Pig is an homage to the "Gastro Pub" trend sweeping Britain, where customers find themselves eating slow-braised beef where they'd expect little more than beer nuts. *Mon-Fri noon-2am, Sat-Sun 11am-2am.* $$ ⓧ𝔽⊟ 314 W. 11th St. (Greenwich St.), 212-620-0393, thespottedpig.com

The Stanton Social* • Lower East Side • New American (G)

Whether it be the loungy upstairs space or the more formal dining area below, this modern ode to the 1940s restaurant/lounge combo wears fashion and function well. Dark-wood furnishings, rounded lamps, clean lines, and industrial fixtures set the stage for a to-share menu that is, appropriately, fare for a social night out. Kobe beef burgers typify the offerings, which also include soup dumplings and pulled barbecued pork sandwiches. The menu is a foodie favorite, though the hipper-than-thou scenester crowd may annoy those sick of the *Sex and the City* routine. *Sun 11:30am-2am, Mon-Tue 5pm-2am, Wed-Fri 5pm-3am, Sat 11:30am-3am.* $$ 99 Stanton St. (Orchard St.), 212-995-0099, thestantonsocial.com

Strip House • Greenwich Village • Steak House
Best Steak Houses Since steak is pretty much the opposite of sexy finger food, few meateries make an attempt at sultriness, settling instead for a solid and powerful design. While Strip House is certainly masculine, it's also pretty sexy. Deep red walls display black-and-white photos of burlesque performers, and what 1890 New York (and the modern-day Bible Belt) probably considered pornography. Unlike most steak houses, Strip House serves excellent side dishes, which are considered more than glorified garnish. As evidence, we submit truffled cream spinach and goose-fat potatoes as exhibits A and B. *Sun 5-11pm, Mon-Thu 5-11:30pm, Fri-Sat 5pm-midnight. The bar closes 1am Sun-Thu, 2am Fri-Sat.* $$$ 13 E. 12th St. (5th Ave.), 212-328-0000, theglaziergroup.com/restaurants/striphouse

Turks and Frogs* • West Village • Turkish
The name derives from the Turkish owners' former antique shop (chock-full of photos and ceramics of frogs). Now they've traded their fusty old trinkets for a liquor license, and stocked the joint with 60-plus Turkish wines, served along with specialty light eats, like lebni (a yogurt dip that bears a slight resemblance to fondue). The most charming feature is that the vases, plates, pictures, and furnishings in this urban *Little House on the Prairie* are for sale. *Sun-Thu 5pm-midnight, Fri-Sat 5pm-4am.* $- 323 W. 11th St. (Washington St.), 212-691-8875

212 Restaurant* • Upper East Side • New American
212 is the area code assigned to Manhattanites (some get 646s, and they're never happy about it). This deco Upper East Side hotspot, with "212" attitude, elegant skylights, and white-oak furnishings, is not only a polished restaurant with a well-regarded, if a bit uninspired, American menu, but also a lively, see-and-be-seen scene. Beyond the juicy burgers and grilled chicken are surprisingly playful desserts, such as mini donuts, butterscotch ice-cream sandwiches, and crepes oozing with Nutella. *Daily noon-midnight.* $$ 133 E. 65th St. (Park Ave.), 212-249-6565, 212restaurant.com

Vento Trattoria • Meatpacking District • Italian
It's hard to miss this triangular landmark building, which occupies one of this area's best-looking corners. Two floors of tightly packed tables host a steady mix of foodies and scene seekers—the latter making up the majority. Vento's walls of windows offer an entertaining view of the busy scene on the cobblestone streets outside. Dishes like venison sausage and shrimp tagliolini are good, but you can't beat the oven-baked pizzas. That rumbling below your feet is the hot nightclub, Level V. *Call for hours.* $$ 675 Hudson St. (14th St.), 212-699-2400, brguestrestaurants.com/restaurants/vento

Hot New York:
The Nightlife

Aer Lounge • Meatpacking District • Nightclub
This vast space of modern design is where one goes to spend an entire evening. Though the cushy sofas in the back of the main room are generally reserved, the primary dance floor is on the public perimeters. A wall of resin-encased butterflies adorns Aer's main bar, while the front of the club, which is more rock than hip-hop, is pretty much the make-out room. The beautiful VIP space downstairs is usually reserved for movie premiere parties and magazine launches, but there's no indication that regular admission requires being well connected. *Thu-Sat 10am-4am.* C≣ 409 W. 13th St. (9th Ave.), 212-989-0100, aerlounge.com

Bounce • Upper East Side • Sports Bar
On the walls of this testosterone-intensive lounge you'll find more than a dozen flat-screen TVs broadcasting sporting events to the 30- and 40-something guys bonding around the shiny zinc-top bar. After the games end, the place buzzes with attractive women in tight-fitting, trendy fashions, looking to mingle and flirt and be showered with free cocktails from Bounce owners and patrons. The kitchen cooks up well-seasoned pub food, while a late-night DJ spins spring-break party tunes. It's a beer commercial come to life, but with a surprising degree of maturity. *Mon-Thu 4pm-2am, Fri 4pm-4am, Sat noon-4am, Sun noon-1am.* F≣ 1403 2nd Ave. (73rd St.), 212-535-2183, bounceny.com

brite bar • Chelsea • Bar
Clubs in West Chelsea can be cruel. Within two blocks of brite bar are superclubs Quo, Cain, Marquee, and Bungalow 8. There's a good chance that, on a busy night, average folks won't get into any of them without a reservation. That's where a neighborly "spillover" spot like brite bar comes in. With Lite-Brite kits (complete with colored pegs and paper), lounge music, and energy-drink specialty cocktails, brite bar is also a good place to meet up with friends before tackling the more-demanding velvet-rope joints. *Mon-Wed 5:30pm-2am, Thu-Fri 5:30pm-4am, Sat 7pm-4am, Sun 8pm-2am.* B≣ 297 10th Ave. (W. 27th St.), 212-279-9706, britebar.com

Bungalow 8 • Chelsea • Nightclub
Best Clubs for Celebrity Sighting On an average week, Bungalow 8's guest list sees more celebrity names than *People* magazine. This celebrated Beverly Hills theme club has a timelessness about it that's part 1960s Social Club and part 2020 hotspot. A big skylight twinkles over green leather crescent booths and palm trees, while a small elevated balcony (partly occupied by the rock and hip-hop DJ) provides a good view for patrons who want to play Name That Olsen Twin. If you want to feel like a celeb, just order the $1,200 plate of Tsar Imperial osetra caviar. Getting into Bungalow 8 is very difficult, so it's highly recommended to have a plan B. *Daily 11pm-4am.* B≣ 515 W. 27th St. (10th Ave.), 212-279-3215

Cain • Chelsea • Nightclub

Best Clubs for Celebrity Sighting Chichi and fun converge at Cain, which is designed to look like a Cape Town game lodge. Thanks to the combined efforts of a celebrated Armani designer and a very able crew that traveled to South Africa to gather materials for Cain's decor, the theme works wonderfully. This rectangular room was a cabstand before designers rolled in a huge boulder (now the DJ booth) and constructed the place around it. Weeknights are the best times to be here, mainly because they attract a party crowd that doesn't need to get up early. *Tue-Sat 10:30pm-4am.* ☰ 544 W. 27th St. (11th Ave.), 212-947-8000, cainnyc.com

Cielo • Meatpacking District • Nightclub

Best Dance Clubs A crowd of European expats and NYC underground music fans pack into Cielo, where tunes range from modern to '80s. Singles mingle at the bar and smoke in a pleasantly heated outdoor space, while the dance floor flashes with strobes and an enormous disco ball. Since Cielo's more about music than celebs, the doorman isn't as brutal as those of nearby clubs, and Fridays are crammed to the hilt. The crowd is stylish in a dressed-down way. Funky hats are OK, but the ball cap simply won't do. *Wed-Sat 10pm-4am.* Ⓒ☰ 18 Little W. 12th St. (9th Ave.), 212-645-5700, cieloclub.com

Crobar • Chelsea • Nightclub

Unless you've been to a Crobar in Miami or Chicago, there's just no way to prepare for this experience. About 2,800 decked-out bodies groove to dance-oriented tracks on two sprawling, monstrous floors. The video-projected images, flashing lights, and occasional bursts of dry ice recall the '80s, when passionate clubbers found anonymity in venues the size of aircraft hangars. Almost everyone gets in, which means a guaranteed good night, not to mention morning. *Thu-Sun 10pm-8am.* Ⓒ☰ 530 W. 28th St. (10th Ave.), 212-629-9000, crobar.com

The Daily Show with Jon Stewart • Midtown • Performance

Best Live Tapings Those who really believe that Rob Corddry is reporting from sites all over the world, or that Stephen Colbert isn't "that" goofy in person, are in for quite a surprise at the 54th Street studio where *The Daily Show* records. Most shows air the night they tape, with the exception of the second Thursday night taping, which airs on the following Monday. After all, life doesn't stop, so why should the fake news? *Live taping starts Mon-Thu 5:45pm.* ☰ 733 11th Ave. (51st. St.), 212-586-2477, comedycentral.com

58* • Midtown • Ultra Lounge

In the early 2000s, this lower-level space was home to Au Bar, a playground of debauchery for high-earning Uptown 30-somethings. As 58, it has a different decor and smaller crowds, but the scene remains the same. A collection of strangely shaped velvet furniture and leather banquettes shares the floor with a few bars, exotic prints, and tall plants. Singles work the scene as a DJ spins house-oriented tunes for those tipsy enough to dance. Frisky patrons get cozy in two private rooms that look like African hunting lodges, complete with fake zebra-skin rugs. *Daily 10pm-4am.* Ⓕ☰ 41 E. 58th St. (Madison Ave.), 212-308-9455, 58newyork.com

HOT

Fifty Seven Fifty Seven • Midtown • Ultra Lounge

The restaurant and bar at the base of the Four Seasons Hotel is known for its hopping evenings, where power players fresh from the financial trenches linger at the bar with their "nieces from out of town." The high vaulted ceilings and brass-and-onyx chandeliers inside this I.M. Pei neo-Gothic building provide a dramatic contrast to the glamorous vivacity at the bar, where the soft lighting helps the well-heeled, well-put-together crowd look even better. The tables by the bar are reserved for hotel guests only. *Mon-Sat 3pm-1am, Sun 3pm-midnight.* ☰ Four Seasons Hotel New York, 57 E. 57th St. (Park Ave.), 212-758-5757, fourseasons.com

Flatiron Lounge • Flatiron • Lounge

This 1930s-style Chelsea cocktail lounge is the junior league for future Bemelmans and Rainbow Room regulars. An art deco main floor provides jazz tunes and possibly the best cocktails in the city for 20- and 30-something scene seekers. The bar gets crowded, so calling ahead to reserve a booth will give you a Clark Gable savoir faire. People don't exactly don fedoras to come here, but showing up in a baseball cap might prove embarrassing. Downstairs, a more modern lounge sports fiber-optic lighting that changes the color of the room nightly. *Sun-Wed 5pm-2am, Thu-Sat 5pm-4am.* ☰ 37 W. 19th St. (5th Ave.), 212-727-7741, flatironlounge.com

40/40 Club • Flatiron • Sports Bar

There are all kinds of players in Jay Z's sleek, two-story sports club, many being major league athletes in town to beat up on the hapless New York teams (Yankees excluded). Ironically, no jerseys or sneakers are permitted. On the main floor, tables revolve around the individual flat-screen TVs suspended from the ceiling, while in the bar, games are projected onto a giant slab of suspended concrete, while hip-hop tunes thump in the background. Autographed paraphernalia graces the walls of the private rooms upstairs. *Mon-Fri 5pm-4am, Sat-Sun noon-4am.* B☰ 6 W. 25th St. (6th Ave.), 212-832-4040, the4040club.com

Frederick's* • Midtown • Ultra Lounge

Midtown has been waiting for a place like this more than its residents realize. At the door, well-groomed doormen in Windsor knotted ties check the reservation list and scrutinize prospective visitors for an untied shoe or unbuttoned sleeve. Then they walk them downstairs to join the bold and the beautiful drinking specialty cocktails in the intimate lounge, designed with chic, sensual curves. The hungry devour small plates of sushi and endless eye candy. *Tue-Sat 5pm-2:30am.* F☰ 8 W. 58th St. (5th Ave.), 212-752-6200, fredericksnyc.com

G Spa & Lounge • Meatpacking District • Lounge

Those staying at the Hotel Gansevoort just might get a glimpse of this subterranean hotspot; if not, it helps to have a name like, say, Hilton. During the day, this spa is open to all, offering manicures, whirlpools, and a juice bar; at night, the doormen come out. Cocktails and sushi are brought in from Jeffrey Chodorow's Ono restaurant upstairs, and entry often becomes a zero sum game of Who-You-Know. Celebrity sightings are common both day and night. *Tue-Sat 10pm-4am.* ☰ Hotel Gansevoort, 18 9th Ave. (13th St.), 212-660-6733

The Garden of Ono* • Meatpacking District • Ultra Lounge

Just because this restaurant/lounge is an adjunct to the Hotel Gansevoort doesn't mean guests are guaranteed admission. And just because this partially enclosed outdoor space shares wall and name with restaurateur Jeffrey Chodorow's Ono doesn't guarantee that reservations at the restaurant will lead to outdoor lounging. To enjoy the cocktails and light sushi entrees, try calling to reserve an outdoor cabana, dress up in velvet-rope club garb, and arrive right on time. The small tents, which are built for four to eight and equipped with small televisions, are where you want to be. *Thu-Sat 10pm-5am.* B≡ Hotel Gansevoort, 18 9th Ave. (13th Ave.), 212-660-6766, hotelgansevoort.com

Gotham Comedy Club • Chelsea • Comedy Club

Spending your night here? Now that's a laugh ... and a pretty hearty one at that. With its oak bars, brass accents, and overwhelming entrance chandelier, Gotham is probably New York's best-looking comedy club. *The Daily Show*'s Lewis Black is a regular here, as is Todd Barry, and onsite comedy classes have given Gotham street cred with hard-working, sneaker-wearing comics. Since the comedians here tend to work more from the script than the hip, fear not the front row. *Showtimes Sun-Thu 8:30pm, Fri 8:30 and 10:30pm, Sat 7:30pm, 9:30pm, and 11:30pm.* CF— 208 W. 23rd St. (7th Ave.), 212-367-9000, gothamcomedyclub.com

Grand Bar and Lounge* • Soho • Hotel Bar

Best Hotel Lounges The Grand Bar and Lounge has the best cocktails of any hotel, anywhere (thanks to prized mixologist Sasha Petraske), and you'll want to have a bed nearby after sampling the menu from top to bottom. The Grand Bar's stylish room is awash in luscious caramel and chocolate tones, where men model European-cut suits sans ties, and fashion-conscious women show off well-exercised legs and backs. How the waitresses walk in those high heels is anyone's guess, but you'll certainly hear them coming. *Sun 7am-midnight, Mon-Thu 7am-2am, Fri-Sat 7am-4am.* B— Soho Grand Hotel, 310 W. Broadway, 2nd Fl. (Grand St.), 212-519-6500, sohogrand.com

Gypsy Tea • Flatiron • Nightclub

Gypsy Tea is the Flatiron's version of Aer Lounge. There's no real theme at work in this smoothly operated club, where two separate floors offer two entirely different evenings to choose from. Upstairs, soft orange light plays on fabric sails above the heads of weekend big spenders and singles gathered at the bar. Downstairs is where people go to move, with a modern neon dance floor and a labyrinthine VIP area, replete with vintage furniture and ornamental fish tanks. *Thu 10:30pm-4am, Fri 11pm-4am, Sat 11pm-noon.* C≡ 33 W. 24th St. (6th Ave.), 212-645-0003, gypsyteanyc.com

Hiro Lounge • Chelsea • Nightclub

Best Rock Clubs On Monday nights, Hiro Lounge becomes the most popular club in town, with guests like Mick Jagger, Famke Janssen, and P. Diddy among the high-profile crowd. This low-ceilinged, Japanese-themed lounge beneath the Maritime Hotel has a fitting underground vibe. The fashion-forward clientele favors tight denim and leather pants for the rock party after midnight. The Asian-themed cocktails are good, but seating is generally reserved for bottle service, which means showing off your platinum LP. *Thu-Sat 10pm-4am.* ≡ The Maritime Hotel, 371 W. 16th St. (9th Ave.), 212-727-0212, themaritimehotel.com

Level V • West Village • Nightclub
Best Singles Scene There's more than a little medieval charm to Level V—an underground lounge of cut stone, iron bars, and minimal lighting. It's not hard to envision the S&M parlor that occupied this space in the '90s. Now, the whips are gone and the only chains to be found are made by Tiffany's. Most reserved tables sit empty while patrons hit the dance floor. Don't like the rock, rap, funk, and soul DJ? Do like the celebs—rent one of the private rooms off the main lounge and plug your iPod into the speaker system. *Sun-Sat 8pm-4am.* B≣ 675 Hudson St. (14th St.), 212-699-2410, brguestrestaurants.com

Marquee • Chelsea • Nightclub
Best Clubs for Celebrity Sighting If you only go to one club, this is it. While Marquee is not as intimate as Cain, nor as wall-to-wall with celebrities as Bungalow 8, it just may be New York's sexiest club scene. In the center of the main room, a chandelier wraps around the spinning disco ball, scattering light over the dancing masses. Downstairs are two great lounges, one sharing with the main floor DJ, the other going rock 'n' roll. Getting in is tough, and the cover depends on the doorman's mood. *Tue-Sat 10pm-4am.* C≣ 289 10th Ave. (26th St.), 646-473-0202, marqueeny.com

MObar • Upper West Side • Hotel Bar
The bar atop the Mandarin Oriental is something to see. More accurately, the city is something to see from the bar atop the Mandarin Oriental. Of course, given MObar's popularity, those who'd rather stretch out at a table than cram around the circular counter are in for a wait. The living room–like lobby area is usually filled with slightly older hotel guests, while singles gravitate to the main bar, where the modern music is louder, and the focus turns from the Central Park view to who's in the room. *Mon-Tue 4pm-1am, Wed-Sat 4pm-2am, Sun 4pm-midnight.* ≣ Mandarin Oriental Hotel, 80 Columbus Cir., (60th St.), 212-805-8826, mandarinoriental.com

One • Meatpacking District • Lounge
This über-trendy spot, with its exposed brick walls, soaring ceilings, flickering candles, and top-shelf (and top-price) liquors, could be the poster child for the Meatpacking District. Velvet ropes are unfurled to protect cool club kids, trendsters, and models, who knock back fusion cocktails and graze on the global tapas menu, from crunchy shrimp tempura to paper-thin slivers of Kobe beef. Intimate nooks also abound, so you can enjoy a romantic tête-à-tête, but the DJ music and cute waitresses may be distracting. *Daily 5:30pm-4am.* $$ F≣ 1 Little W. 12th St. (9th Ave.), 212-255-9717, onelw12.com

Pink Elephant • Chelsea • Dance Club
Best Dance Clubs In its original Meatpacking District locale, this electronic and house music club gained a reputation as a favorite for the well-heeled with disco fever. After reopening on 27th Street in March '06, Pink Elephant's filling out its new, considerably bigger digs quite nicely. The long, dramatic hallway gives everyone the chance to make an entrance, and the podiums placed behind the booths give off a "dancing on the tables" kind of vibe. Things get rolling on the early side. Show up at 11:30pm and entry will be faster. Thursday nights are the hippest. *Tue-Sat 11pm-4am.* $$$ C≣ 527 W. 27th St. (10th Ave.), 212-463-0000, pinkelephantclub.com

Plunge • Meatpacking District • Ultra Lounge

Calling a rooftop lounge Plunge might give people crazy ideas. Fortunately, this sky-high penthouse bar gives patrons a good reason to live. Fifteen floors above the Meatpacking District, the Hotel Gansevoort hotel bar has four semienclosed lounges with views of the Hudson so jaw-dropping, it almost justifies the vertiginous price of the drinks. Tourists and chic local beauties coexist around the pool, and drink cocktails on the flower-laden wrap-around patio. *Mon-Sun 11am-4am.* ⊟ Hotel Gansevoort, 18 9th Ave. (13th St.), 212-206-6700, hotelgansevoort.com

PM • Meatpacking District • Nightclub

PM is like a velvet-rope party in Port au Prince. The colorful, Haitian-themed room is designed by Robert McKinley (of Armani and Donna Karan), with high vaulted ceilings, red tables, green leather banquettes, and imported art. The ultrahot crowd that makes it past the bouncers is a mix of the owners' high-rolling, laid-back, island-easy friends, and Wall Street types nostalgic for their last Caribbean vacation. Fresh fruits and top-shelf liquors infuse tropical cocktails with PM's irresistible *belle île* theme. *Mon-Sat 8pm-4am, Sun 10pm-4am.* B⊟ 50 Gansevoort St. (Greenwich St.), 212-255-6676, pmlounge.com

Quo • Chelsea • Nightclub

Best Dance Clubs Manhattan posh and Miami energy combine in this fashionable Chelsea club. From scantily clad go-go dancers to slinky outfits in the crowd, this scene sees more skin than Miami Beach. Clusters of neon-lit beautiful people gather at the white-sand bar, or sweat it out on the unambiguous dance floor, which, oddly, is rare in New York. A pounding sound system plays bass-heavy dance music, with the occasional familiar rock song chorus to get the crowd involved. Thump, thump, (break), "I love rock 'n' roll ..." *Wed-Sun 10pm-4am.* C⊟ 511 W. 28th St. (10th Ave.), 212-268-5105, quonyc.com

Rhone • Meatpacking District • Wine Bar

Best Wine Bars It's hard to strike a compromise between a wine bar and a nightclub. Happily, there's Rhone, a hybrid hotspot in the nightlife-obsessed Meatpacking District. As many as 30 wines are available by the glass at any given time, while over 3,000 bottles are stowed in the 160-square-foot cellar. From Bordeaux to Maipo, the staff knows its wine, and can answer all of your questions with just the right pronunciation and accent. Groups are encouraged to call and reserve a table. *Sun-Sat 5pm-4am.* B⊟ 63 Gansevoort St. (Greenwich St.), 212-367-8440, rhonenyc.com

Snitch • Flatiron • Nightclub

Best Rock Clubs Snitch rock star co-owners Scott Weiland, Duff McKagan, and Brett Scallions have created a music-loving, informal hangout, with waitresses in vintage concert tees and a hip, guitar-worshipping crowd. On most nights the atmosphere is chilled, with modern rock on the sound system and music videos playing on flat-screen TVs. Of course, when McKagan, Weiland, and Velvet Revolver are in town, the velvet ropes go up, and average folks get locked out. In true night-owl fashion, Snitch serves breakfast after last call on weekends. *Mon-Thu 5pm-4am, Fri-Sun 24 hours.* CB⊟ 59 W. 21st St. (6th Ave.), 212-727-7775, snitchbar.com

How to Get in to New York's Most Exclusive Clubs (or at Least Raise Your Chances)

New York City nightclubs are strange animals. Everybody who comes wants to have a good time and everyone's willing to spend a little money, yet doormen seem to decide indiscriminately who makes the cut and who takes a walk. Psssttt .... here's a little secret—there's a method to the madness.

First off, call and reserve a table. This usually requires buying a bottle, which means your group of four should plan on splurging for a $400 bottle of vodka that comes with all the mixings. Sure, millionaires, models, and movie stars can just "pop in" wearing their pajamas, but mere mortals like the rest of us are likely to get turned away.

Secondly, dress like a big spender. Showing up in a suit—tie optional—shows that gentlemen take this outing seriously. Ladies who work out should show off those well-toned physiques to a tasteful degree; note that this does *not* work for guys. Macho men in muscle shirts imply trouble for the bouncers. Sexy women in "wife beater" tees are often seen as cool.

The third and biggest tip is making sure your group's gender ratio is even, or skews female. As Crobar doorman Gilbert Stafford once said, "Guys will get a few drinks in them, they'll start grabbing and pinching girls, and when they're not getting attention, they'll start fighting with other guys—even with each other." Gentlemen, if your pride permits, hold hands with each other when you enter. This shows you're not riding a testosterone high into the competitive pickup scene. It also shows duo spending power and says your intentions aren't to deplete the much-coveted single women pool. "Six gay guys walk in a lot faster than six straight guys," Stafford insists.

There are a few other key things to know: Clubs get busy at midnight, but they generally open around 11pm. Show up somewhere in between and deprive doormen the privilege of putting you into a popularity contest. Also, always keep your cool. If you ask a doorman straight off, "Is this going to happen?" they'll generally appreciate it, and, either way, they'll almost always tell you the score.

Furthermore, "Which party are you with?" is door speak for "No way." Don't take it personally, and don't worry—there's a reasonable chance that the "hotspot" will be out of business within a year.

Hot New York:
The Attractions

Bethpage State Park • Farmingdale, NY • Golf Course
Beware these competitive grounds, where tricky winds wreak havoc, sand traps abound, and Tiger sightings are not uncommon. Bethpage State Park's Black Course is widely regarded as one of the East Coast's most impressive golf courses, which is why it was asked to host the 2002 U.S. Open (and will do so again in 2009). Par 71 on this 7,065-yard course is no easy feat, but getting there is half the fun. (There are also four smaller courses.) At 585, the long seventh hole is a tough goal with its five stroke expectation. *Mon-Sun 6am-6pm, schedule changes with season and the weather.* $$$$ 99 Quaker Meeting House Rd. (Puritan Ln.), 516-249-0700, nysparks.state.ny.us

Big Onion Walking Tours • Brooklyn • Tour
Big Apple's the town, Big Onion's the tour. If you're with us so far, following the instructions of the history professors that lead this procession should be a breeze. On Thursdays, Fridays, and Saturdays, these smarty-pants guides lead curiosity-seekers through the city's most interesting neighborhoods, often attaching themes, like "Gangs of New York," to their 2-hour, $15 per person dalliances with the city they know and love. *Tours: Thu-Sat 1-3pm.* $ 476 13th St. (8th Ave.), 212-439-1090, bigonion.com

Bliss Soho • Soho • Spa
Best Spas Indulgence is Bliss. That's not how the saying goes? Who cares! Bliss Soho and its Uptown sister, Bliss 57, provide facials, massages, and every kind of wrap but chicken, and they do it in one of the hottest shopping districts on the planet. These health and beauty experts understand the need to make everything from midriffs to ankles presentable. After all, who knows what this season's fashions will force you to reveal? *Mon-Fri 9:30am-8:30pm, alternate Wed 12:30-8:30pm, Sat 9:30am-6:30pm.* $$$$ 568 Broadway, 2nd Fl. (Houston St.), 212-219-8970, blissworld.com

Cooper-Hewitt, National Design Museum • Upper East Side • Museum
Cooper-Hewitt is the only museum in the United States devoted exclusively to historic and contemporary design. This New York member of the Smithsonian is divided into four areas: Applied Arts and Industrial Design, Drawings and Prints, Textiles, and Wall Coverings. In addition to 60,000 books, the museum houses blueprints for crucial works of architecture, decorative arts, gardens, interiors, and more. Some fine examples of the Cooper-Hewitt's collection include rare Michelangelo drawings for a candelabrum, and furniture design sketches by renowned architect, Frank Lloyd Wright. *Tue-Thu 10am-5pm, Fri 10am-9pm, Sat 10am-6pm, Sun noon-6pm.* $ 2 E. 91st St. (5th Ave.), 212-849-8400, cooperhewitt.org

Jeffrey New York • Meatpacking District • Shop

Having the best wardrobe in the über-chic, fashion-obsessed Meatpacking District is tough, but Jeffrey is a good place to start. Its impressive collection of haute couture for both men and women has earned this small department store a big reputation. For the shoe fetishist, this is must-stop shopping, offering Fendi, Gucci, and all the big names with heels that, though they're an accident waiting to happen on these cobblestone streets, are an essential part of the dress code in the neighborhood's hottest clubs. *Mon, Tue, Fri 10am-8pm, Thu 10am-9pm, Sat 10am-7pm, Sun 12:30-6pm.* 449 14th St. (Washington St.), 212-206-1272

Liberty Helicopter Tours • Chelsea • Tour

This might be the most expensive way to legally spend $849 for a 15-minute experience—even in Manhattan. There are multiple helicopter tours to choose from, each running seven days a week. The popular Big Apple tour costs $108 per person for a 10-to-12 minute ride over the Statue of Liberty, Empire State Building, and Central Park, while the high-end Romance Over Manhattan tour rents the entire chopper for 15 minutes. Romance tour notwithstanding, Liberty has to fill all six passenger seats to make these flights happen, so have a backup plan. *Office: Daily 9am-9pm; Downtown: Mon-Sat 9am-7pm.* $$$$ Office: W. 30th St. (12th Ave.), Chelsea, 212-967-6464 / 800-542-9933; Downtown: East River Pier (West Side Hwy.), 212-967-6464, libertyhelicopters.com

Museum of Modern Art • Midtown • Art Museum

Founded in 1929, the Museum of Modern Art was an instant classic that challenged the stuffy ideals of museums past. A decade later, MoMA found its current, recently expanded home in Midtown. The $20 cover charge has upset many art patrons, but when you consider that the newly added 630,000 feet alone take an entire afternoon to see, the cost per hour is less than that of a Stallone film, and the experience considerably more rewarding. *Sun, Mon, Wed, Thu, and Sat 10:30am-5:30pm, Fri 10:30am-8pm.* $$ *(free Fri 4-8pm)* 11 W. 53rd St. (6th Ave.), 212-708-9400, moma.org

Museum of Television and Radio • Midtown • Museum

Best Unusual Museums The Museum of Television and Radio must be seen and heard. On the bottom floor is an operating theater that shows episodes of classic TV shows, while the Radio Listening Room replays historic radio broadcasts, like Orson Welles' *War of the Worlds*. Visitors who have been spoiled by TiVo can check in at the front desk and reserve tapes and a private console, selecting from the collection of 50,000-plus options. You'll laugh, you'll cry, and, most important, you'll be wonderfully entertained. *Fri-Wed noon-6pm, Thu noon-8pm, Winter: closed Mondays. Ticket booth closes one hour before the museum.* $ 25 W. 52nd St. (5th Ave.), 212-621-6800, mtr.org

Solomon R. Guggenheim Museum • Upper East Side • Art Museum
Perhaps the most impressive piece of art at the Guggenheim is the museum itself. Designed by Frank Lloyd Wright and completed in 1959, this landmark structure saw numerous renovations before the turn of the century. Though Wright was reluctant to build such a spectacular museum in crowded old New York, today it's hard to imagine it anywhere else. The Guggenheim's expansive art collection includes works by Picasso, Van Gogh, Degas, Chagall, and Kandinsky. The museum's spiraling rotunda also hosts regular jazz performances, lectures, and a film series. *Sat-Wed 10am-5:45pm, Fri 10am-8pm.* $ 1071 5th Ave. (89th St.), 212-423-3500, guggenheim.org

The Spa at Mandarin Oriental • Upper West Side • Spa
This Asian-influenced spa brings together health and beauty in the most posh of environments. As though the 35th-floor view of the Central Park area weren't tranquil enough, the 14,500 square feet of comfort includes a naturally lit indoor lap pool spanning 75 feet. A sauna, fireplace, and cozy tearoom make losing an entire day here quite easy. Full body massages are recommended for those who've spent too much time in the state-of-the-art fitness center. *Daily 9am-9pm.* Mandarin Oriental, 80 Columbus Cir. (60th St.), 212-805-8880, mandarinoriental.com

Stella McCartney • Meatpacking District • Shop
Rumor has it this designer's dad was in a band or something, but for fashion lovers, it's all about Stellaaaaaa! Known for its airbrushed, rock-flavored tees, McCartney's collection also includes tank tops, boots, jewel-encrusted sunglasses and bags, and texturally sweet ribbon-and-bow sweaters seen in the suburbs as well as Meatpacking hotspots. McCartney has more than a famous name—Stella learned her trade while working for Chloe and Gucci, among others. Madonna, Gwyneth Paltrow, and Britney Spears are among her fans. *Mon-Sat 11am-7pm, Sun 12:30-6pm.* 429 14th St. (10th Ave.), 212-255-1556, stellamccartney.com

Trapeze School New York • Upper West Side • Activity
It's never too late to run off and join the circus. Some like to watch, while others want to be part of the act, and when summer comes, both are welcomed at this Hudson Riverside school, guaranteeing thrills, chills, and safety-padded spills. The courses are taught by Jon Gulick, who has chalked up more than 200 performances in Florida, New York, and London, where he spent a year at the famed "Circus Space." Trapeze classes generally run two hours and cost $45 to $60. *Classes are weekend afternoons and some weekday evenings.* $$$$ Hudson River Park, West St. (between piers 34 & 26), 917-797-1872, trapezeschool.com

United Nations • Midtown • Site
Tour 191 countries in an hour on this 18-acre, flag-laden stretch of Manhattan that serves as headquarters to the multinational organization founded in 1945 with the idea of maintaining world peace. The General Assembly Building, conference buildings, and Dag Hammarskjöld Library comprise the United Nations complex, which took 11 architects to build and boasts a stained-glass window by Marc Chagall, a Foucault pendulum, and a Japanese peace bell. *Tours every half hour Mon-Fri 9:30am-4:30pm only during January and February, also Sat-Sun 10am-4:30pm the rest of the year.* $ 1st Ave. (46th St.), 212-963-8687, un.org/tours

Whitney Museum of American Art • Upper East Side • Art Museum
The Whitney is a top-caliber modern museum, and it also has a bit of an edge that the most jaded of Soho gallery owners can appreciate. Where else might one see Hopper's 75-plus-year-old *Early Sunday Morning* painting on the wall, then five minutes later catch a Kenneth Anger short film about gay bikers? (The original Whitney was built way downtown in 1931. This became its home in 1966.) There are original masterpieces among the Whitney's 12,000 piece collection, many by artists including Arshile Gorky, Reginald Marsh, and Roy Lichtenstein. (Photography and video are forbidden here, but many replicas can be purchased in the gift shop.) Touring the Whitney can take three or four hours, and those wishing to avoid school groups should try to come after 2pm, which leaves four hours of prime browsing time. The museum is open until 9pm on Fridays. *Wed-Thu 11am-6pm, Fri 1-9pm, Sat-Sun 11am-6pm.* $ 945 Madison Ave. (75th St.), 212-570-3676, whitney.org

Cool New York

Cool is comfortable. A break from the heat. Not too hot and not too cold, Cool New York is all about fun places to go where you'll never have to compete with a long line of well-connected, name-dropping locals. This is where you meet people without having to worry whether everyone's getting in. This is where you can have a great dining experience without having planned three months in advance. While the "in crowd" and celebs are most often associated with hotter venues, these are the ones they hit when they want to cocktail sans flash bulbs.

*Note: Venues in bold are described in detail in the listings that follow the itinerary. Venues followed by an * asterisk are those we recommend as both a restaurant and a destination bar.*

Cool New York:
The Perfect Plan (3 Days and Nights)

Highlights

Thursday
Mid-morning	Chelsea Galleries, Chelsea Market
Lunch	BLT Fish
Mid-afternoon	Bryant Park, *Sex and the City* Tour
Pre-dinner	The Dove
Dinner	Lure Fishbar*, Public*
Nighttime	MercBar, Canal Rm.
Late-night	Church Lounge

Friday
Breakfast	Cafe St. Bart's
Mid-morning	Soho Shopping
Lunch	Boom, Dos Caminos
Mid-afternoon	*Conan O'Brien*, Museum of Sex
Dinner	Biltmore Room*, Town*
Nighttime	Iridium Jazz, Whiskey Blue
Late-night	Hudson Bar, AVA

Saturday
Breakfast	Cafeteria
Mid-morning	Chelsea Piers
Lunch	Blue Water Grill*
Mid-afternoon	American Folk Art, Madison Sq. Garden
Pre-dinner	44 Restaurant*, Flûte*
Dinner	Estiatorio Milos, Sushi Samba 7*
Nighttime	Duvet*, Upright Citizens Brigade Theatre
Late-night	Earth NYC*, Bar Veloce

Morning After
Brunch	Balthazar*

Hotel: W New York

Thursday

10am Head straight to art scene central—in Chelsea. Long city blocks are filled with enough galleries, including **Paul Kasmin Gallery** and **Paul Morris Gallery**, to satisfy the most avid art lover.

11:30am The nearby **Chelsea Market**, a fancy piece of artwork in its own right, is a ten-minute stroll from the heaviest-density gallery area. This design spectacle has bakeries, craft shops, and all things fitting for the Food Network and Oxygen studios, both of which operate in the building's offices.

12:30pm Lunch Lunchtime can be a lively affair in this part of town, especially at **BLT Fish**, which is only a 10- or 15-minute walk east of the primary gallery zone. Depending on what you're wearing, you can choose between the two dining areas here: the casual or the more upscale. If the weather is nice, you should head up to the stylish **Bryant Park Grill**, which is like Tavern on the Green for the younger set.

2pm Join the hundreds, if not thousands, of others in taking a breather in **Bryant Park**, before heading off for the *Sex and the City* **Tour**. The bus journey begins in Central Park and makes the shopping, restaurant, and lounging rounds. Sure, it's touristy, but the HBO show was spot-on in portraying cool New York.

7pm **The Dove** may not be directly on the route to your dinner spot, but the cocktails (and ambience) are worth a stop.

8:30pm **Dinner** With a regular following of foodies, celebs, and well-heeled neighborhood locals, **Lure Fishbar*** is the darling of this area's restaurant scene. Three blocks away, the Australian-influenced **Public*** offers a meatier dining alternative. **BondSt***, with its sushi-loving hipsters, is located just north of Houston Street in the neighborhood called Noho. The upstairs restaurant can start your evening, while the downstairs lounge often leads to cocktailing late into the evening.

11pm Across the street from Lure Fishbar is the quirky lounge **MercBar**, where the clientele are almost as good-looking as the staff. For more high-voltage fun, take a cab to Tribeca and check out the **Canal Room**, where you'll either find reunited '80s bands playing, or dance-oriented DJs running the floor. Three minutes

from Public is Russian-themed **Pravda**, with its endless lists of imported vodkas. If you're craving a light bite with your cocktails, take a walk through Little Italy to **Odea***, a great little lounge that also offers tasty late-night fare.

1am For a nightcap follow-up to Odea, there's nearby **Church Lounge** in the Tribeca Grand Hotel. If you've got your dancing shoes on, check out **Embassy**. Rarely will one find a club this cool with a velvet rope so lax.

Friday

9am When a hotel breakfast won't do, **Café St. Bart's** has a cool patio space along Park Avenue, which lets you linger over coffee in the morning air.

10am It's a Soho morning. Shops including Helmut Lang, Emporio Armani, Betsey Johnson, Marc Jacobs, Kenneth Cole, and Cynthia Rowley are just the start. Stop at the **Apple Store**, the mother lode for techies, or check out the photography at the **Morrison Hotel Gallery**, which is a rocker's dream.

1pm **Lunch** If you're wondering who's buying all those painfully hip Soho clothes, have lunch at the fashionable **Boom** and take a look around you. For good-weather dining, **Dos Caminos Soho** has a spectacular patio space and guacamole made at your table.

3pm With luck you've wrangled tickets to a taping of New York's own *Late Night with Conan O'Brien*. Otherwise, you'll have time for **The Fashion Institute of Technology Museum**, which displays two city blocks of sartorial splendor. Though it's not as raunchy as its name suggests, you'll find out what's underneath all those clothes in the **Museum of Sex**.

8pm Dinner The Biltmore Room's* cool marble and mirrored interior is a chic place to enjoy some of the best cuisine in New York City. There's no need to change clothes after postmuseum cocktails—semicasual wear is fine here. Further south in Soho, **Cipriani Downtown*** means pulling out the black outfits for trendy Italian food. If you feel like dressing to the nines, try the ultrachic **Town*** restaurant in the Chambers Hotel.

10pm You might have to rush dinner a bit to make the show at the **Iridium Jazz Club**, designed in part by guitar legend Les Paul. If you're antsy for a fish-in-a-barrel singles scene, **Whiskey Blue** midtown is definitely the spot. Head to the Hudson Hotel for cocktails in front of a fire or over a game of pool in the sedate **Hudson Library**.

Midnight You needn't leave the Hudson Hotel for one last drink. Just skip over to the **Hudson Bar**, which isn't just any old hotel lounge—this one is owned by former Studio 54 operator Ian Schrager, so you're sure to find a little late-night debauchery. High atop the Dream Hotel, the **AVA Lounge** and AVA Garden rooftop provide intoxicating cocktails with a sobering view straight down Broadway.

Saturday

9am Fuel up at the popular and modern 24-hour diner, **Cafeteria**, where late-night clubbers and freshly risen hipsters meet.

10am To get your blood pumping, head west to **Chelsea Piers**, for running, bowling, basketball, or driving golf balls. Just south of Chelsea in the West Village is **Integral Yoga**, which offers individual classes, or have a luxurious morning with a facial or a massage at **Metamorphosis Day Spa**.

12:30pm Lunch Right at the edge of the Union Square market is the **Blue Water Grill***, a stylish way to enjoy the freshest of fish. Just on the other side of the square is Todd English's **Olives*** restaurant.

COOL

2:30pm Cab to Midtown where the **American Folk Art Museum** houses 18th- and 19th-century quilts, fashions, and artwork—but there's nothing old-fashioned about this place. Within walking distance, at the **International Center of Photography**, see the city through the eyes of renowned shutterbugs. Sports fans will want to check out **Madison Square Garden**, which offers daily tours of the famed sports arena, as well as the Knicks, Rangers, and Liberty locker rooms.

6:30pm Midtown's **44 Restaurant*** starts your night off with a nibble and cocktails in a sexy off-the-lobby setting. Or perhaps bubbly is in order—you can't do better than **Flûte***, on the edge of the Gramercy Park area.

8pm Dinner Estiatorio Milos is no dance-on-the-table Greek restaurant, but it does hold up Greece's reputation for serving the very best fish. In the mood for meat? The Brazilian **Churrascaria Plataforma** is an upscale, spirited place for the gluttonous. For a totally different Brazil-influenced experience, go downtown to **Sushi Samba 7***.

11pm In West Chelsea, nightlife is hot. In central Chelsea, it's cool, which means shorter lines and less name-dropping. Climb into bed at the Miami-themed **Duvet***—a more relaxed version of B.E.D. Of course, you'll be missing cutting-edge sketch and stand-up comedy at the **Upright Citizens Brigade Theatre**.

1am The place in Chelsea for happy feet and sharp dressers is **Earth NYC**, which packs in a hip clientele, and where nights run very late. But you may prefer to end your weekend with a postshow champagne supernova at the laid-back, romantic wine spot, **Bar Veloce**.

The Morning After
Whether you're still roaming the streets of Soho in your evening attire, or you've slept off your buzz at the hotel, the restaurant **Balthazar*** is your best bet for one of the hippest and most satisfying brunches in town.

Cool New York:
The Key Neighborhoods

Chelsea While West Chelsea is hot as can be, the bars, clubs, and lounges in the heart of this nouveau, upscale, gay-friendly area are cool and refreshing. The area's residences are, for the most part, young, single, and willing to part with their disposable incomes.

Gramercy/Murray Hill These interchangeable eastside neighborhoods are chock-full of half-hip, half-fancy restaurants for up-and-coming bankers, advertising folks, and general office workers who live comfortably between their midtown offices and downtown culture.

Midtown Think W Hotel, and you've got Midtown. In addition to serving the great masses of people who congregate here for work, there are hotels, restaurants and even nightlife that appeal to those who are looking for something with a cool vibe.

Soho For the most part, the A-list has moved uptown (relatively speaking), but Soho's reputation as a sophisticated, trendy shopping and nightlife scene carries on with some of the city's best stores, restaurants, and lounges.

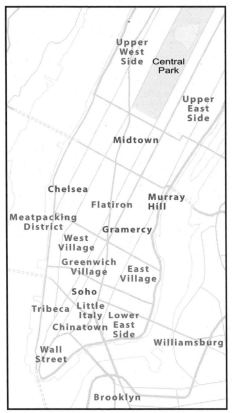

Cool New York:
The Shopping Blocks

Soho

An interesting amalgamation of big-name chains and independent boutiques, Soho is a pioneer of "bourgeois cool." Broadway below Houston Street is the main drag, but it's packed with chain stores and tourists. Walk along Spring Street, then wander onto Greene Street, Mercer, and West Broadway for more unique offerings.

A.P.C. Unisex French hipster staples come surprisingly starched, especially the cult-status denim, all in a no-pressure sales environment. 131 Mercer St. (Prince St.), 212-966-9685

Apple Store This mother lode of hip gizmos also hosts free tech classes and live music performances by artists who worship at the altar of Apple. (p.106) 103 Prince St. (Greene St.), 212-226-3126

Flying A Cutesy-kitschy accessories mingle with op-art print dresses at this eclectic boutique. There's even a small section of vintage finds that could pass for contemporary designs. 169 Spring St. (W. Broadway), 212-965-9090

Kirna Zabête For girls, but not girly: avant-garde indie and big-name designers have made this a trendsetting boutique. 96 Greene St. (Spring St.), 212-941-9656

Marc Jacobs The kingpin of cool manages to woo fashion editors, celebrities, and common people with his ready-to-wear and accessories. Marc's empire is cemented by the fact that he owns three stores, all in a row. Women's accessories: 385 Bleecker St. (Perry St.), 212-924-6126; men's and women's clothing (p.108): 403-405 Bleecker St. (W. 11th St.), 212-924-0026

Moss Purveyor of quirky modern design for every room and nook in the house, Moss has enough imaginative housewares and decorative objects to make an aesthete swoon. 146 Greene St. (Houston St.), 212-204-7100

Sunrise Mart Offering one of the most comprehensive assortments of Japanese foods—from fish cakes to every type of noodle under the sun. There's also household goods, lovely ceramics, and even videos perfectly arranged in the bright, cheerful space. 494 Broome St. (W. Broadway), 212-219-0033

Via Bus Stop This Japanese export brings a little slice of Tokyo to Soho, stocking quirky high-end designers for fashion obsessives with platinum Visas. 172 Mercer St. (Houston St.), 212-343-8810

Vivienne Tam With snow-white walls and black floors, this stylish Soho shop is almost as sleek as Vivienne Tam's Asian-influenced dresses. The Canton-born designer has spent significant periods in Hong Kong, London, and New York City, so while her designs have traditional Chinese overtones, the look is undeniably Western. 99 Greene St. (Spring St.), 212-966-2398

We include a small area known as **NoLita** in the Soho neighborhood. Hard to define in terms of location (the moniker stands for North of Little Italy), it's easy to see why NoLita has become one of the city's hottest shopping spots. It offers an edgier alternative to Soho, and a quieter, European feel. Stroll around Mott, Mulberry, and Elizabeth Streets between Houston and Spring for cutting-edge boutiques.

Eva This artfully spare boutique is the perfect backdrop for fearless women's clothing (Vivienne Westwood, Rick Owens, Sass & Bide) with a rock 'n' roll edge. 227 Mulberry St. (Spring St.), 212-925-3208

I Heart Marked only by a pink neon heart, this subterranean boutique carries hard-to-find imported designers along with a hip selection of art, music, and books. 262 Mott St. (Houston), 212-219-9265

Resurrection Forget the musty and the moth-eaten, Resurrection stocks pristine, pricey vintage designer clothing and accessories. 217 Mott St. (Prince St.), 212-625-1374

Sigerson Morrison The eponymous line of modern women's footwear that fills this shop has an art school sensibility, yet manages to remain office appropriate. There's a newly opened handbag boutique down the block. Shoes: 28 Prince St. (Mott St.) 212-219-3893, Handbags: 242 Mott St. (Prince St.), 212-941-5404

West Village

Amidst flower shops, bakeries, and celebrity-owned brownstones, these streets have a quaint charm. Amazingly the West Village manages to stay somewhat off the grid while stocking the city's hippest wares. Hit up Christopher, Bleecker, and Hudson Streets for shopping, and grab cupcakes at the cult favorite, Magnolia Bakery (401 Bleecker Street)—that is, if you don't mind waiting in line.

Aedes de Venustas Perfume junkies, get your fix. This shop's decadent array of rare and hard to find fragrances, lotions, and soaps make it easy to get hooked. 9 Christopher St. (Sixth Ave.), 212-206-8674

Albertine Find wispy dresses and earthy jewelry by up-and-coming designers at this on-trend boutique. 13 Christopher St. (Greenwich Ave.), 212-924-8515

Zachary's Smile Stylists and fashion editors know the greatness that lies within— well-priced, expertly edited vintage, as well as a house brand of reworked vintage pieces. Men and women can both go retro. 9 Greenwich Ave. (Christopher St.), 212-924-0604

COOL

Cool New York:
The Hotels

Bryant Park Hotel • Midtown • Trendy (130 rms)
It's hard to imagine how a hotel could be more stylish than this one. World-famous hair stylist Rick Pipino even keeps a salon here, and his clients, which include Naomi Campbell and Sarah Wynter, barely stand out from the chic hotel clientele. Once the American Radiator Building (New York City's first skyscraper), this boutique hotel is rumored to be Leonardo DiCaprio's favorite place to crash in the city. With red padded lobby walls and a 70-seat screening room for media industry types, this place was built for cool. While the hotel is all about models during Fashion Week, the rest of the year draws producers, high-rolling attorneys, and deal makers. Make no mistake—this place is even better for pleasure than it is for work, with its Cellar Bar and one of the hippest places to be in New York—Koi restaurant. Of the hotel's 130 rooms, 11 offer park view terraces. The 4th floor Deluxe rooms overlooking the park are the most spacious. As you might expect, the hotel is very accommodating, and the rooms are stocked with high-tech amenities. $$$ 40 W. 40th St. (5th Ave.), 212-869-0100, bryantparkhotel.com

Dream Hotel • Midtown • Trendy (220 rms)
The New Age-y Dream Hotel, chock-full of the latest in technological amenities, is hotelier Vikram Chatwal's latest creation. An interesting, odd, and comfortable place, the hotel practically buzzes with diffused neon lighting, which even emanates from beneath the beds, like a kind of *Star Wars* hovercraft. In each of the 220 large rooms is a 42-inch plasma TV and a preprogrammed iPod. Ask for a King Deluxe room with a view of Broadway. The halls are aglow with chic, Patrick Nagel–like art, and in the lobby, fluorescent Chinese fish drift ethereally around a tall cylindrical tank guarding the Technicolor Dream Lounge. On top of the building is the AVA Penthouse—a popular rooftop lounge named after actress Ava Gardner. A glass elevator descends from the lobby to an Ayurvedic healing arts center, informed by guru Indian physician Deepak Chopra. $$$$ 210 W. 55th St. (7th Ave.), 212-247-2000, dreamny.com

Hudson Hotel • Midtown • Trendy (1,000 rms)
The Hudson Hotel manages to be both egalitarian and supercool. With many less expensive (and very small) rooms, the Hudson draws a creative, artsy crowd who want to be near the Theater District, but can't otherwise afford the swanky Midtown rates. Why so cool? It's operated by former Studio 54 co-owner and conspirator Ian Schrager, who knows how scene-y and social a fun hotel should be. This hotel knows how to bring people together, whether they're drinking beneath the towering trees of the outdoor "town square" or refueling at the buzzing Hudson Cafeteria. If you're looking for a bit more space, try to snag a double double Deluxe room (the highest floors have river views). That said, with a chic onsite bar, a rooftop garden, and a private park, who wants to hide out in their room? $$$ 356 W. 58th St. (9th Ave.), 212-554-6000 / 800-606-6090, hudsonhotel.com

The Lowell • Upper East Side • Timeless (70 rms)
There's nothing modern, much less corporate, about the Upper East Side's Lowell, which allows guests to get a taste of life in a stately manor. The decor is all plush and old world, with gilt-framed art, marble floors, and a mahogany desk in the lobby. Many suites feature functioning fireplaces, libraries, and fully equipped kitchens, and the Garden Suite even has a pair of manicured terraces with flower beds and a fountain. There are a few modern touches at the Lowell as well, like the flat-screen TVs at the foot of bathtubs, and an exercise suite with its own private gym. The hotel's informal Pembroke House is open all day, and the more upscale Post House offers exquisite high-end cuisine. Guests of the Lowell also enjoy signing privileges at the fabulous French bistro across the street, Le Bilboquet. The Lowell Kings are generously-sized non-suites (11C is quiet and bright, plus the only one with a working fireplace). $$$$$ 28 E. 63rd St. (Madison Ave.), 212-838-1400 / 800-221-4444, lowellhotel.com

The Maritime Hotel • Chelsea • Trendy (125 rms)
In 1966, this building was constructed to house the National Maritime Union for hosting visiting sailors. Today, with its patio of lawn tables and white, loungy lobby, visitors might think they've ended up in Miami. But this Chelsea favorite is pure New York, often hosting entertainment industry bigwigs. Preserving the Union's original nautical theme, this hotel offers 125 small, cabinlike rooms, porthole windows and all (rooms above the 5th floor enjoy a river view). Fortunately, the Maritime's decor reaches beyond the sea, with custom Japanese fabric headboards, flat-screen TVs, video game consoles, and CD/DVD players. The bathrooms are nothing short of luxurious, with waterfall shower-heads and marble floors. Of course, it's tempting for guests to spend all of their time in one of the hotel's two fantastic restaurants, Matursi and La Bottega, or the ultrahip, Japanese-themed nightclub, Hiro Lounge, in the basement. For downtime away from the New York hustle and bustle, the Maritime boasts more outdoors space—10,000 peaceful square feet—than any other hotel in the city. $$$ 363 W. 16th St. (9th Ave.), 212-242-4300, themaritimehotel.com

Paramount Hotel New York • Midtown • Trendy (592 rms)
Formerly the Century Paramount, this once deteriorating hotel now boasts a cutting-edge, ultramodern decor by renowned interior designer Philippe Starck. The pop-nuevo–inspired lobby sports a chessboard checkered rug and an arrangement of unusually shaped, painfully hip sofas and chairs. In the Paramount Bar, known for its cosmos, flat-screen TVs display video art commissioned from several international artists, giving the place a cache so cool, even the locals come here to drink. The stark white rooms are best known for the headboards, with reproductions of 17th-century Vermeer paintings. The gilded frames and Dutch art are a funky contrast to the contemporary lamps and gray-and-white checkered carpets featured in each room. Ask for one of the considerably larger Deluxe Corner Rooms with a street view. There is a 24-hour gym for insomniacs who don't dig the bar scene, complete with fresh fruit and stocks of bottled water. The Paramount is located only steps away from Broadway and the throbbing masses of Times Square. $$ 235 W. 46th St. (7th Ave.), 212-764-5500 / 888-956-3542, paramountnewyork.solmelia.com

COOL

Royalton Hotel • Midtown • Trendy (205 rms)

Conceived and executed by the team behind the Paramount Hotel, the Royalton claims to have invented the "art of Lobby Socializing." Philippe Starck's sleek, ultramodern design combines minimalism with theatrical extravagance, and plenty of space to schmooze. The lobby's 20-foot-long marble Library Table is a great place to have a drink and peruse one of the books from the hotel's collection, which includes selections about art, fashion, and film. The 44 restaurant looks like something out of an Austin Powers movie, with curved, lime-green velvet banquettes and New American cuisine. Yeah, baby. The Round Bar, nestled into an innocuous corner of the lobby, was modeled on Hemingway's favorite bar at the Ritz in Paris. The Royalton is a good spot for spacious rooms with working fireplaces, five-foot custom bathtubs, flat-screen TVs, and stocks of Dean & DeLuca chocolates. Be sure to ask for a Deluxe room that looks onto the street. $$$ 44 W. 44th St. (6th Ave.), 212-869-4400 / 800-697-1791, royaltonhotel.com

Soho House • Soho • Trendy (24 rms)

So sleek. So stylish. So exclusive. This Soho House, known as VIP quarters for London and New York, is named for the eponymous neighborhood east of the Atlantic. Its New York location in the oh-so-fashionable Meatpacking District is a private club for dues-paying jet setters who want only the best. Happily for the rest of us, 24 bedrooms have been set aside so that regular visitors may enjoy the rooftop pools and James Bond ambience while in town. The three 950-square-foot "playground suites" are the best of the lot. Equipped with state-of-the-art perks, these airy lofts with exposed brick walls and high ceilings are the perfect place to bring the party after the clubs have closed. The restaurant, lounge, and drawing room are open to nonmembers, as is the game room (complete with billiards and foosball) and the rooftop pool. Great views abound, but the best rooms face east, which sees the most street action in this busy neighborhood. $$$$$ 29-35 9th Ave. (13th St.), 212-627-9800, sohohouseny.com

W New York • Midtown • Modern (688 rms)

The lobby design of New York's first W Hotel exudes modernity, with lots of glass and multicolored lights, yet it also maintains an earthy serenity. An oasis in a hectic city, the W New York was designed by architect David Rockwell with nature's elements in mind: earth, wind, fire, and water. There's almost always a buzz around the public areas on the main floor, especially at Rande Gerber's plush Living Room bar and lounge area, adjacent to the check-in counter (which makes for great people-watching). Though, as in most of New York's hotels, the rooms at the W are too small, there is a reasonable selection of amenities, including a DVD player, a CD player (with guest CDs), large desks, and free internet. Ask for the Corner Spectacular Room. Whiskey Blue, on the hotel's ground floor, is by far the city's coolest whiskey lounge. The best rooms are those with a view of Times Square. $$$$ 541 Lexington Ave. (49th St.), 212-755-1200 / 888-625-5144, whotels.com

Cool New York:
The Restaurants

Asia de Cuba* • Murray Hill • Asian-Cuban
Asia de Cuba is one of those rarest of places that starts out hip and stays that way. The room is easy on the eyes, with dreamy white curtains and modern accents of color. On this unique fusion menu, Asian and Latin spices mingle, with fantastic results. Honey rum roast pork may sound a little strange, but does it work? *Sí.* Tuna tartare with Spanish olives? *Jesús.* The long, communal marble table provides a worthwhile pickup scene, giving Asia de Cuba a lounge-style cachet as well. *Sun 5:30-11pm, Mon-Wed noon-11pm, Thu-Fri noon-midnight, Sat 5:30-midnight.* $$$ ⟨Y⟩⟨B⟩⟨≡⟩ 237 Madison Ave. (38th St.), 212-726-7755, chinagrillmanagement.com

B Bar and Grill* • Greenwich Village • Seafood
The black-and-tan banquettes give this hip eatery a retro-diner feel, but the bar's shimmering gold light and the pale orange lanterns that hang like pumpkins from the rafters bring B Bar into the new millennium. The gorgeous garden space can rival any alfresco dining in town. Lunch here is steady, especially in the summer, when models and showbiz types stop in for seafood and salad. Tuesday night's gay party is wildly popular, and random karaoke nights pop up from time to time. The partially enclosed space between the dining room and the patio offers the best of both worlds. *Mon 11:30am-midnight, Tue-Fri 11:30am-1am, Sat 10:30am-1am, Sun 10:30am-midnight.* $ ⟨B⟩⟨≡⟩ 40 E. 4th St. (Bowery St.), 212-475-2220, bbarandgrill.com

Balthazar* • Soho • French
Best Always Trendy Restaurants Balthazar is the mature older brother of owner Keith McNally's successful triplets (along with Pastis and Schiller's Liquor Bar). A mix of yuppies and bohemians lounges in red leather banquettes, complaining about the crowds in this ever popular eatery. High ceilings, faded yellow walls, and that Parisian fondness for mirrors gives Balthazar the feel of an authentic old-style brasserie. Five different menus apply to different times of the day, starting with breakfast, which features soft-boiled organic eggs, and ending with "late night" fare, featuring macaroni au gratin and an extensive list of over 300 wines. *Mon-Thu 7:30am-1am, Fri 7:30am-2am, Sat 8am-4pm and 5:45pm-2am, Sun 8am-4pm and 5:30pm-midnight.* $$ ⟨F⟩⟨≡⟩ 80 Spring St. (Crosby St.), 212-965-1785, balthazarny.com

Barça 18 • Gramercy • Spanish
Restaurants along Park Avenue South tend to cater to the neighborhood's well-heeled 9-to-5 crowd, which prefers a lifestyle of no alarms and no surprises. Smoothly operated and expertly thought out, this high-frills, no-thrills eatery is a combined effort of prominent restaurateur Steve Hanson, Le Bernardin's four-star chef Eric Ripert, and cocktail designer extraordinaire Eben Klemm. Faux leather tablecloths and matching leather upholstery and menus give Barça 18 a modern but conservative flair. The informal Iberian cuisine is among the city's best. The Spanish tapas and swordfish are not to be missed. *Mon-Thu 11:30am-*

midnight, Fri-Sat 11:30am-1am, Sun 10:30am-midnight. $$ ▣ 225 Park Ave. S. (18th St.), 212-533-2500, brguestrestaurants.com

The Biltmore Room* • Chelsea • Asian Fusion

Best Informal Upscale Restaurants This may be the coolest restaurant in town where one can turn up in jeans (though patrons tend to wear them with $400 tee shirts). With low rafters, dark tones, and plenty of wide leather chairs, the Biltmore Room took the surviving remnants from the historic Biltmore Hotel fire and re-created an old-time supper club. No one combines scene and cuisine quite like this. The French-American-Asian menu includes an unusually complex rack of lamb, and a giant prawn spiced and prepared with impossible care. The lounge is sexy and warm, providing an excuse to arrive at 7:15 for an 8pm reservation. *Mon-Thu 5:30-10:30pm, Fri-Sat 5:30-11:30pm, Sun 5:30-10pm. The lounge stays open until 4am daily.* $$$ ▣▣ 290 8th Ave. (25th St.), 212-807-0111, thebiltmoreroom.com

BLT Fish • Flatiron • Seafood

Up and coming "it" chef Laurent Tourendel (put Bistro before his name to get BLT), cooks up good times for a healthy-looking clientele that probably runs a mile for every calorie consumed. There's a heavy New England slant to BLT Fish, and special attention is paid to the oysters, Maryland crab cakes, and Boston clam chowder. The dramatic, retractable glass roof combined with the warm glow from the kitchen is at once grand and cozy. The scene transforms as you ascend the trilevel space, with the casual main room featuring a raw bar, and a top tier that is more formal than fashionable. *Daily 5pm-midnight.* $$$ ▣▣ 21 W. 17th St. (6th Ave.), 212-691-8888, bltfish.com

BLT Steak • Midtown • Steak House

A copper-topped bar and light caramelized colors give BLT Steak a classier tone than the traditional dark wood and white linen chop house. Top-notch steaks are prepared with a variety of sauces, and the usual sides have a decidedly French spin. The rounded booths against the back wall provide the best people-watching, but are reserved for larger groups. The wine list is exceptional. *Mon-Fri 11:45am-2:30pm and 5:30-11pm, Sat 5:30-11:30pm.* $$$ ▣▣ 106 E. 57th St. (Park Ave.), 212-752-7470, bltsteak.com

Blue Water Grill* • Flatiron • Seafood

Situated in a converted bank, Blue Water Grill offers a raw bar, a sushi bar, a mouthwatering selection of cooked dishes, and some of the most inventive cocktails in town. Though vault rooms are still utilized, the main space is airy, with huge French windows and high, ethereal ceilings. Celebrity sightings are common, both in the main dining room and the downstairs jazz room, which features nightly live acts. If you can't fit another dinner into your trip, the Blue Water has a great Sunday brunch, with or without a side of jazz. *Mon-Thu 11:30am-midnight, Fri-Sat 11:30am-12:30am, Sun 10:30am-11:30pm.* $$ ▣▣▣ 31 Union Square W. (16th St.), 212-675-9500, brguestrestaurants.com

BondSt* • Greenwich Village • Sushi

Best Restaurant Lounges This two-story, Japanese minimalist restaurant and lounge has some of the coolest fish around. Upstairs, a spacious and earthy room welcomes foodies and scene seekers to sit down elbow-to-elbow and dine on highly seasoned sushi. Amid sleek lines, shimmering candles, and black-framed mirrors, the downstairs scene pulsates with Uptowners, out-of-towners, and a big weekend crowd that does its best to dress like the celebrity crowd that reigned here in the '90s. The diaphanous sirens serving the sushi are as lovely as ever. *Restaurant: Mon-Sat 6pm-midnight, Sun 6-11pm. Lounge: Mon-Sat 5pm-2am, Sun 6pm-1am.* $$ ⓍⒷ≡ 6 Bond St. (Broadway), 212-777-2500

Boom • Soho • New American

Behind Boom's raw wood exterior is a well-appointed room with masculine chandeliers and candles aplenty. The nouveau sauces and seafood-heavy menu is aggressively prepared for a lively late-night scene of investment bankers, socialites, gallery hoppers, and shoppers. Fridays host live Brazilian music, and Saturdays get the speakers thumping with hip-hop DJs. *Sun-Thu noon-midnight, Sat-Sun noon-1am.* $$ Ⓑ≡ 152 Spring St. (Wooster St.), 212-431-3663

Brasserie • Midtown • Brasserie

Though *très* popular and romantic, Brasserie is more *Star Trek* than Toulouse-Lautrec. Shiny and polished, with stark white chairs, concealed ceiling lights, and bottles of booze that seem to suspend magically behind the bar, this chic bistro is the ultimate urban refuge. Brasserie's brunch is notable, with creative options, like black truffle scrambled eggs and Prince Edward Mussels and frîtes. The bar seats are great for seeing and being seen. If you want to get cozy with your paramour, reserve one of the coveted intimate booths. *Mon-Thu 7am-midnight, Fri 7-10am and 4:30pm-1am, Sat 11am-1am, Sun 11am-10pm.* $$ Ⓑ≡ 100 E. 53rd St. (Park Ave.), 212-751-4840, rapatina.com/brasserie/

Brasserie 8¹ᐟ² • Midtown • Brasserie

The honey-lit bar of this modern brasserie comes across as an ideal date spot for nouveau riche, scene-seeking Midtowners, but the kitchen is more intent on impressing seasoned foodies. Traditional French entrees like filet mignon au poivre work for more-conservative diners, while Mediterranean- and Asian-influenced dishes like Spanish mackerel tartare and yellowtail sashimi provide a little spice. Though the lounge area is a busy place to eat, the banquettes closest to the main room's walls provide greater privacy. *Mon-Fri 11:30am-3pm and 5:30-11pm, Sat 5:30-11pm, Sun 11am-3pm and 5:30-9pm.* $$$ ▭ 9 W. 57th St. (6th Ave.), 212-829-0812, rapatina.com/brasserie8/

Bryant Park Grill • Midtown • American

Stylish, geographically blessed Bryant Park Grill has its seasonal permutations—a sun-speckled patio in summer, and a heated white tent in winter—but the potent cocktails and sexy singles crowd flirt under the stars year-round. On standing-room-only Thursday nights, the circular bar does a roaring trade in cosmos, imported suds, and pickup lines. The hit-or-miss American fare is less enticing than the clientele, so stick to the straightforward options, like the perfectly tangy Caesar salad and tender herb-roasted chicken. With all the eye candy around, you may not even notice what's on your plate. *Sun-Mon 11:30am-3:30pm and 5-9:30pm, Tue-Wed 11:30am-3:30pm and 5-10:30pm, Thu-Sat 11:30am-3:30pm and 5-11pm.* $$ Ⓑ≡ 25 W. 40th St. (5th Ave.), 212-840-6500, arkrestaurants.com

COOL

Café St. Bart's • Midtown • New American

Praise be St. Bart—patron saint of alfresco dining. Throughout the summer this lively cafe occupies the sprawling garden terrace of St. Bartholomew's Church, which overlooks the midtown bustle of Park Avenue. Live jazz bands play, people sip glasses of wine, and grilled dishes, like roasted leg of lamb with rosemary, make the rounds. The cuisine is mostly American, but with a distinctive Southwestern flair. If you decide to top off the meal with one of St. Bart's sinful black cow ice cream floats, you won't have far to go to confess. *Winter Mon-Fri 9am-3pm. Summer Mon-Fri 9am-10pm, Sun 11:30am-4pm.* $$$ ▭ 109 E. 50th St. (Park Ave. S.), 212-888-2664, cafestbarts.com

Cafeteria • Chelsea • New American

Best All-Night Restaurants Not only is this softly whitewashed, clubby restaurant always open, but it's always abuzz. For years, Cafeteria has managed to maintain its status as the staple eatery of the ever-changing fabulous and fashionable club scene. When the local gay and straight clubs close, Cafeteria is packed. When nightlifers wake up at noon, it's packed again. The menu dabbles in soul food, but for the most part sticks with American comfort cuisine, spanning from macaroni and cheese to waffles. *24/7.* $ F≡ 119 7th Ave. (17th St.), 212-414-1717

Candela • Gramercy • International

Candela is one of the city's more romantic restaurants for several reasons, not the least of which is its abundance of candles. The thick tapers flicker sensually in every corner of the room, including in the overhead chandeliers. More hodgepodge than fusion, the Asian, Italian, Middle Eastern, and Americana menu ensures that diners get exactly what they want. The less sentimental may think Candela overreaches a tad. The less cynical will count it among their favorite restaurants. *Call for hours.* $$ B≡ 116 E. 16th St. (Irving Pl.), 212-254-1600, candelarestaurant.com

Churrascaria Plataforma • Midtown/Tribeca • Brazilian

Best Steak Houses In Portuguese, Churrascaria Plataforma very well may translate into "long cumbersome name no one can remember." Still, it's safe to say that once you've eaten at this Brazilian steak house, you won't forget the experience. Servers buzz about the place toting mounds of meat for anyone who hasn't flipped the placard by their plate. Those who don't know the custom risk exploding. The setting of white tablecloths, leather chairs, and polished brick walls is rather formal, but the roving samba and Brazilian jazz bands on weekends turn dinner into Carnaval—minus the thongs. *Daily noon-midnight.* $$ ≡ 316 W. 49th St. (9th Ave.), 212-245-0505, churrascariaplataforma.com

Cipriani Downtown* • Soho • Italian

Best Always Trendy Restaurants The Downtown installation of the Cipriani family of restaurants draws a younger, hipper crowd. This is more about the people than the risotto or veal Milanese. The capacious space of oversized paintings, walls of windows, and sidewalk seating has one of the best lunch scenes in town. At night, the Euros and Euro-looking come out to sip Bellinis (Cipriani's staff swears the champagne-and-peach-based Bellini was invented in their Venetian locale) on the outdoor deck while waiting for the upstairs VIP club to open. *Daily noon-11pm.* $$ ⒯F≡ 376 W. Broadway (Broome St.), 212-343-0999, cipriani.com

Craft • Gramercy • New American (G)
The name is meant to be read as a verb, as in "to craft," since the menu lists groups of food, and diners form meals of their liking. It's no more complicated than combining tapas or ordering side dishes, and while there's technically no wrong way to do it, waiters may dissuade customers who put together things like roasted halibut and applesauce. The high ceilings and leather walls provide a chic setting for the well-appointed crowd, which leans toward the hipper side of the socialite scene, with more than a few hard-core foodies. *Sun-Thu 5:30-10pm, Fri-Sat 5:30-11pm.* $$$ Ⓑ≡ 43 E. 19th St. (Park Ave. S.), 212-780-0880, craftrestaurant.com

DB Bistro Moderne • Midtown • French
Is it still a burger when stuffed with foie gras and black truffles? Run by celebrity chef Daniel Boulud (of four-star restaurants Daniel and Boulud), DB is his most accessible and least pricey venture to date. Though limited, the menu is never weak or without imagination (as the bacon-veiled monkfish tail illustrates). DB's tables and chairs are modeled on African wood carvings, and the room's design is a color explosion—red walls with massive paintings of shocking red flowers—providing a sexy element of canned heat. *Call for hours.* $$ Ⓕ≡ City Club Hotel, 55 W. 44th St. (6th Ave.), 212-391-2400, danielnyc.com

Dos Caminos Soho • Soho • Mexican
Steve Hanson operates highly lauded venues like NoHo Star, Blue Water Grill, Vento Trattoria, and Ruby Foo's, to name a few, yet the nouveau Mexican Dos Caminos is one of his most popular joints. The cuisine isn't four-star, but the vibe is always young and energetic. In the summertime, the patio is the place to be, and margaritas are a must (especially considering the collection of 150 tequilas). Inside the two dining rooms, skylights brighten the Southwestern stone decor. The entrees are straightforward, the desserts are decadent. *Call for hours.* $$ Ⓕ≡ 475 W. Broadway (Houston St.), 212-277-4300, brguestrestaurants.com

Ess-a-Bagel • Gramercy/Midtown • Deli
Best Bagels You can find the same thick, meaty bagels at either location, where piling on the lox and other toppings for a fully loaded "sandwich" will put you around the $3 mark. The Nine-Grain with Honey is the newest thing to hit the long standing traditional menu. Ess-a-Bagel rolls all of their bagels by hand, and everything they sell is guaranteed kosher. Gourmet flavored coffees and espresso drinks are also served, and an array of cakes, pastries, rugelach, and cookies are baked fresh daily. *1st Ave.: Mon-Sat 6:30am-9pm, Sun 6:30am-5pm; 3rd Ave.: Mon-Fri 6am-9pm, Sat-Sun 7am-5pm.* $- ≡ 359 1st Ave. (22nd St.), 212-260-2252; 831 3rd Ave. (50th St.), 212-980-1010, ess-a-bagel.com

Estiatorio Milos • Midtown • Greek (G)
Opa! Estiatorio Milos may be one of the finest Greek restaurants this side of the wine-dark sea. Toss a plate if you must, but if it contains one of the menu's excellent helpings of octopus, it would not only be a waste, it could cause you a hernia. These near-perfect entrees come in portions so generous, not even Zeus could eat it all in one sitting. The dramatically lit, minimalist space is big, too, with rounded Acropolis-like walls and white mesh curtains. *Mon-Fri noon-2:45pm and 5-11:30pm, Sat 5-11:30pm, Sun 5-10:45pm.* $$$$ Ⓑ≡ 125 W. 55th St. (6th Ave.), 212-245-7400, milos.ca

Félix • Soho • French Bistro

Best French Bistros Félix is a fantastic, upscale bistro, inside and out (literally), with an old-fashioned bar complete with arched mirror, and tall French doors that open onto the sidewalk in warm weather. Well-cooked steaks frites are served on the outdoor patio, or in the polished-yet-rustic dining room, which draws Soho's trendiest regulars. Dress is fashionably informal, with men combining expensive jeans and blazers, while ladies don snug denim and of-the-moment heels. The late crowd is about lingering over specialty cocktails. When weather permits, the outside tables fill up fast. *Mon-Fri noon-midnight, Sat 11:30am-midnight, Sun 11:30am-10:30pm.* $$ B≡ 340 W. Broadway (Grand St.), 212-431-0021, felixnyc.com

Harry Cipriani • Midtown • Italian

Best Chic Restaurants Jet-setters (and jet owners) are already familiar with Harry Cipriani's older cousin in Venice, Harry's Bar, which has inspired this Midtown favorite's menu of exquisite Venetian fare. Harry Cipriani's offerings are as rich and worldly as its international clientele, featuring pastas in heavy cream sauces, and a calamari risotto that will leave you full for a week. The small room is dark and thoughtful, with picture windows overlooking the Empire State Building. Men in gold-buttoned navy blazers nurse stiff martinis at the small bar. *Daily 7am-10:30am, noon-3pm, and 6-10:45pm.* $$$$ ▢ 781 5th Ave. (59th St.), 212-753-5566, cipriani.com

Hudson Cafeteria • Midtown • American

When the designer-restaurateur dream team of Ian Schrager and Jeffrey Chodorow opened Hudson Cafeteria, its door policy was as elitist as the Ivy League prep school it was modeled after. Though the gleaming mahogany and dark-wood decor still has a *Dead Poets Society* feel, the overall place has dropped its pretensions. Communal, candlelit tables look onto the open kitchen, where white-clad chefs bustle around a fire-dancing stove. The comfort food comes with a twist, like mac and cheese topped with shrimp or foie gras, and spaghetti with tuna balls. *Mon-Wed 6:30am-11:30pm, Thu-Fri 6:30am-12:30am, Sat 6:30am-12:30am, Sun 6:30am-11:30pm.* $ ▢≡ Hudson Hotel, 356 W. 58th St. (8th St.), 212-554-6500, hudsonhotel.com

Indochine* • Greenwich Village • French-Asian

Best Asian Dining Indochine no longer enjoys the extreme popularity it saw in the early 2000s, and in many ways, that's not a bad thing. Now people can actually get reservations on the day they want them. The French-Asian menu suggests a post-colonial reconciliation, with items like sole in coconut milk curry representing the East, and the filet mignon acting as ambassador of the West. Indochine's dining room is lush, with majestic green banquettes and a palm leaf decor. The bar scene is lively to overflowing, with elbow-rubbing cocktailers spilling into the dining area in later hours. *Sun-Mon 5:30-11:30pm, Tue-Sat 5:30pm-2am.* $$ ▨≡ 430 Lafayette St. (4th St.), 212-505-5111, indochinenyc.com

La Bottega • Chelsea • Italian

Fancy chicken under a brick? La Bottega serves up rustic *cucina italiana* amid gleaming white-tiled walls, buttery leather seats, and a quirky "wallpaper" of Cinzano bottles. Though this Tuscan-chic eatery draws a trendy, boutique-hotel crowd, it also manages to maintain a casual, trattoria vibe. The chatty waitstaff keeps the wine flowing, and the down-home Italian fare not only satisfies, it also pulls off a few surprises, such as the thin, flaky pizza of ribiola cheese drizzled in aromatic white truffle oil. *Daily 6pm-midnight.* $ ▤ The Maritime Hotel, 363 W. 16th St. (9th St.), 212-242-4300, themaritimehotel.com/bottega.html

Lure Fishbar* • Soho • Seafood

Best Of-the-Moment Dining It didn't take this nautical-themed Soho restaurant long to reel in the hippest Downtowners, with its spit-shined interior and exotic maritime menu. Awash in polished wood, brass accents, and white leather, this underground space is as cozy as a billionaire's yacht, with porthole windows to boot. Creative culinary twists include fried calamari with sweet and sour chili glaze, and tempura shrimp with black-bean mayonnaise. The straightforward raw bar is as fresh as it gets. Lure's little lounge-bar has a happening scene, but is not conducive to conversation. *Mon-Fri noon-11pm, Sat-Sun noon-3pm and 5:30-11pm.* $$$ 🍸⟟▤ 142 Mercer St. (Prince St.), 212-431-7676, lurefishbar.com

Matsuri • Chelsea • Japanese

The sleek, hipster Maritime Hotel is a fitting backdrop for the airy, Asian-kissed Matsuri. In a city where space is at a premium, Matsuri's soaring dining room is a pleasant anomaly, with paper lanterns strung across high vaulted ceilings. The dark-wood tables, plush banquettes, and giant vases of bamboo afford a soothing Zen-like vibe that compliments (and complements) the delectable Japanese sushi, including sake-marinated black cod, and silky salmon topped with lotus root. The staff and crowd, decked out in designer duds, are easy on the eyes, too. *Sun-Wed 6pm-12:15am, Thu-Sat 6pm-1am.* $$ ▤ The Maritime Hotel, 363 W. 16th St. (9th St.), 212-242-4300, themaritimehotel.com/matsuri.html

Mercer Kitchen • Soho • Mediterranean

With a hotel as cool as the Mercer, only a Jean-Georges kitchen will suffice. These days, the Mercer Kitchen gets a lot less hype than the superchef's newer venues, which is just why you should come (though reservations are still highly recommended). The dining room is in the basement, with lavender banquettes and a translucent glass ceiling. The Franco-Mediterranean cuisine is predictably excellent. *Daily 7-11am, noon-3pm, 6pm-2am.* $$ ⟟▤ 99 Prince St. (Mercer St.), 212-966-5454, jean-georges.com

Olives* • Gramercy • Mediterranean

Chef Todd English (who has restaurants all over the United States, in Tokyo, and aboard the Queen Mary 2) has been named Restaurateur of the Year as well as one of *People* magazine's 50 Most Beautiful People. His restaurant, Olives, housed in the bustling lobby of the W Hotel Union Square, offers a nightly five-course tasting menu of artfully prepared homemade pastas, heartier fare like short ribs and duck, and delicate seafood dishes. Lunch is a good time to sample English's legendary gourmet burger. *Mon-Thu 7-10:30am, noon-2:30pm, and 6-10:30pm, Fri 7-10:30am, noon-2:30pm, and 6-11pm, Sat 10am-2:30pm and 6-11pm, Sun 10am-2:30pm and 5:30-10pm.* $$ 🍸⟟▤ W Hotel Union Square, 201 Park Ave. S. (17th St.), 212-353-8345, toddenglish.com

Otto* • Greenwich Village • Pizzeria
Best Pizza Leave it to Mario Batali to reinvent a New York staple like pizza. Otto's classic Italian, ultrathin crust pies include familiar ingredients like pepperoni, and esoteric suggestions like raw fennel and bottarga (Italian caviar). In addition to its variety of pies, Otto offers a selection of cured meats and cheeses, inventive vegetable side dishes, homemade pastas, and exquisite desserts. The wine list is extensive and carefully chosen with the menu in mind (many vintages are also available in generous quartinos). The back dining room faces tranquil Washington Mews, a car-free cobblestone street of revamped Victorian stables. *Daily 11:30am-midnight.* $ ⅩF☰ 1 5th Ave. (8th St.), 212-995-9559, ottopizzeria.com

Public* • Soho • Australian
Best Always Trendy Restaurants This ultracool Australian/New Zealand-inspired restaurant's design hints at a Depression-era public house, with concrete floors, lofty ceilings, exposed piping and rafters, and iron lamps. The menu not only features treats from Down Under, like kangaroo medallions (and many a Shiraz on the wine list), but a few Asian-infused dishes as well. The small den in back is for nursing cocktails and conversing in front of a roaring fire. *Mon-Thu 6-11:30pm, Fri-Sat 6pm-12:30am, Sun 6-10:30pm, Fri-Sat the bar stays open until 3am.* $$ ⅩB☰ 210 Elizabeth St. (Prince St.), 212-343-7011, public-nyc.com

Sushi Samba 7* • West Village/Gramercy • Sushi
Best Sushi There are two Sushi Sambas in Manhattan, and while the menus are pretty much the same, their personalities are quite different. The original locale on Park Avenue South, with a more corporate clientele, is a little more "sushi." Sushi Samba 7 in the West Village, with a more bohemian clientele, is a tad more "samba." The most relaxed scene is in the Village, where diners sip caipirinhas on the rooftop and listen to live jazz. What both places share is a fun and creative fusion of Japanese food and Brazilian spices. *The Park: Mon-Wed 11:45am-1am, Thu-Sat 11:45am-2am, Sun 1pm-midnight. 7th Ave.: Mon-Wed 11:45am-1am, Thu-Sat 11:45am-2am, Sun 12:15pm-midnight.* $$ ⅩF☰ 87 7th Ave. S. (Bleecker St.), 212-691-7885; 245 Park Ave. S. (19th St.), 212-475-9377, sushisamba.com

Tabla • Gramercy • Indian Fusion (G)
For the past seven years, Tabla has shown Gotham gourmands the true meaning of fun fusion via well-merged American and Indian cuisine. Thanks to the nearby green market, the menu is always fresh, with exotic inventions like crab with tamarind chutney and seared scallops with tandoori cauliflower. Tabla's interior space is stunning, if complicated, with stained wood, green walls, and an almost theaterlike decor. The service is impeccably efficient. On the ground floor, Bread Bar serves exceptional home-style Indian cuisine. Note to trivia buffs—a "tabla" is a pair of Indian hand drums. *Mon-Fri noon-2pm and 5:30-10:30pm, Sat 5:30-10:30pm, Sun 5:30-10pm.* $$$ F☰ 11 Madison Ave. (25th St.), 212-889-0667, tablany.com

Tao* • Midtown • Asian Fusion
This is Billionaire Buddhism à la Richard Gere, and it looks as good as it tastes. *Sex and the City* did an episode here a few years back, and immediately the cool factor (which was already high) went through the roof. A 16-foot Buddha presides over the massive, multilevel space. The chronically scene-y crowd dresses to impress, and one can only hope the kitchen's awe-inspiring Pan-Asian cuisine isn't going unnoticed. The corny theme cocktails are a little hard to forgive, but you have to give the bar credit for knowing its crowd. *Mon-Wed 11:30am-midnight, Thu-Fri 11:30am-1am, Sat-Sun 5pm-1am.* $$$ ☕≡ 42 E. 58th St. (Madison Ave.), 212-888-2288, taorestaurant.com

Town* • Midtown • New American
Never mistake refinement for blandness, as there's much fun to be had at this elegant trilevel haunt. The New American cuisine at Town is as colorful as the restaurant is subtle, designed in gray tones and amber light. Downstairs, it's all about dining, and the wildly ranging menu features entrees like octopus, quail, vela tongue, and duck steak. Over 300 wines are offered on the two upper floors overlooking the dining room, but the "on the Town" folks decked out in semi-formal threads generally accessorize with specialty cocktails that change seasonally. *Daily 7-10:30am, noon-2:30pm, and 5:30-10:30pm, Sun 11am-2:30pm.* $$$ ☕≡ Chambers Hotel, 15 W. 56th St. (5th Ave.), 212-582-4445, townnyc.com

Tribeca Grill* • Tribeca • New American
The once über-hot upscale tavern, Tribeca Grill, is still very popular, though once the trend-seeking hordes realized they wouldn't be pounding shots with co-owner Robert De Niro, they moved on. Once a coffin factory, the spacious dark-wood and exposed-brick interior now hosts a spirited mix of locals and celebs (especially Hollywood big shots who come to visit the Weinstein brothers in their Miramax offices upstairs). Mediterranean-inspired surf and turf entrees round out an otherwise solid, though predictable, menu. *Mon-Fri 11:30am-11:30pm, Sat 5:30-11:30pm, Sun 11:30am-3pm and 5:30-10pm.* $$$ ☕≡ 375 Greenwich St. (Franklin St.), 212-941-3900, myriadrestaurantgroup.com/tribecagrill

COOL

Cool New York:
The Nightlife

Angel's Share • East Village • Lounge
In this unmarked second-floor lounge, cocktailing is rarely the end of a date, if you get my drift. Located on a quiet East Village side street, Angel's Share is nothing if not romantic. The solemn Japanese staff refuses entry to groups of five or more, and new patrons are only admitted when seating is available. Shouting is not allowed, perhaps to avoid distracting the alchemists mixing cocktails behind the bar. Sake and whiskey are the spirits of choice, with a menu of late-night fare, like sashimi and dim sum, to sate a late-night palate. *6pm-2:30am.* B☐ 8 Stuyvesant St. (3rd Ave.), 212-777-5415

AVA Lounge • Midtown • Ultra Lounge
In the summertime, AVA's rooftop is a popular after-work hangout for 9-to-5ers, as well as hip out-of-towners who flood the place in the late evening. Off season, it's a good idea to call ahead to request a table near the big southern-exposed windows overlooking the Ed Sullivan Theater and a dazzling sea of neon. While this ultracool venue could do the velvet-rope thing, AVA opts for an egalitarian admissions policy, and there's nothing wrong with that. *Sun-Wed 5pm-2am, Thu-Sat 5pm-4am.* ☰ Dream Hotel, 210 W. 55th St. (Broadway), 212-956-7020, avaloungenyc.com

Bar Veloce • East Village • Wine Bar
Best Wine Bars It doesn't take much to fill this attractive East Village wine bar, with quarters so snug, if you didn't come with a date, you'll probably leave with one. The scene is a cool and evenly mixed gay and straight crowd, basking in Veloce's radiant pink glow while sipping everything from basic reds and whites to grappa, sake, and cognac. Bartenders clad in perfectly tailored suits are earnest and knowledgeable, offering pressed sandwiches and a wine for every taste. *Sun-Sat 5pm-3am.* B☰ 175 2nd Ave. (11th St.), 212-260-3200, barveloce.com

Canal Room • Soho • Nightclub
Canal Room is always a nice little club, but when artists big and small host listening parties, it's truly the coolest joint in town. An elevated, eye-level VIP table faces the stage across the room, overlooking the lounge of leather sofas, the parquet dance floor, and the state-of-the-art DJ booth, which is always occupied by a top-notch DJ and a sound engineer. The music depends on the night, but while the room is modern, the sound system is all about the '80s. *Mon 11pm-4am, Thu-Sat 9pm-4am.* C☰ 285 W. Broadway (Canal St.), 212-941-8100, canalroom.com

Church Lounge • Tribeca • Ultra Lounge

Church Lounge is one of the city's coolest hotel lounges, especially when big fashion-related events are in town, and designers and models fill the Tribeca Grand Hotel. The high-ceilinged, sofa-lined lounge is decorated in honey tones, and its long, well-attended bar twinkles with a wall of electric candles. Both the Tribeca Grand Hotel and the Church Lounge are very dog-friendly, so expect to see visiting socialites accessorizing with lap dogs and colored cosmos. Scenesters come out in droves on weekends, and with them, the velvet rope. *Mon-Sun noon-3am.* B≣ Tribeca Grand Hotel, 2 6th Ave. (White St.), 212-519-6677, tribecagrand.com

Cub Room* • Soho • Restaurant Lounge

This trendy lounge built in 1994 hosts a well-to-do and mature Soho "it" crowd for after-work cocktails and candlelight dinners. This probably isn't the kind of place where people meet their future spouse, but it's a sufficiently romantic place to take the current one. *Sun-Wed 11am-2am, Thu-Sat 11am-4am.* F≣ 131 Sullivan St. (Prince St.), 212-677-4100, cubroom.com

The Dove • Greenwich Village • Bar

Best Cocktail Mixologists Red parlor wallpaper, white columns, and an old fireplace provide the backdrop to pretty, rock-chic bartenders who serve up exotic concoctions of soymilk and honey, pints of imported beer, and wine from an extensive list (one of the owners also operates a wine store). In the after-work hours, the iPod stereo's classic jazz songs create a speakeasy vibe. As night falls, the rock tunes take over. The big booth by the French windows is the best place to camp out for an evening, and can be reserved with a phone call. *Daily 3pm-4am.* ≣ 228 Thompson St. (Bleecker St.), 212-254-1435

Duvet* • Flatiron • Restaurant Lounge

The bed trend in nightclubs has grown a bit tired, but unless you live here or in Miami, where it started, dining in the company of dozens of reclining couples is a unique experience. The neon shades and heavy stylization bring South Florida to mind. Duvet's seafood menu is serviceable, just avoid eye contact with the starfish in the tank downstairs. The crowd may not make the A-list cut at the city's super-chichi hotspots, but when it comes to a chic night on the town for mere mortals, Duvet has it covered. *Mon-Thu 5:30pm-midnight, Fri-Sat 5pm-4am.* F≣ 45 W. 21st St. (6th Ave.), 212-989-2121, duvetny.com

Earth NYC* • Chelsea • Nightclub

You don't need posters of Gandhi and camels to get the Bombay vibe at this bi-level, Indian-themed lounge, with red and tangerine walls, low sofas, purple curtains, and bejeweled candleholders. Westernized Indian beats play while couples cavort downstairs, and semi-socialite party types dance on the half-balcony overhead. The Indian appetizers are more street food than four-star, mainly kabobs and spicy cocktail weenies. Earth does have a rope, but it's not nearly as VIP as the neighboring Meatpacking District and West Chelsea scene. *Thu 5-11pm, Fri-Sat 5pm-4am.* F≣ 116 10th Ave. (17th St.), 212-337-0016, earth-nyc.com

Embassy • Flatiron • Nightclub

Embassy is one of those clubs that's equally conducive to dancing and lounging. The doorman is mostly looking to keep the male-female ratio even, perhaps paying some attention to what patrons are wearing, but not to the point of condescension. If you made reservations, you're getting in. If not, your chances are still good. Earth-toned floors and walls combine with elaborate chandeliers to create a cozy denlike vibe. House music is played at levels loud enough to provide energy, but the crisp sound system makes conversation possible. C≣ *Thu-Sat 11pm-4am.* 28 W. 20th St. (5th Ave.), 212-741-3470

Flûte* • Gramercy • Wine Bar

These are two of the most romantic lounges in town, or maybe it's just the champagne talking. Actually, if champagne could talk, this place would be a-chattering, as Flûte stocks more than 100 varieties (10 by the glass), elegantly served in Baccarat crystal. The 54th Street locale is a former speakeasy that still has a bit of misbehavin' spirit. The Park Avenue locale is livelier, even bringing in a DJ on weekends. Whichever you choose, and that's not to say you're limited to one, try some of the handmade chocolates imported from Paris. *Sun-Wed 5pm-2am, Thu 5pm-3am, Fri-Sat 5pm-4am.* F≣ 40 E. 20th St. (Park Ave. S.), 212-529-7870; 205 W. 54th St. (Broadway), 212-265-5169, flutebar.com

44 Restaurant* • Midtown • Hotel Lounge

The lounge adjunct to the Royalton Hotel's 44 Restaurant is a destination spot in its own right, thanks to an oh-so-posh decor designed by Philippe Starck in the late '80s. The bar area buzzes with well-to-do 35-plus power players always looking to seal a deal, while the surrounding linen-covered tables host couples snacking on French-influenced New American cuisine. The nearby lobby's Round Bar is a nice option for those struck with a sudden need for privacy. *Mon-Fri 7am-3pm and 5:45-10:30pm, Sat-Sun 8am-2pm and 5:45-10:30pm.* B≣ Royalton Hotel, 44 W. 44th St. (5th Ave.), 212-944-8844, royaltonhotel.com

Happy Ending • Soho • Theme Bar

Best Theme Bars Upon entering this seemingly derelict building, an old security monitor displays looped black-and-white footage from when the underground space housed a seedy massage parlor, known for its "happy endings." There's still plenty of action going on inside, but today it's all legal. A good-looking, friendly crowd comes for rock and funk in the two downstairs lounges, complete with old linoleum-lined steam rooms left over from those "gratifying" old days. *Tue 10pm-4am, Wed-Sat 7pm-4am.* ≣ 302 Broome St. (Forsyth St.), 212-334-9676, happyendinglounge.com

Henrietta Hudson • West Village • Dive Bar

Best Gay/Lesbian Bars Guys, if you're having no luck at this bar, it really isn't you. Ladies, if you're having no luck here, well ... maybe it's time to rethink the hairdo. Henrietta Hudson is one of the city's most beloved lesbian bars, known for its something-for-everyone appeal. A crowd of professionals, artists, fashionistas, and locals is quick to fill the front room bar and the pool table area in back (not to mention every other nook and cranny). Occasionally, there's a minimum cover for the DJs, who get things going around midnight. *Mon-Fri 4pm-4am, Sat-Sun 1pm-4am.* C≣ 438 Hudson St. (Morton St.), 212-924-3347, henriettahudsons.com

Hudson Bar • Midtown • Hotel Lounge

Best Hotel Lounges Hotel bars don't get much livelier than this one, but what else would you expect from the man behind Studio 54? Hotel, restaurant, and nightclub ingenue Ian Schrager certainly didn't earn his party-throwing reputation with subtlety, and Hudson Bar is proof. The floor is lit from beneath, à la *Saturday Night Fever*, and furnished with Louie XV chairs. Colorful murals walk the line between tacky and showy, as does the well-heeled crowd (particularly on weekends). Hotel guests should use their "influence," as should guests of sister lodgings, the Royalton and Gramercy. *Daily 4pm-4am.* ⬚ Hudson Hotel, 356 W. 58th St. (8th Ave.), 212-554-6500, hudsonhotel.com

Hudson Library • Midtown • Lounge

One could indeed get some reading done in this glorified study, which feels like the den of an exclusive members-only club. Sparsely stocked bookshelves surround game board–topped cocktail tables, and a billiard table covered in purple felt. The cozy fireplace stirs up cravings for cognac and quiet conversation. The Hudson Library bar often serves as a warm-up for those waiting for the hotel's considerably more animated main bar to pick up steam later in the evening. *Sun-Mon noon-4am.* ⬚ 356 W. 58th St. (8th Ave.), 212-554-6317, hudsonhotel.com

Iridium Jazz Club • Midtown • Jazz Club

Best Jazz Clubs Though Iridium itself isn't one of those charming, basement-level jazz clubs that's been sitting around since the beginning of time, its neighborhood hosted many such venues before Disney moved in. This busy, relatively new jazz club has an excellent sound system that was, in part, designed by Monday Night's resident guitar legend, Les Paul. It may be too young to be considered an institution, but Iridium books some of the biggest names in jazz, and there isn't a bad sight line in the house. *Fri-Sat 6:30pm-1am, Sun-Thu 6:30pm-midnight.* ©🄵▤ 1650 Broadway (51st St.), 212-582-2121, iridiumjazzclub.com

Late Night with Conan O'Brien • Midtown • Performance

If offbeat comedy is your game, then Conan's the name. The free tickets to *Late Night* can be tough to come by, albeit easier than those for *Letterman*. You may be able to score standby tickets at the 49th Street entrance to 30 Rockefeller Plaza, where the line starts to form at 9am, when the box office opens (but get there by 8am). That said, there are no guarantees. Fans of the Max Weinberg Band can sometimes catch them playing at Chelsea's Cutting Room (19 W. 24th St.). *Tapings Tue-Fri 5:30-6:30pm. Those with tickets should arrive by 4:30pm.* ▤ 30 Rockefeller Plz. (49th St.), 212-664-3056, nbc.com

Lotus* • Meatpacking District • Ultra Lounge

Best Restaurant Lounges A nightclub that's relatively historic (having started up in 2000, which, by New York nightlife standards, is ancient) and still somewhat chic, Lotus packs in big crowds. Pioneer of the out-of-control Meatpacking District club scene, this trilevel space served as a model for everything that followed in its designer footsteps. The rather unfunky vibe works well for corporate types who prefer the supper club schedule to the postmidnight starting time that you'll find in newer hotspots. *Kitchen: Tue-Sat 7-11:30pm; Club: Tue-Sun 11pm-4am.* ©🄵▤ 409 W. 14th St. (10th Ave.), 212-243-4420, lotusnewyork.com

Lucky Strike* • Soho • Restaurant Lounge

When Soho was the city's hottest neighborhood, this was one of its hottest locations. Now decidedly cooler, this late-night eatery is still humming with life. Owned by Keith McNally, who runs a string of popular faux French hotspots throughout the city, Lucky Strike serves a mix of French and American comfort food and strong, supersized cocktails. Of course, people go to Lucky Strike for the scene, which has the vibe of both a neighborhood bar and a hip bohemian hangout. *Sun-Wed noon-3am, Thu-Sat noon-4am.* F≣ 59 Grand St. (W. Broadway), 212-941-0772, luckystrikeny.com

MercBar • Soho • Ultra Lounge

Yes, there's a doorman and a velvet rope outside MercBar, but that's just to prevent overcrowding. Anyone who's going to pass judgment is already drinking at the bar. It's hard to guess the theme at work. The canoe and antlers hanging about suggest a house-in-the-woods schtick, but the sleek modern design, and attractive, black-clad staff, are all Downtown Manhattan. In the summer, the front windows open and become the place to be seen. *Sun-Mon 5pm-1:30am, Tue-Wed 5pm-2am, Thu 5pm-2:30am, Fri-Sat 5pm-3:30am.* ≣ 151 Mercer St. (Houston St.), 212-966-2727, mercbar.com

Odea* • Soho • Lounge

Best Restaurant Lounges It's not often that something new and hip hits Little Italy, and it's an Odea whose time has come. Too nice to be a bar and too small and laid-back to be a club, Odea throws open its doors to Downtowners, who pack tightly around the underlit onyx bar. In back, four canopied group seating areas offer U-shaped booths holding six to eight people each. Unless you're looking for close contact, the best way to lounge here is to book one of those areas and show up with a group. *Tue-Wed 6pm-2am, Thu-Sat 6pm-4am.* F≣ 389 Broome St. (Mulberry St.), 212-941-9222, odeany.com

Pravda • Soho • Lounge

Is it the best vodka lists not written out in Cyrillic, or the stylish Soho crowd of art dealers, Wall Streeters, and potato juice aficionados, that makes Pravda a downtown mainstay? More than 70 vodkas from a dozen Eastern Bloc nations are paired with fine caviar in this low-ceilinged, dimly lit setting. Just a few years ago, Keith McNally's Pravda was so popular, the queue outside looked like a bread line in Communist Russia. Things have since calmed down, and getting inside no longer involves a frustrating wait. *Mon-Tue 5pm-1am, Wed-Thu 5pm-2am, Fri-Sat 5pm-3am, Sun 6pm-1am.* ≣ 281 Lafayette St. (Prince St.), 212-226-4944, pravdany.com

Session 73 • Upper East Side • Bar

Best Easy Local Vibe It's a tried-and-true formula that attracts postcollegiates and balding middle-aged locals alike—a live band plays and nobody pays. Between a small, innocuous dining room and a TV-dominated lounge, Session 73 stretches long, facing the stage where cover bands jam out popular rock tunes. No one seems too interested in the occasional original song slipped into the set list, but given that the music is always live and free seven nights a week, the business-casual crowd of regulars doesn't complain. *Sun-Wed 5pm-2am, Thu-Sat 5pm-4am.* F≣ 1359 1st Ave. (73rd St.), 212-517-4445, session73.com

Upright Citizens Brigade Theatre • Chelsea • Comedy Club

Cofounded by *Saturday Night Live* star Amy Poehler, the Upright Citizens Brigade Theatre is New York City's most cutting-edge improv house. The oddball sketch comedy that's come out of this place also spawned a popular Comedy Central series. It's unlikely you'll have to endure the indescribable pain of bad comedy at this grassroots venue, where it isn't uncommon to see accomplished comics like Dave Berry honing his skills. Sunday night's "Asssscat 3,000" is quickly becoming one of the popular shows on the docket. *Daily showtimes vary, beginning as early as 7pm and as late as midnight.* ⓒ 307 W. 26th St. (7th Ave.), 212-366-9176, ucbtheatre.com

Whiskey Blue • Midtown • Hotel Lounge

Best Singles Scene There are as many whiskey bars in New York City as Wal-Marts in the rural South. Why? Because there's a market for them. At Whiskey Blue, where a reservable bed sits front and center, there's more character than one might expect from an upscale-ish franchise watering hole. A surprisingly flirtatious Park Avenue after-work set packs the place after 5pm, leaves around 8pm, and often returns refreshed and reenergized when the pickup scene continues later in the night. *Daily 4pm-4am.* ⊟ W New York—Union Square, 541 Lexington Ave. (49th St.), 212-407-2947, midnightoilbars.com

COOL

Cool New York:
The Attractions

American Folk Art Museum • Midtown • Museum

This sizable museum, only steps from the park, boasts 4,000 diverse works of creative inspiration, produced from the 19th century to the present day. Defying the rigid categories of fine art, these sculptures, quilts, paintings, and weather vanes, among many other pieces, are kept in context to tell American stories that would otherwise go untold. The Contemporary Center features self-taught individuals who create "outsider" art of the late 20th and early 21st centuries. The museum also hosts symposiums, guided tours, and workshops, as well as a certificate program in folk art. *Tue-Sun 10:30am-5:30pm, Fri 10:30am-7:30pm.* $- 45 W. 53rd St. (5th Ave.), 212-265-1040, folkartmuseum.org

Apple Store • Soho • Shop

That's right—this computer store is too cool. Not only can visitors pop in to check their email, they can stay for the free instructional classes on computer tricks taught by techno-hip guests like DJ LES, who records on iTunes and mixes on iPods. You don't have an iPod? Odds are someone here can help in that department as well. As cool as this place is, the Genius Bar isn't much of a pick-up spot. *Sun 10am-7pm, Mon-Wed 9:30am-8pm, Thu-Fri 9:30am-9pm.* 103 Prince St. (Greene St.), 212-226-3126, apple.com

Bryant Park • Midtown • Park

Best Outdoor People-Watching If it weren't for Central Park, this is where everyone in New York would hang out. Occupying most of the block behind the Public Library, Bryant Park's expansive lawn is where thousands of Midtown shoppers and office workers tan their fluorescent bulb–blanched faces at lunchtime. *Good Morning America*–sponsored concerts in the park usually start around 7am, and have featured superstars like Stevie Wonder, Jessica Simpson, and *American Idol* Ruben Studdard. In the summer, the park hosts a romantic Monday night movie series. 500 5th Ave. (42nd St.), 212-768-4242

Chelsea Market • Chelsea • Shop

This city isn't big on malls, but Chelsea Market is as close as it gets. Forget the Gap store or Orange Julius; this beautiful industrial design features rows of restaurants and small shops, where you'll find fresh produce, gourmet cooking ingredients, kitchen supplies, and flowers. The Food Network, whose offices are upstairs, sometimes films on-the-spot pieces here. Also housed in the building above are Oprah Winfrey's Oxygen Studios, which the Queen of Daytime TV visits whenever she's in town. *Mon-Sat 7am-9pm, Sun 10am-8pm.* 75 9th Ave. (W. 17th St.), 212-243-6005, chelseamarket.com

Chelsea Piers • Chelsea • Health Club

This sports complex makes a nice neighborhood. Seriously, an afternoon spent walking around the expansive collection of gyms, fields, and, yes, piers, will provide more exercise than most people get in a year. The glass-enclosed lap pool nearly touches the Hudson. City bowlers (who fancy themselves athletes of sorts) take advantage of the AMF Chelsea Piers Lane, and golfers slice it up at Pier 59's driving range. The sprawling complex also offers batting cages, skating rinks (roller and ice), and basketball courts. Are you tired yet? *Mon-Sun 6am-midnight during the summer. Hours vary in the winter.* W. 23rd St. (the Hudson River), 212-336-6666, chelseapiers.com

Chrysler Building • Midtown • Site
For one glorious year, before its neighbor, the Empire State Building, was finished in 1931, the 77-story Chrysler Building was the world's tallest. In the opinion of many architecture buffs, it's still the coolest. The amazing seven-story art deco spire was literally built inside the tower, then raised through the roof. That tower once housed a speakeasy known as the Cloud Room, now closed to the public ... or is it? OK, we're just messin' with you. It is. But there's nothing like standing at the foot of this formidable structure and looking straight up. *Mon-Fri 8:30am-5:30pm.* 405 Lexington Ave. (42nd St.), 212-682-3070

Exit Art • Midtown • Art Gallery
Enter expensive retailers, exit Exit Art. Such is the story of Soho, where this hip gallery was a shining star for the unconventional painters, photographers, and sculptors of the 1980s art explosion. Now housed in a bigger space in the Midtown outskirts of Hell's Kitchen, Exit Art is inviting musicians and filmmakers to share their visions, too. This organic gallery is not the Guggenheim, and may not work for those who aren't into conceptual art. Don't expect priceless displays of stained glass—unless it's been "altered." *Tue-Thu 10am-6pm, Fri 10am-8pm, Sat noon-8pm. The Cafe: Fri-Sat noon-8pm, Sun noon-6pm.* $- 475 10th Ave. (36th St.), 212-966-7745, exitart.org

Integral Yoga • West Village • Health Club
When you have to have your hatha, Integral Yoga is the place to go. The daily classes and workshops on the second floor welcome walk-ins, but reservations are recommended. This place draws 6,000-plus students monthly. Luckily, there are courses aplenty, including a free deep relaxation course from 5:30 to 6pm every day. Levels of classes range from beginning to advanced, and starting times range from 9:30am to 8pm. The vibe here is very laid back, and the crowd is more meditative than aerobic. *Mon-Fri 7:15am-9:30pm, Sat 9:15am-8:30pm, Sun 10:15am-6:30pm. Closed on Sundays in August.* $$ 227 W. 13th St. (7th Ave.), 212-929-0586, iyiny.org

International Center of Photography • Midtown • Museum
Not nearly as broad in scope as the MoMA or the Whitney, the International Center of Photography caters to a specific breed of artists and admirers. The ICP is mightily influenced by the respected school across the street, so the lecture series and exhibitions tend to attract more practicing shutterbugs than photography fans. Both modern and contemporary, the permanent collection leans toward vérité snapshots, with more than a small nod to photojournalism. The cafe downstairs is modest and bohemian. *Tue-Thu 10am-6pm, Fri 10am-8pm, Sat-Sun 10am-6pm.* $ 1133 Avenue of the Americas (43rd St.), 212-857-0000, icp.org

Madison Square Garden • Chelsea • Site
Did you know that the Knicks actually practice? They do, and if you take a one-hour MSG tour, offered daily, you just might see it happening. Depending on the

day's events, this all-access walk-around takes visitors through the Knicks, Liberty, and Rangers locker rooms, shows how the basketball court is laid over the ice rink, and explains the backstage workings behind the huge concerts that happen here regularly. This tour has enough magic for a 13-year-old, and enough substance for a 30-something. *Daily 11am-3pm.* $ 4 Pennsylvania Plz. (W. 31st St.), 212-465-6741, thegarden.com

Marc Jacobs • Soho • Shop
From the outside, this chic shop looks like a fashion speakeasy. Despite the high-profile Marc Jacobs label, his Soho store keeps a very low profile. His designs follow suit, with a worn-to-comfort look that savvy fashionistas easily recognize and die-hard fans won't go without. Accessories like hats and bags sell really well here, and you can say, "These Marc Jacobs heels? I got them in Soho." You'll find a smaller men's collection here as well. *Mon-Sat 11am-7pm, Sun noon-6pm.* 163 Mercer St. (W. Houston St.), 212-343-1490, marcjacobs.com

Marcoart • Lower East Side • Art Gallery
Best Galleries Viewing thought-provoking pop art is fun. Owning it is even better. This quintessential Soho painter sold his work on street corners for years before opening a gallery to display his vibrant cartoon art (reminiscent of the work of fellow Soho artist, the late Keith Haring). Though Marco has decorated a line of guitars for Gibson and painted portraits of NBA Hall of Famers for the 2004 U.S. Olympic Committee, local collectors still come to this gallery to see what they might hang on their apartment walls. *By appointment.* 181 Orchard St. (Stanton St.), 646-479-2263, marcoart.com

Metamorphosis Day Spa • Midtown • Spa
Best Spas This well-operated Park Avenue spa prides itself on grooming and relaxation treatments for the weary and the fabulous. Most of the patrons of this tranquil urban retreat are female, but the male clientele make a surprisingly strong (if metrosexual) showing. Airbrush tanning is a popular feature, and the facials and hair removal draw a fiercely loyal, not to mention soft and smooth, clientele. *Mon-Fri 10am-9pm, Sat 10am-6pm.* $$$$ 127 E. 56th St., 5th Fl. (Park Ave.), 212-751-6051, metspa.com

Michelle Nevius • Tour
Those with a strong sense of curiosity, good walking shoes, and about four hours to spare should check out the Michelle Nevius tour known as the "Manhattan Sampler," a jaunt that covers Broadway from the bottom of Manhattan to Central Park (including the occasional subway ride past certain less visitor-friendly parts of town). Those with a sense of purpose can customize tours to fit their schedule. Guided walks are especially useful downtown, where the grid doesn't apply. (Good luck finding the intersection of Waverly Street and Waverly Avenue.) *Call for tour times.* $$$$ 877-572-9719, walknyc.com

Morrison Hotel Gallery • Soho • Art Gallery
Rock art and memorabilia groupies won't want to miss this celluloid backstage pass to a half century of unbelievable photography. Some of the work is for sale, some is just to dream about, but it's all worth a look. Many cool shows pass through this modest Soho storefront, including the recently lauded Jim Marshall and Henry Diltz exhibit, which featured photos of the Beatles, the Rolling Stones,

the Doors, Crosby, Stills, Nash, and Young; and Jimi Hendrix, to name a few. Exhibits are always changing. *Gallery: Mon-Tue 11am-6pm, Wed-Sat 11am-8pm, Sun noon-6pm. Show openings usually start at 7pm.* 124 Prince St. (Wooster St.), 212-941-8770, morrisonhotelgallery.com

The Museum of the Fashion Institute of Technology • Chelsea • Museum

FIT is where future runway stars learn to strut, and the school's museum sets the bar for future Fendi models. The permanent display relies heavily on costumes and textiles, with a look at fashion's historical significance, as well as what's to come. A steady rotation of shows covers such themes as fashion in film, the styles of featured eras and decades, and, occasionally, individual designers. *Tue-Fri noon-8pm, Sat 10am-5pm.* 7th Ave. (27th St.), 212-217-5970, fitnyc.edu

Museum of Sex • Flatiron • Museum

Best Unusual Museums Strangely, the Museum of Sex isn't really perverse at all—at least not intentionally. Fortunately, it's not boring or clinical either. The emphasis is on how sexuality evolves in a fast-moving culture insistent on PG ratings, and with exhibits like "Vamps & Virgins: The Evolution of American Pinup Photography 1860–1960," this museum both educates and entertains. The two floors of tasteful, and sometimes comical, pictures, statuettes, and vintage memorabilia can be covered pretty thoroughly in a couple of hours, and, while kids probably don't need to be here, it wouldn't be at all awkward to bring a friend who's quick to blush. Oh, behave. *Sun-Fri 11am-6:30pm, Sat 11am-8pm.* $ 233 5th Ave. (27th St.), 212-689-6337, museumofsex.org

Paul Kasmin Gallery • Chelsea • Art Gallery

Paul Kasmin's collection includes multiple works by legendary artists, including Frank Stella, Robert Indiana, Joe Zuck, and Andy Warhol, as well as prized pieces from some of the most accomplished artists of today. Despite being a native Brit, Mr. Kasmin's collection is very American, as highlighted by the ten Warhols. Go ahead and get dressed up for this place—it's more than OK (though it isn't mandatory). *Tue-Sat 10am-6pm.* 293 10th Ave. (W. 27th St.), 212-563-4474, paulkasmingallery.com

Paul Morris Gallery • Chelsea • Art Gallery

Paul Morris is one of the more important photo galleries among West Chelsea's celebrated art scene, with several works from cartoonist Robert Crumb highlighting its modern, and occasionally controversial, collection. Other artists include Ewan Gibbs, Julian Schnabel, and David Seidner. *Mon-Fri 11am-6pm or by appointment.* 530 W. 25th St., 5th fl. (10th Ave.), 212-727-2752, paulmorrisgallery.com

Sex and the City Tours • Midtown • Tour

Best City Tours Whether this long-running HBO series helped many of the city's hipper restaurants and lounges, or only ruined them for the rest of us, is debatable. One thing's for sure—any venue that appeared on this program was destined to change forever. The three-hour, $35 *Sex and the City* tour, which meets in front of the Pulitzer Fountain at Fifth Avenue and 58th Street, revisits the places where Carrie and her girls discussed groundbreaking topics like pointy shoes, gay straight men, and the correlation between ice cream and heartbreak. *Tours: Mon-Fri 11am and 3pm, Sat-Sun 10am, 11am, and 3pm.* $$$ 5th Ave. (58th St.), 212-209-3370, sceneontv.com

COOL

Original New York

They say that imitation is the highest form of flattery, and no place inspires copycats like New York City. From the Las Vegas casino's Statue of Liberty to the oft-touted "New York style" pizza (or cheesecake, or deli, or steak house, or ...), American life as we know it began here in the Big Apple. Where else can you explore the pre-served tenements of the country's immigrant pioneers, lunch at the birthplace of punk rock, sing along with the cross-dressing divas at Lucky Cheng's, and laugh at the legendary comedy of *Saturday Night Live?* Only in New York, baby!

Note: Venues in bold are described in detail in the listings that follow the itinerary. Venues followed by an * asterisk are those we recommend as both a restaurant and a destination bar.

Original New York:
The Perfect Plan (3 Days and Nights)

Highlights

Thursday

Morning	Statue of Liberty
Lunch	teany
Mid-afternoon	Tenement Museum, Chinatown, Little Italy
Pre-dinner	Verlaine
Dinner	Schiller's, Elephant
Nighttime	Tenement*, Slipper Room
Late-night	Three of Cups*, BiNY

Friday

Breakfast	Pink Pony*
Mid-morning	Christine Chin Spa, East Village
Lunch	Katz's, Veselka
Mid-afternoon	Shop East Village
Pre-dinner	Mannahatta*
Dinner	Five Points, Raga
Nighttime	Marion's Continental*
Late-night	Lucky Cheng's, 6's & 8's

Saturday

Breakfast	Great Jones Café
Mid-morning	Rock Junket NYC
Lunch	Diner*
Mid-afternoon	Williamsburg Art & Historical Center
Dinner	Lucien
Nighttime	*Saturday Night Live*
Late-night	Libation*

Morning After

Breakfast	Prune

Hotel: **Hotel on Rivington**

Thursday

9am Cab down to Battery Park, where ferries depart for the **Statue of Liberty** and Ellis Island. For a significant percentage of New York's population, life in America began here.

1pm Lunch Many early immigrants settled in the Lower East Side, where today musician Moby's restaurant **teany** satisfies vegans.

2:30pm Explore the history of the Lower East Side, once home to Little Italy, Little Poland, and Jew Town, at the **Tenement Museum**, a converted tenement filled with artifacts documenting the lives of the immigrants who built New York. Of course, New York history also includes Warhol, Haring, and most every pop artist of the past half-century. Catch a glimpse of a most unusual emerging artist at **Zito Studio Gallery**.

5pm Chinatown and Little Italy butt up against each other at several points, most clearly around Mott Street. At the bottom of Chinatown is serene Columbus Park, where locals play dominos and practice Tai

Chi. Visible from the park is the **Museum of Chinese in the Americas**, where visitors learn about the neighborhood.

7pm On your way out of Chinatown, have a cocktail layover at the French-Thai–influenced **Verlaine**, where specialty drinks are mixed with house-infused liquors.

8pm Dinner A block away from Verlaine, and still a little French, is **Schiller's Liquor Bar**, one of the Lower East Side's most popular restaurants. Ten short minutes uptown on First Street, the festive French-Thai restaurant **The Elephant**, and its romantic Mediterranean/Middle Eastern neighbor **Ludo***, add some spice to the neighborhood's culinary melting pot.

11pm If the Tenement Museum is the Lower East Side's past, **Tenement*** is its future. Among this area's first upscale restaurant-lounges, this bilevel hotspot halfway between Schiller's and the other two dinner options, serves traditional American fare with flair, then brings in the DJs who play upbeat lounge tunes. Around the corner and less modern, the Lower East Side gets the quasi-hip, old-fashioned burlesque shows at **Slipper Room**.

1am Head ten minutes north to the central East Village where **Three of Cups*** turns the Nirvana tunes

up to 11. In nearby Soho, also a ten-minute jaunt, **BiNY** summons would-be rock stars to try their luck at one of the city's most spirited karaoke scenes.

3:30am Never go to bed on an empty stomach—or so says the crowd at **Diner 24**.

Friday

9:30am **Pink Pony***, a French cafe-meets-bistro operated by the owner of Lucien, is a favorite for artists and intellectuals.

10am Pampering after breakfast? **Christine Chin Spa** is ready to serve you; just make sure you booked your treatment with the boss. Once refreshed, begin a leisurely stroll around the immigrant-built East Village.

1pm Lunch It's hard to beat **Katz's Delicatessen** for traditional Yiddish food. Those skittish about mile-high sandwiches might opt for **Veselka**, which serves Eastern European comfort cuisine just two minutes away. The burgers you smell wafting in from two blocks down are frying on the corner of Sixth and A's **Sidewalk Café***.

2:30pm Just a quick jaunt from lunch is **St. Mark's Place**, known as the birthplace of New York City's punk rock movement. Today it's a less-edgy-but-still-hip stretch lined with numerous record stores, clothiers, and kitschy snack shops.

3pm There's plenty of shopping to be done in the area, and a lot of it is, well, discounted. **Gabay's** outlet is where the city's major department stores dump their Manolo Blahnik and Prada overstock at up to 70% off the original price.

6:30pm **Mannahatta***, in Greenwich Village, works well for lounging and cocktailing with tapas before and after dinner.

8pm Dinner There's nothing more satisfying than coming across one of those places local Manhattanites want to keep for themselves. In the Noho area, the New American **Five Points** is just the find you're looking for. If you're digging the East Village vibe, follow Sixth Street's Indian Row to its crown ruby, **Raga**, where Indian cuisine is creatively fused with French fare, only a block away from the curry scurry of the nightlife scene.

11pm Nearby is the resurrected **Marion's Continental***, with a 1950s retro-glam supper club motif. **Dick's Bar** is a modest gay haunt offering a less intrusive alternative scene.

1am For late-night fun, **Lucky Cheng's** greets visitors with a song—literally—all sung by the cross-dressing staff. Nearby, **Rififi** delivers a different kind of show—art films on a pull-down screen. Don't worry—they have beer, too. If you're in the mood to rock, **6's & 8's** provides an upscale backstage feeling, with fashion models in the audience and Grey Goose bottles behind the bar.

Saturday

9am Those nursing a hangover in the East Village should visit the **Great Jones Café** for a bit of New York charm and New Orleans spice. Or begin a day of gallery-hopping with breakfast in Williamsburg at **Anytime**, or the bohemian and resourceful train-car-turned-diner, **Relish**.

10:30am Note: The only argument for staying in Manhattan is taking the **Rock Junket NYC** tour, which comprehensively covers the late '70s rock scene in the city. Otherwise, walking the mile-long Williamsburg Bridge is a worthwhile summertime activity, especially on Saturdays when the Hasidim, who are not allowed to drive on the Jewish Sabbath, pour across in droves. Over the bridge in Williamsburg, the **Realform Girdle Building** (which used to be a girdle factory) sells music, clothing, and locally produced art. For a more substantial purchase, check out

ORIGINAL

northside JUNK, where vintage jukeboxes, pinball machines, and home furnishings are cleaned up and resold.

1pm Lunch Sitting under the Williamsburg Bridge is **Diner***, the aptly named eatery that started the area's train-car craze. There are countless other restaurants down North Bedford Street running a mile north to the old Polish neighborhood of Greenpoint.

3pm Going to Williamsburg without visiting a gallery is like going to the library without looking at books. **Momenta Art** and the versatile **Williamsburg Art & Historical Center** are great places to start. Those wanting to stay on the Big Island can visit the **Anthology Film Archives** to see 35mm film versions of classic and rare movies.

8pm Dinner If you're still in Williamsburg, **Planet Thailand** has a huge menu matched only by its hip clientele. For a fantastic dinner on the East Village–Lower East Side border, head to **Lil' Frankie's Pizza***, a Roman wine bar and pizzeria, or cross First Avenue for the straight-out-of-Paris **Lucien**.

10:30pm With planning and luck you've secured tickets to *Saturday Night Live*. Otherwise, hang out in Williamsburg at **Pete's Candy Store**, one of the area's most popular, least pretentious venues, with acoustic performances in back, and Scrabble tournaments up front. Nostalgic gamers should opt for **Barcade**, where vintage '80s video games still cost a quarter per play.

11:30pm Late nights in the 'burg are lively, as you'll see in the semi-divey **Union Pool** where bands are loud and good. The much smaller, modern-Moroccan **Black Betty*** sometimes has jazzy bands and a hip crowd.

12:30am For a hopping singles scene, quench your thirst at **Libation***, a refurbished building that looks like a Trump tenement.

The Morning After
Brunch at the hip and funky **Prune**, with New American cuisine as eclectic and original as your stay in New York.

Original New York:
The Key Neighborhoods

We've combined two contrasting notions of Original in this chapter—the cutting-edge, soon-to-be hotspots, along with the neighborhoods where the first immigrants settled. Strangely enough, they're both the same.

East Village German, Irish, Jewish, and Polish immigrants made this area their home during the early part of the last century. A little gritty and a bit bohemian (as it's been since the 1950s), the East Village is probably best known as the original home of the New York City rock music scene. Whereas in the 1970s only the brave visited this part of town, today's restaurants and nightlife bring in the crowds.

Lower East Side There's an undeniable and inevitable gentrification going on in this hipster-bohemian epicenter, where divey rock bars are turning into coffee shops and boutiques. Still, walking past the converted tenements on Ludlow Street, one can see and smell the Manhattan of 100 years ago.

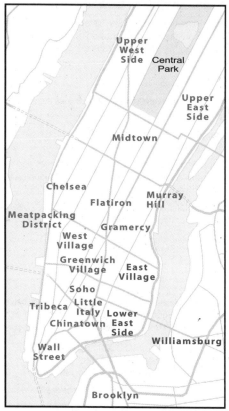

Williamsburg When people find that the East Village is becoming too expensive, their next stop is Williamsburg, just across the bridge. Williamsburg is as close to the edge (that is, funky) as we go—for art, eating, and drinking. Think 1960s Berkeley meets 1980s Soho, then throw in a bit of rock star attitude, and you've got a feel for the 'Burg.

Original New York:
The Shopping Blocks

East Village

Vintage shops and tiny boutiques carry eclectic indie designers, music, and books. For holdovers from the punk era, walk down St. Mark's Place. Otherwise stick to the cluster of stores that lines East 7th and 9th Streets.

Gabay's Outlet A no-frills outlet offering designer goods for up to 70% under original price. (p.131) 225 1st Ave. (13th St.), 212-254-3180

St. Mark's Bookshop Scruffy hipsters and professor types support this indie with an impressive array of photo and art books, and handmade zines. 31 3rd Ave. (9th St.), 212-260-7853

Tokio 7 Prada, Dior, and Gucci devotees love this basement level store with second-hand designer clothing and accessories. 64 E. 7th St. (1st Ave.), 212-353-8443

Trash and Vaudeville In memory of the Ramones and the Sex Pistols, who used to roam this street, Trash and Vaudeville stocks true punk threads—including the skinniest jeans and bondage pants. 4 St. Mark's Place (3rd Ave.), 212-982-3590

Lower East Side

The official hotbed of hipsterdom this side of Williamsburg has no obvious signage, so it's best to stick to Rivington and Ludlow Streets.

Babeland The ultimate adult kink shop, with an educational bent. (p.130) 94 Rivington St. (Ludlow St.), 212-375-1701

Edith and Daha Opinionated salespeople make sure modernized vintage pieces and a sublime selection of vintage accessories flatter and fit, adding to the "shopping in your sister's closet" ambience. 104 Rivington St. (Essex St.), 212-979-9992

Some Odd Rubies Celebrities come for reworked vintage pieces and accessories by quasi-celebrities-turned-designers. 151 Ludlow St. (Stanton St.), 212-353-1736

TG-170 This is the destination for girls looking for quirky labels like United Bamboo and Grey Ant. 170 Ludlow St. (Stanton St.), 212-995-8660

Williamsburg

An enclave of young artists, musicians, and designers has made this part of Brooklyn *the* place for under-the-radar cool. Stick to Bedford Avenue, Berry, and North 6th Streets for the best hipster sightings and the hottest music venues, bars, and shops.

Saved Gallery of Art & Craft A museum of hip peculiarities, seemingly curated by Edgar Allan Poe, including restored furniture, taxidermy delights, jewelry, and fashion from emerging designers. 82 Berry St. (N. 9th St.), 718-388-5990

Sleep Linens and lingerie are housed in what appears to be a flapper-era boudoir. 110 N. 6th St. (Berry St.), 718-384-3211

Original New York:
The Hotels

Blue Moon Hotel • Lower East Side • Timeless (22 rms)
There's a historical grittiness to the Lower East Side, where poor Jewish immigrants once overcrowded dank, dilapidated buildings. Today, the gentrifying winds of change blow strong. The Blue Moon Hotel straddles the line between this neighborhood's former blue-collar spirit and the blue blood of the new upscale scene. Located in a renovated tenement house, this posh hotel finds chic charm in shabby details, reinstalling the original 19th-century oak wainscoting and pine moldings, while leaving the nail holes unfilled. The original fire escapes have been reattached as balconies, and old irons, bottles, and other discarded ephemera are now proudly displayed in the Blue Moon's decor. Even the hotel menu resurrects the neighborhood's past, featuring the old-world recipes of the owner's Grandma Ida. Of course, there's nothing humble about the rooms, where the amenities and views are pure posh. The cozy Duke Ellington and Deluxe Benny Goodman rooms are on the corner, affording lovely views of the Williamsburg Bridge. $$$$ 100 Orchard St. (Broome St.), 212-533-9080, bluemoon-nyc.com

Dylan Hotel • Murray Hill • Trendy (107 rms)
The elements all add up in this former home to the Chemist's Club of New York, where the Alchemy Suite used to serve as a meeting place for renowned masterminds, such as Dr. Morris Loeb, Dr. Frederic Schweitzer, and Professor Charles F. Chandler. (Yeah, we've never heard of them either.) Now a posh, sleekly designed boutique hotel, the recently revamped 1903 Beaux Arts building is awash in the muted colors of tinted lamplight, which give it a cocktail lounge vibe. Thanks to the 11-foot-high ceilings, these smallish rooms feel relatively spacious, and they provide comfortable bathrobes and slippers. Ask for one of the Executive King rooms on the upper floors with a view of 41st Street. The sensually lit lounge and restaurant, the Chemists' Club Grill (once the Chemists' Club Grand Hall), is a well-appointed, dramatic room, with impossibly high ceilings and reputable New American cuisine. $$$ 52 E. 41st St. (Madison Ave.), 212-338-0500, dylanhotel.com

Hotel on Rivington • Lower East Side • Trendy (110 rms)
Back in the day, if you tried to build a nice hotel on the Lower East Side, no one would've stayed there. Now, this once-dodgy neighborhood is home to scores of hip bars and restaurants, not to mention sophisticated hotels like the Rivington, completed in late 2004. Located halfway between Wall Street and Midtown, this hotel suits the business traveler, but its main attraction is being the first comfortably modern hotel in a hip neighborhood. The Rivington boasts floor-to-ceiling glass walls in every room, many balconies, and even a few showers with a view. Designed by Paris-based India Mahdavi, these unique, elegant, ample-sized rooms pamper guests with velvet furniture, flat-screen TVs, and heated bathroom floor tiles (there's even one with a three-person shower). Thor, the Rivington's masculine-sounding hotel restaurant, serves seasonal European fare for room service, or in its attractive, elegant space. $$$$ 107 Rivington St. (Ludlow St.), 212-475-2600 / 800-915-1537, hotelonrivington.com

ORIGINAL

Hotel QT • Midtown • Modern (140 rms)

Courting Uma Thurman isn't hotelier Andres Balazs's only impressive feat. He also has a way with properties. (Balazs also operates the Mercer downtown and the Chateau Marmont in Los Angeles.) Over the past year or so, QTs have been popping up in all the right places, and with its stellar Times Square location, this one is truly a find. A minimalist version of the W Hotel chain, sans the celebs and superposh lounges, QT attracts a stylish crowd more interested in spending time on the town than in kicking around in their hotel room. Though colorful and tidy, the rooms here are small. Still, not an inch is wasted—there are no cheesy murals, no frivolous extras; just a bed, a flat-screen TV, and, in some cases, bunk beds. The hip lobby bar has a nightly DJ, and the pool has underwater music and a terraced lounge. Often labeled "chic but cheap," the Hotel QT is a bargain at any rate. The "B" rooms vary slightly; ask for the largest one with the most light. $$$ 125 W. 45th St., (Broadway), 212-354-2323, hotelqt.com

Hotel Roger Williams • Murray Hill • Trendy (191 rms)

If paying more than this boutique hotel charges will make you feel better about the place, go right ahead, but this is simply a charming hotel with relatively easy rates. The fashionable crowd here consists of freelance types who are on all of the big guest lists, but couldn't get "the magazine" to pick up the tab. There's no in-house club, but there is a wine bar. Without a restaurant, the guest lounge serves coffee and beyond-serviceable breakfasts overlooking the modern lobby of soothing green walls. Higher-level rooms facing north offer views of the Empire State Building. If the weather is nice, opt for one of the slightly smaller rooms with a terrace. $$$ 131 Madison Ave. (31st St.), 212-448-7000 / 888-448-7788, hotelrogerwilliams.com

The Muse Hotel • Midtown • Modern (200 rms)

Fittingly, the Muse Hotel prides itself on being an inspirational place to stay, limiting its palette to light, earthy tones, which don't cloud the imagination. Inside the limestone-and-brick facade of the Leavitt Building, a large mural of the nine muses invites guests into the lobby. Though touted as being 50 square feet larger than standard New York hotel rooms, the accommodations here are still rather small, though nicely laid out and tended to by a genuinely friendly staff. Beige walls bring the Technicolor beddings into focus, and, if the lighting in the rooms is too low, the big-screen TVs will more than make up for it. Ask for one of the slightly larger rooms in the "11" line. The Restaurant District next door opens its theatrical curtain for diners on their way to or returning from one of the many Broadway shows in the area, or moving on from the intimate hotel lounge, Mini-Bar. $$$ 130 W. 46th St. (Broadway), 212-485-2400 / 877-692-6873, themusehotel.com

Original New York:
The Restaurants

Anytime • Williamsburg • Diner
When is a good time to visit Anytime? Never mind—that's too easy for this place, which, like its shaggy hipster neighborhood, is built on irony. How else might one explain a menu that includes tater tots, schwarma, salmon, veggie burgers, lasagna, and pork burritos? Anytime has a couple of coveted booths in the back, and a surprisingly good happy hour. Clocks cover the artsy diner's walls, which is appreciated by this club-hopping crowd that's never really sure whether the sun is rising or setting. *Sun-Thu 6pm-2am, Fri-Sat 6pm-4am.* $ F☰ 93 N. 6th St. (Wythe St.), 718-218-7272, anytimeny.com

Diner* • Williamsburg • Diner
Though Diner looks like it was built for postcard photography, its menu is three-dimensional. With the Brooklyn Bridge as its neighbor and the Manhattan skyline as a backdrop, this picturesque train-car restaurant is a favorite of hung-over hipsters. Empathetic, hung-over servers deliver Bloody Marys at a leisurely pace, along with eggs benedict and more absorbent lunch-y items. At night, DJs set up, pints start to flow, and regulars with short-term memories begin the cycle again. *Daily 11am-2am.* $ ☲F☰ 85 Broadway (Berry St.), 718-486-3077, dinernyc.com

Diner 24 • Chelsea • New American
Best All-Night Restaurants Diner 24 is unassuming enough for a family luncheon, but its kitschy menu of Disco Fries and Duck Meatloaf was probably designed with urban hipsters in mind. The specialty cocktails are good enough to make Diner 24 a nightlife destination spot itself. Cut stones cover the walls and orange lighting implies sunlight for the 4am crowd, who may have forgotten what morning feels like. There's a late '50s to early '60s influence behind the aesthetic, especially with the tongue-in-cheek addition of TV dinners to the menu. *24/7.* $ F☰ 102 8th Ave. (W. 15th St.), 212-242-7773, diner24.com

The Elephant • East Village • French-Asian
The Elephant is found on a colorful street clearly unconcerned with the troublesome details of zoning laws. At the base of a residential building, this unique, apartmentlike restaurant puts out a serious European vibe, packing the patrons into a playfully gauche interior of gilded red-trimmed walls, disco balls, and leopard prints. Most of the French-Thai fusion offerings, like cinnamon roasted chicken and curly fries, are meant to be shared, which makes The Elephant a great place for groups and double dates. *Mon-Thu noon-3:30am and 5:30pm-midnight, Fri-Sat noon-3:30am and 5:30pm-1am, Sun 5:30-midnight.* $ F☰ 58 E. 1st St. (1st Ave.), 212-505-7739, elephantrestaurant.com

Five Points • Greenwich Village • Mediterranean
Best Informal Upscale Restaurants Although this restaurant is named after the legendary Five Points area where the "Gangs of New York" once roamed, it's neither rugged nor near the former Five Points neighborhood. In fact, it's a highly underrated restaurant whose sleepy street location is less its weakness than its charm. Inside, a wood-burning oven serves up traditional, yet inventive, American cuisine

to a large brunch and dinner crowd. The vibe is homey and serene, enhanced by a babbling fountain and sunny skylight. In the warm weather, Five Points drags a few tables and a grill outside, which tends to pull in an even bigger crowd still. *Mon-Fri noon-3pm and 6pm-midnight, Sat 11:30am-3pm and 6pm-midnight, Sun 11:30am-3pm and 6-10pm.* $$ F≡ 31 Great Jones St. (Lafayette St.), 212-253-5700, fivepointsrestaurant.com

Fornino • Williamsburg • Pizzeria

Williamsburg has always had a late-night pizzeria, where bar-goers could grab a midnight slice when they just as easily would've eaten a shoe. Then came Fornino. A wood-burning oven in the back of the room bakes classic and nouveau pies whose ingredients are grown in the tiny restaurant's backyard greenhouse. (The semi-outdoor seating near the greenhouse is highly recommended in warmer months.) This menu is divided into unusual sections, one of which features pies that are officially recognized by the Italian Agriculture Ministry. *Sun-Thu noon-11pm, Fri-Sat noon-midnight.* $ ≡ 187 Bedford Ave. (N. 6th St.), 718-384-6004

Great Jones Café • East Village • Cajun

Even if the scene has shifted from the über-bohemian Basquiat crowd of yore, the famous jukebox and widely lauded Bloody Marys ensure that the Great Jones Café is still one-of-a-kind. Located in a tiny shack painted orange (inside and out) on the opposite corner from Andy Warhol's old apartment, Great Jones Café has a subtle New Orleans spirit, sans the Beale Street memorabilia and wet tee-shirt contests. Crowds get happy while mingling around the jukebox and basking in the retro feel of the old-style menu handwritten on the wall. The jambalaya is *magnifique*, the burgers divine, and the pies down-home delicious. Arrive early, because the Jones doesn't take reservations. *Mon-Thu 5pm-midnight, Fri 5pm-1am, Sat 11:30am-4pm and 5pm-1am, Sun 11:30am-4pm and 5pm-midnight.* $$ F≡ 54 Great Jones St. (Bowery), 212-674-9304, greatjones.com

Horus Café* • East Village • Mediterranean

Since the smoking ban passed in 2002, hookah bars have become all the rage in New York, and Horus is one of the most unique. This smokers' haunt offers tobacco flavors like mango and melon, while offering a lunch and dinner menu that spans from hamburger to hummus. Inside, crafted wood furniture, like tables carved out of tree stumps, creates a kitschy-hip enchanted forest. In warm-weather months, the crowd fights for sidewalk tables to puff away under the stars. *Daily 11am-4am.* $ �XF≡ 93 Ave. B (6th St.), 212-777-9199, horuscafe.com

John's of Bleecker Street • West Village • Pizzeria

Best Pizza This city is the pizza capital of the western hemisphere, and John's of Bleecker Street is one of its best. For more than 75 years these brick-oven pizzas have been drawing crowds with their finest mozzarella and thin crusts. That local Al Pacino is a regular of John's is all the proof you need that this New York institution is true italiano. Visitors usually have to wait in the inevitable line out front, but it tends to move quickly along (though stopping by at conventional dinner hours is guaranteed to keep you waiting 20 minutes or more). *Daily noon-11:30pm.* $$ ≡ 278 Bleecker St. (Jones St.), 212-243-1680, johnsofbleeckerstreet.com

Katz's Delicatessen • Lower East Side • Deli

Best Delis With all due respect to Woody Allen, when you think Jewish and New York, you think Katz's Deli. Upon entering this nearly 120-year-old institution, get a ticket and enter the cafeteria-style food line. (Here's a tip: tip! Money in the jar means bigger portions for you.) Some take their pastrami and corned beef to go, but most grab one of the many tables, labeled to indicate which famous people sat where. (The midroom spot, where Meg Ryan faked her famous orgasm in *When Harry Met Sally*, is a favorite.) *Mon-Tue 8am-10pm, Wed, Thu, and Sun 8am-11pm, Fri-Sat 8am-3am.* $- ▯≣ 205 E. Houston St. (Ludlow St.), 212-254-2246, katzdeli.com

Lil' Frankie's Pizza* • East Village • Pizzeria

There is a kind of hipster kitsch about Lil' Frankie's, with gilded mirrors, exposed brick, and an oven reputedly constructed from the lava of Mount Vesuvius. The crowd is mostly 20-somethings, and the vibe is more *The Daily Show* than *Cinema Paradiso*. Since the crispy thin pizzas are noticeably small, there's space for more inexpensive oven-baked goodies, like roasted eggplant and chicken with mashed potatoes. The next-door Internet radio station, EVR, pipes in indie tunes for the lively bar scene. *Sun-Thu 11am-1am, Fri-Sat 11am-3:30am.* $ ▯≣ 19 1st Ave. (1st St.), 212-420-4900, lilfrankies.com

Lucien • East Village • French Bistro

Downtown fashionistas, bohemians, and intellectuals will wait a half hour for a seat at little Lucien while the half-dozen restaurants a Renault-length away are completely empty. Authentic dishes, like frogs' legs and cassoulet, are served up in these cozy (some say cramped) quarters where, but for the friendly wait-staff, you'd think you were in Paris. Definitely make reservations here (few people do, or even know they can), and ask for a table in the back of the room where the waiting masses won't be breathing down your neck. *Daily 10am-1:30am.* $$ ▯≣ 14 1st Ave. (1st St.), 212-260-6481, luciennyc.com

Ludo* • East Village • Middle Eastern

Formerly Chez Es Saada, one of NYC's hottest date destinations, this Middle Eastern eatery has cooled things down with its relaxed ambience and romantic setting. The stylish, laid-back crowd hanging out in the upstairs lounge is filled with refugees from the neighborhood's rock 'n' roll scene. Downstairs, a second bar separates two spacious dining rooms of exposed brick walls, candles, and lush, low-slung furnishings. The menu is heavy on Mediterranean fish and less-beefy meats, all of which go great with a glass of sangria. *Daily 6pm-3am.* $$ ▯≣ 42 E. 1st St. (2nd Ave.), 212-777-5617, ludonyc.com

Peanut Butter & Co. • Lower East Side • American

You guessed it. This beloved specialty joint makes peanut butter sandwiches more ways than your mother could fathom, combining everything from bananas to bacon. Got milk to get that stuff off the roof of your mouth? Peanut Butter & Co. has more flavors and varieties of milk (including rice, soy, and Lactaid) than you can shake a cow at. With vintage jam ads and tins on the walls, this very small place is fun, if nothing else, and you're sure to be in and out in a "jiffy." *Sun-Thu 11am-9pm, Fri-Sat 11am-10pm.* $- ≣ 240 Sullivan St. (Bleecker St.), 212-677-3995, ilovepeanutbutter.com

Peter Luger Steak House • Williamsburg • Steak House
There's little argument that Peter Luger (now nearly 120 years old) is the city's best-known steak house. Tradition here is strong—the only sauce served and the only credit card accepted both have the restaurant's name on the front. The exposed beams, bright lighting, and loud acoustics give Peter Luger a working man's charm. Large groups celebrating birthdays and office events are common. If you want the full Peter Luger experience, start with a gin martini, order the porterhouse, and finish with a slice of cheesecake. *Mon-Thu 11:30am-9:45pm, Fri-Sat 11:30am-10:45pm, Sun 1-9:45pm.* $$$ ◨ 178 Broadway (Driggs Ave.), 718-387-7400, peterluger.com

Pink Pony* • Lower East Side • Brasserie
Before condos and hotels started popping up on the Lower East Side, entrepreneurs could open storefronts where musicians played at night, poets sipped coffee during the day, and chefs could experiment with new dishes that hipsters would try, so long as they were cheap. Unfortunately, none has survived the LES gentrification ... except the Pink Pony. Large front windows flood the room with light by day, while cheerful globe lanterns dangling from the high tin ceiling keep things rosy by night. In the larger, louder back dining room, French-American entrees are surprisingly pleasant, even when the staff isn't. *Mon-Sun 10am-2am.* $ ⵙⴼ◨ 178 Ludlow St. (Stanton St.), 212-253-1922

Planet Thailand • Williamsburg • Thai Fusion
Hipster restaurant Planet Thai (as it's often called) is located in a former warehouse where three kitchens churn out hundreds of Japanese and Thai treats. This place is always abuzz, so you should grab a seat wherever you can find it. The playful decor includes a funky wine-bottle chandelier and a rowboat sculpture hanging from the heights; the high brick walls give way to a gleeful mustard yellow. The windowless back room is good for privacy, but this is the kind of joint where people want to see and be "scene." Cash only. *Sun-Thu 11:30am-1am, Fri-Sat 11:30am-2am.* $ ⴼ◨ 133 N. 7th St. (Berry St.), 718-599-5758

Prune • East Village • New American/French
This is a quaint brunch joint that tourists always cherish like a sentimental souvenir of their trip to Manhattan. "What was that quaint little town and country-like place we went to in the East Village where the staff wore pink shorts and the big pancakes were covered in fruit?" Of course, no one really forgets a cheeky name like Prune. Just ask the brunch nuts who wait for as long as an hour for one of the 30 or so seats that never get cold. *Mon-Thu 6-11pm, Fri 6pm-midnight, Sat 10am-3:30pm and 6pm-midnight, Sun 10am-3:30pm and 5-10pm.* $$ ⴼ◨ 54 E. 1st St. (2nd Ave.), 212-677-6221

Raga • East Village • Indian
There's a longstanding myth that the dozen or so Indian restaurants on Sixth Street share a single kitchen. No matter what people say, there's no denying that Raga's kitchen crew, who cook up less-than-traditional, American-infused cuisine, are one of a kind. Just one short block east of Little Bombay, Raga manages to capture the authenticity of India without the card readers and sitar players that distract tourists from culinary mediocrity. The cozy dining room is decked out in mustard yellow and red, with tealights flickering. The downstairs lounge is great for martinis. *Tue-Sun 6-11pm.* $$ ⴼ◨ 433 E. 6th St. (Ave. A), 212-388-0957, raganyc.com

Relish • Williamsburg • Diner

Unlike Diner, the successful train-car diner just a couple streets away, Relish has a wonderful outdoor space overlooking the row of Harley Davidsons lined up outside the repair shop across the street. No one in this neighborhood gets up early, so the 11am breakfast menu at Relish is like an early-bird special. The eggs with cheddar grits are fun, while the always-appropriate cheeseburgers are the main draw. Should you be catching the night train, try one of the well-mixed sidecars. *Sun-Thu 11am-11:30pm, Fri-Sat 11am-12:30am.* $ F≡ 225 Wythe Ave. (N. 3rd St.), 718-963-4546, relish.com

Schiller's Liquor Bar • Lower East Side • French-American

Critics might compare Schiller's to a bad actor wearing a beret and faking a French accent, but the faux distressed decor in this gimmicky but fashionable bistro/brasserie is done with a wink. The wines are labeled cheap, decent, and good, and dinner reservations book up faster than a Jerry Lewis film festival in Cannes. Since brunch is a little too early for Schiller's regular night owls, it's a good time to get in sans hassle. Keith McNally, who owns Schiller's, also runs similar themed hotspots Balthazar and Pastis. *Mon-Wed 11am-1am, Thu 11am-2am, Fri 11am-3am, Sat 10am-4pm and 6pm-3am, Sun 10am-4pm and 6pm-1am.* $ F≡ 131 Rivington St. (Norfolk St.), 212-260-4555, schillersny.com

Sidewalk Café* • East Village • Diner

The Sidewalk Café is part neighborhood bar, part music venue, part restaurant. The loyal, action-seeking crowd divides its time between the long bar and the live performances on the tiny stage around the corner. There's never a cover at the Sidewalk, which is a good thing, considering that some of the local acts are, shall we say, "experimental." The other half is an all-night diner, serving comfort food at a leisurely pace (especially when your server is more into their band than into your burger). *Sun-Thu 7:30am-4am, Fri-Sat 24 hours.* $ TF≡ 94 Ave. A (6th St.), 212-473-7373

teany • Lower East Side • Vegetarian

What's short, bald, smart, and doesn't eat meat? Well, there are those strange designer cats, but we were going for Moby, who owns this popular vegetarian restaurant. Ironically, this building used to house a hair salon. It isn't unheard of to spot A-list musicians and actors noshing fake ham and cheese in teany's rather tiny confines, but despite the fact that "We Are All Stars," celebrity is not what this place is about. Grab a seat near the windows (most of them are), and the Lower East Side becomes a motion picture. *Fri-Sat 10am-2am, Sun 10am-8pm.* $- F≡ 90 Rivington St. (Orchard St.), 212-475-9190, teany.com

Thor* • Lower East Side • New American (G)

Thor is the Norse god of thunder, but more importantly he is married to Sif, a fertility goddess. That pretty much describes the vibe at this very loud (thunder), sexy (fertility) and original (menu and design) restaurant. (Note: Thor is also the acronym for The Hotel On Rivington.) The menu covers all the basic foods, which are then reinvented by Austrian chef Kurt Gutenbrunner. The lounge scene and music are integrated with the restaurant, but the mood coup de grâce is the glass-wall view of the tenement buildings next door. *Daily 7am-3pm, Sun-Wed 5:30pm-midnight, Thu-Sat 5:30pm-1am.* $$ TF≡ The Hotel on Rivington, 107 Rivington St. (Ludlow St.), 212-796-8040, hotelonrivington.com

ORIGINAL

Veselka • East Village • Eastern European

This Eastern Bloc eatery is a popular late-night stop for hipsters post–closing time, especially in the warm-weather months when tables are set up around the property's perimeters. Veselka's menu is hearty enough to get hungry revolutionaries through a Siberian winter, though it offers fruit-plate alternatives for those trying to stay Bolshoi light. The crowd is so hip and fashionably mussed, it's hard to tell if they just woke up or have been out all night. *24/7.* $ F≡ 144 2nd Ave. (9th St.), 212-228-9682, veselka.com

Yatagan Kebab House • West Village • Middle-Eastern

Yatagan is a chart topper on everyone's "quick eats" list, even if most of its customers have no idea what the place is called. There are a few rickety tables inside, but the vast majority of Yatagan's patrons order their food through a pick-up window, which sees an endless outflow of lamb, chicken, and beef kebabs. These servings are very, very big, and while eating them on the move has resulted in many a stained shirt, there are plenty of benches and rest stops in the area, including Washington Square Park. *Mon-Sun 10am-5pm.* $ ≡ 104 MacDougal St. (W. 3rd St.), 212-677-0952

Yonah Schimmel's Knishes Bakery • Lower East Side • Bakery

In 1910, Bulgarian rabbi Yonah Schimmel opened shop in this little storefront, and nearly a century later the knishes are as fresh as ever. Schimmel's family still handcrafts these softball-sized pastries, stuffed with anything from cheese and fruit to potato, and bakes them daily in brick ovens. Wander east down Houston Street and you'll also find Russ & Daughters fish and specialty store (1914) and Katz's Delicatessen (1888), two equally charming classics. *Daily 8:30am-7pm.* $ ≡ 137 E. Houston St. (Eldridge St.), 212-477-2858, yonahschimmel.com

Original New York:
The Nightlife

Arthur's Tavern • West Village • Club

For the price of one drink, music lovers can gather around the small stage at Arthur's Tavern and groove to the tunes of excellent up-and-comers and accomplished stage musicians. Anything less is legally considered loitering. This intimate basement-level venue feels like something yanked from 1950s Harlem, where the musicians dress in jazzy suits and hats, and break into chaotic Thelonious Monk–like riffs, occasionally taking requests from the crowd. Despite the sartorial display onstage, patrons are encouraged to wear what they like. *Mon 8pm-2:30am, Tue-Thu 7pm-2:30am, Fri-Sun 7pm-4am.* C≣ 57 Grove St. (7th Ave.), 212-675-6879, arthurstavernnyc.com

Barcade • Williamsburg • Theme Bar

Best Theme Bars Centipede, Mario Bros., and Frogger are back, and this time you're old enough to drink while you play. At this slightly out-of-the-way former warehouse space, friendly, grungy locals jingle around the long room with more quarters in their pockets than you'd find in the local laundromat. Surprisingly, Barcade attracts an even number of men and women, so you can still try to impress that special someone by blasting aliens into oblivion and getting your initials at the top of the screen. *Mon-Sat 5pm-4am, Sun 5pm-2am.* ≣ 388 Union Ave. (Ainslie St.), 718-302-6464, barcadebrooklyn.com

BiNY • Soho • Karaoke

There's something inexplicably magnetic about this nerdy karaoke bar, where earnest Asian crooners mix with a trendy Soho set. Baseball fans watch the game at the divey bar, while a roving singer with a wireless mic belts out "Crazy Train" in front of a wall-sized projection TV. Obviously, most of the performers at BiNY are one drink away from falling down, and two from doing another song. Needless to say, no one leaves here proud. Private rooms can be booked, but you don't come here to hide away. *Daily 5pm-4am.* B≣ 8 Thompson St., 2nd Fl. (Canal St.), 212-334-5490, biny.com

Black Betty* • Williamsburg • Nightclub

There was a time when Jackie Gleason and other heavy hitters would turn up at this shack near the foot of the Williamsburg bridge, drinking, joking, and playing the piano. The space has reinvented itself many times since, most recently emerging as Black Betty, a pumpkin-colored Moroccan-esque lounge, where DJs spin funk, South American jazz, and music that is more rockin' than Middle Eastern. Occasionally live bands perform, ranging from rock to flamenco. A Mediterranean fusion menu is available, offering the ever-popular "pitza." *Daily 6:30pm-4am.* C F≣ 366 Metropolitan Ave. (Havemeyer St.), 718-599-0243, blackbetty.net

Dick's Bar • East Village • Bar
Best Gay/Lesbian Bars For those who only know gay New York from the boas, Cher impersonators, and backless chaps of the Gay Pride parade footage they see on TV, Dick's Bar will come as a surprise. Aside from the kitschy Hollywood B-flicks on the TV above the bar, Dick's is gimmick free. With a pool table, a pinball machine, and a new digital jukebox, Dick's is a laid-back alternative to the high-energy gay party scene. That said, Show Tunes Monday is still an absolutely fabulous good time. *Mon-Sun 4pm-4am.* ▤ 192 2nd Ave. (12th St.), 212-475-2071

Duplex • West Village • Piano Bar
Best Piano Bars A long time ago, Bette Midler worked the cabaret room atop Duplex, which hosts off-Broadway shows, musical reviews, and the occasional comedy sketch group. In the Piano Bar downstairs, a supportive crowd eggs on amateurs at the nightly open mic, where accolades abound, and no one gets blamed for the obvious lack of voice lessons. Outdoor seating wraps around the lower level, providing insulation from the looky-loos stealing peeks from the street. Tourists and greenhorns fill up the intimate table area, while Broadway pros often linger around the bar. *Daily 4pm-4am.* ▤ 61 Christopher St. (7th Ave. S.), 212-255-5438, theduplex.com

Libation* • Lower East Side • Lounge
Best Singles Scene Formerly a restaurant named Torch (which poetically burned down), Libation combines an upscale, trilevel club with a practical restaurant. While the diner-priced afternoon menu and delivery option go over well in the Lower East Side, the velvet rope–governed late-night scene is the kind of thing that can end in egg-stained windows. That hasn't stopped the frisky singles scene of attractive bourgeois-bohemians from filling the floors, suggesting that, like it or not, this neighborhood may someday become the new Meatpacking District. *Daily noon-4am.* F▤ 137 Ludlow St. (Stanton St.), 212-529-2153, libationnyc.com

Living Room • Lower East Side • Nightclub
Best Easy Local Vibe The original (and much smaller) Living Room was right around the corner from its new locale, and is best known for having launched Norah Jones. This laid-back music venue hosts live folk, light alt, and song-writer-oriented acts in the rear space, while local drinkers sit at the long bar up front. The performances are cheap or free, and many of the up-and-comers here seem on the verge of making it big. Tables are first come, first serve, so arrive about half an hour before the music starts (generally around 8pm). *Sun-Thu 6pm-2am, Fri-Sat 3pm-4am.* ▤ 154 Ludlow St. (Stanton St.), 212-533-7235, livingroomny.com

Lucky Cheng's • East Village • Cabaret
While this kitschy restaurant and lounge serves passable Chinese cuisine, Cheng's is best known for the drag queen waitresses who serve all entrees with a little "sauce." Though every night is entertaining, karaoke Thursdays are especially popular, known to bring in celebrity fans like Britney Spears and Al Roker. Beware the weekends when screechy bachelorette parties often overwhelm the room. For Grandma, there's Monday night bingo, run by some of Cheng's most flamboyant trannys. *Mon-Thu 6pm-midnight, Fri 6pm-4am, Sat 5:30pm-4am, Sun 6pm-2am.* CF▤ 24 1st Ave. (2nd St.), 212-995-5500, planetluckychengs.com

Mannahatta* • Greenwich Village • Lounge
From top to bottom and front to back, Mannahatta is the perfect place for dining lightly, cocktailing moderately, and effortlessly soaking up the vibe. Outdoor seating melds into the main floor lounge, while the social scene buzzes at the long bar, where a squeaky-clean urban office crowd chatters over ambient house tunes. The women, mostly *Cosmo* readers and drinkers, survey the room in the mirrors behind the bar. Downstairs, a spirited, clubby space spins hip-hop and dance tunes. *Mon-Sat 5pm-4am.* B≡ 316 Bowery (Bleecker St.), 212-253-8644, mannahatta.us/index_flash.html

Marion's Continental* • Greenwich Village • Lounge
In the '50s, when the Bowery was a seedy stretch of brothels and bawdy theaters, famed European model and socialite Marion Nagy opened Marion's Continental. It was an instant hit with slumming celebrities who'd stay up late eating, drinking, and misbehaving. When it closed in 1973, the over-the-top Golden Age decor was stripped, sold, and destroyed. Now, thanks to Marion's son, the Continental has been re-created in its original form. Part kitsch, part glam, this resurrected restaurant lounge is a huge hit with the John Waters variety of patrons. *Mon-Sun 6pm-2am.* F≡ 354 Bowery (4th St.), 212-475-7621, marionsnyc.com

Max Fish • Lower East Side • Dive Bar
Much to the chagrin of the devoted regulars, Max Fish is about as popular as an "underground" bar can be. Jaded rockers, struggling actors, and tourists converge to drink cheap booze in this brightly lit watering hole, where it's hip to be square (though Huey Lewis should not be quoted). Local artists exhibit their work on the walls, and students shoot pool in back, giving the place a kind of bohemian geek chic. Pinball machines and video games offer an alternative to eyeing the room or gazing thoughtfully into your beer. *Mon-Sun 5:30pm-4am.* ≡ 178 Ludlow St. (Stanton St.), 212-529-3959, maxfish.com

Pete's Candy Store • Williamsburg • Bar
Cozy, smart, and hip, this former candy shop is where Williamsburgers of the less scene-y set like to go. This modest two-room hangout has nooks and crannies aplenty, and a small stage in back. Tuesday is Bingo night, Saturdays are Scrabble pairings, and Wednesday night is "Quiz Off." Every other Monday Pete's hosts a spelling bee, where contestants vie for prizes. Toasted sandwiches are available to soak up the extralarge martinis. *Sun-Wed 5pm-2am, Thu-Sat 5pm-4am.* B≡ 709 Lorimer St. (Frost St.), 718-302-3770, petescandystore.com

Pianos • Lower East Side • Club
Best Easy Local Vibe This former piano store turned performance venue was wildly popular with the bohemian hipsters of the Lower East Side when it opened in 2002. Despite being nearly commercialized by a sudden wave of Upper East Siders, Pianos remains a cutting-edge place to see live comedy and music. The kitchen stays open late, the entertainment is fresh (and cheap), and the minimalist space exudes maximum character with a minimum of effort. *Daily 3pm-4am.* CF≡ 158 Ludlow St. (Stanton St.), 212-505-3733, pianosnyc.com

ORIGINAL

Red Rock West • Chelsea • Theme Bar

Best Theme Bars Red Rock West rocks the Wild West Side of Manhattan to its racy core. When does it open? A better question would be "When does it close?" A honky-tonk jukebox rattles Southern rock classics as bawdy bartenders dance atop every surface in the joint. The pool table in back is a refuge for the rhythmless, as dudes show their moves, begging the attention of sideline damsels. Avoid ordering anything "cute," as the barmaids have megaphones, and they know how to use them. *Daily 11:30am-4am.* ≣ 457 W. 17th St. (10th Ave.), 212-366-5359, redrockwestsaloon.com

Rififi • East Village • Club

This ain't the Cineplex. At Rififi, an indie film crowd comes not only for the music and beer, but for the foreign, artsy, and/or black-and-white flicks playing inside. Used to being gouged at the concession stand? Here, pints start at $3, and the admission price can't be beat. It's free! Screenings are generally on Mondays, with random specials during the week, so calling before going is highly recommended. When movies aren't playing, the back room is used for stand-up comedy, burlesque shows, and live music. *Sun-Thu 6pm-2am, Fri-Sat 6pm-4am.* ☐≣ 332 E. 11th St. (1st Ave.), 212-677-1027, rififinyc.com

Saturday Night Live • Midtown • Performance

Best Live Tapings "Live from New York ... it's one of the toughest tickets in town!" *SNL* is career-launching central for some of the best-known comic actors around, from Chevy Chase and Bill Murray to Eddie Murphy and Billy Crystal, and everybody wants a piece of the action. The show is taped live (obviously) every Saturday night (again ...), and there's also a live dress rehearsal from 8pm-9:30pm (the same lottery determines ticket dispersal for each). Send an email to snltickets@nbc.com to try your luck. Stand-by tickets are sometimes available at the studio around 7am on Saturday. *Tapings Sat 11:30pm-1am.* ≣ 30 Rockefeller Plz. (49th St.), 212-632-3975, nbc.com

6's & 8's • Lower East Side • Nightclub

Best Rock Clubs At 6's & 8's, don't count on hearing your father's rock 'n' roll. That's not to say the occasional Stones song doesn't slip by, but the models want to dance, and they don't remember the '60s. Come to think of it, neither do the Stones. Upstairs, circular leather banquettes occupy one side of the room, while a long bar and DJ booth hold down the other. In between, denim-clad 20- and 30-somethings dance under dim chandeliers. Downstairs, a party rages to a Las Vegas theme until the wee morning hours. *Mon-Sat 6pm-4am.* ≣ 205 Chrystie St. (Stanton St.), 212-477-6688, 6sand8s.com

Slipper Room • Lower East Side • Cabaret

You'll find a little bit of everything at the Slipper Room, where an authentic vaudeville/cabaret show provides a wide range of entertainment. Although the skit comedy can go awry at any time, the small cover charge is money well spent. Weekends sometimes see live bands, and occasionally comedians take the stage, but burlesque is a given. The booths in the back of the room are more comfortable, but the view can be a problem when the standing-room crowd pours in. Your best bet is to grab one of the tables near the stage. *Tue-Sat 8pm-4am, Sun-Mon depending on event booked.* ☐≣ 167 Orchard St. (Stanton St.), 212-253-7246, slipperroom.com

Tenement* • Lower East Side • Restaurant Lounge

An homage to the residencies that once lined Ludlow Street, Tenement merges the area's old and new, carefully dodging the pitfalls of condescension. Concrete walls and ceilings are stylishly lit, with a collection of small tables that succumb to a cozy, carpeted back-room lounge. (The wrought-iron fencing and old street lamp add a nice touch.) American dishes, like Hudson Valley duck and maple bourbon chicken, dominate the menu. Tenement may be the only OK place to slip your date a "Mickey"—it's actually on the drink menu. *Sun-Wed 5pm-2am, Thu-Sat 5pm-4am.* F☰ 157 Ludlow St. (Stanton St.), 212-766-1270, tenementlounge.com

Three of Cups* • East Village • Dive Bar

The basement bar at Three of Cups feels like the teenage-dominated rec room of a suburban home, with KISS posters, novena candles, and Christmas lights. With a laid-back atmosphere and rockin' speakers, this haunt is a local favorite. The neon "Lounge" sign outside looks like it was lifted from an old bowling alley, but downstairs, the scene is all rock 'n' roll. When the kids in the basement get hungry, they can always run upstairs, where Three of Cups' considerably more subdued restaurant serves up good pasta and pizza. *Mon-Sun 8pm-4am.* F☰ 83 1st Ave. (5th St.), 212-388-0059, threeofcupsnyc.com

Union Pool • Williamsburg • Dive Bar

According to legend, the former owners of Union Pool, once a swimming pool supply and critter control superstore, lost the business in a card game to a suave dude with a handful of aces and a dream. Today, headlining bands and up-and-comers perform for the crowd of rockabilly pseudo punks and bed-headed rockers drinking cheap beer and feigning boredom. In the summer, try a cheap cocktail by the fountain out back. And bring cash—Union Pool is way too hip for plastic. *Mon-Sun 5pm-4am.* ☰ 484 Union Ave. (Meeker Ave.), 718-609-0484, myspace.com/unionpool

Verlaine • Lower East Side • Lounge

Best Cocktail Mixologists Named after the poet Paul Verlaine, this golden-hued cocktail lounge attracts a crowd of writers, artists, and film types looking for a glamorous-but-relaxed vibe. The Asian-themed drink menu features house-infused, vodka-heavy cocktails made with the freshest ingredients. Behind the long, well-staffed bar are bottles of fermenting onions, apples, and pears waiting to put stars in the eyes of the hopeful couples sitting at intimate tables, or sprawled on the comfortable, furry-pillowed sofas. *Mon-Wed 5pm-1am, Thu 5pm-2am, Fri 5pm-4am, Sat 6pm-4am, Sun 6pm-1am.* B☰ 110 Rivington St. (Essex St.), 212-614-2494

ORIGINAL

Original New York:
The Attractions

Angelika Film Center • Greenwich Village • Cinema
The films that play at the Angelika Film Center tend to pop up around Oscar time to the 48-state refrain of "I've never heard of that movie." Its focus is on smaller American movies, popular foreign films, indies, and others that won't play in the Midwest for six to eight months (along the lines of *Reservoir Dogs* and *Amélie*). Though Manhattan doesn't offer matinee prices, afternoon movies are pretty popular Downtown. The theater's cafe is a hip venue in itself, attracting people who couldn't care less about what's playing. *Sun-Thu 10:30am-10:30pm, Fri-Sat 10:30am-midnight.* $ 18 W. Houston St. (Mercer St.), 212-995-2000, angelikafilmcenter.com

Anthology Film Archives • East Village • Cinema
Specializing in restoring and screening 16mm and 35mm negatives from films that might otherwise be lost, Anthology Film Archives is regarded as a godsend by the accomplished directors, producers, and film buffs whose donations keep it rolling. Located in Manhattan's former Second Avenue Courthouse, the Film Archives building also includes two motion-picture theaters, a reference library, and a gallery showing the works of filmmakers who dabble in art and photography. Most screenings take place at night, though afternoon festivals are not uncommon. *Hours vary with show times.* $- 32 2nd Ave. (2nd St.), 212-505-5181, anthologyfilmarchives.org

Babeland • Lower East Side • Shop
No, Rabbit Habit, Nubby G, Silver Bullet, and Diamond Ring aren't rapper names. They're the best-selling items in this heady adult toy store. While Toys in Babeland has plenty of kink, the main objective is getting people to think, which is why they offer more than 60 classes, ranging from "Frugal Bondage Enthusiast" to "Introduction to Sex Toys" (also offered in Spanish). The female-oriented shop provides a welcome break for husbands and boyfriends long feigning an interest in Soho shoe-shopping. *Mon-Sat noon-10pm, Sun noon-7pm.* $$ 94 Rivington St. (Ludlow St.), 212-375-1701, babeland.com

Brooklyn Brewery • Williamsburg • Site
Around the turn of the century, there were nearly 50 breweries operating in Brooklyn. Eventually each one closed down, unable to compete with the weak, cheaply produced beers of the Midwest. In 1984, a former AP correspondent longing for the full-flavored European ales he'd enjoyed while living abroad, founded the Brooklyn Brewery with a friend. Together they resurrected the high standards of the German brewers of yore with their lagers, pilsners, and ales. Each tour includes a complimentary tasting. *Tours Sat at 1pm, 2pm, 3pm, 4pm.* 79 N. 11th St. (Kent Ave.), 718-486-7422, brooklynbrewery.com

Christine Chin Spa • Lower East Side • Spa
The Lower East Side is a rapidly changing neighborhood where unrefined-but-hip is suddenly, and in some case grudgingly, becoming purified. When Christine Chin moved her red-hot Soho spa to Rivington Street in 2002, bringing with her such

superclients as Gisele Bundchën and Hilary Swank, the neighborhood got a lot prettier. Best known for their facials and microdermabrasion treatments, this subtle and slightly modest spot offers customers the option of being treated by the owner herself at a price 20% above regular rates. (Appointments are in high demand, particularly with Ms. Chin.) There are four treatment rooms upstairs, and nails are done on the main level, where things can become rather scene-y. It's there that Christine Chin also sells eponymous products that are quite popular. *Daily 10am-7pm.* $$$ 79 Rivington St. (Allen St.), 212-353-0503, christinechin.com

Dyker Beach Golf Course • Brooklyn • Golf Course
A golf course in New York City? Believe it. Granted, Dyker Beach Golf Course is about as far outside of Manhattan as you can get without crossing city limits, but hey, golf isn't really an inner-city sport. With a view of the Verrazano Bridge to their backs and 6,548 yards of green spread before them, businesspeople and city natives alike shoot for the tough par 71. As it's a public course where families often learn to play, things here can move slowly. Booking an early tee time is advisable. *Daily sunrise-sunset.* $$$$ 86th St. (7th Ave.), 718-836-9722, americangolf.com/foresight.cfm

Gabay's • East Village • Shop
In the 1920s, Sam Gabay began his business by selling garment-factory extras from a pushcart on the Lower East Side. Now, this unassuming, family-owned shop is the mother lode of discount items, where major department stores (including Bergdorf Goodman and Henri Bendel) dump their overstock of designer handbags, shoes, and accessories. The goods piled onto mismatched racks and unfinished shelves are often sold for up to 70% under their original retail prices. While a bit of fishing is sometimes required, there's always a good catch in these waters. *Mon-Sat 10am-7pm, Sun 11am-7pm.* 225 1st Ave. (13th St.), 212-254-3180, gabaysoutlet.com

Hudson River Greenway • Chelsea • Park
Eleven miles is a long way in Manhattan, and this scenic stretch extending from Battery Park to the George Washington Bridge is vast indeed. A bike trail running from the bottom of the island follows the Hudson River into New Jersey and beyond (bikes can be rented at a facility near the USS Intrepid Air & Space Museum). Joggers, tourists, and cyclists alike use the Greenway, slowing down in the mid-20s near Chelsea Piers, where food and beverage stands attract sunbathers, families, freaks, and people from every imaginable walk of life. *Daily from sunrise to sunset.* hudsongreenway.state.ny.us

Manhattan Rickshaw Company • Central Park/Greenwich Village • Tour
In New York, a rickshaw ride is both practical and recreational. First off, you need to get around town, and while cabs are faster, they can be too fast for some. Second, both conventional cabbies and pedicabbies tend to work up a smelly sweat, and the convertible pedicabs are out in the fresh, open air. Averaging $15-$20 per ride, these leisurely transports can be found near Central Park and Greenwich Village, or they can be called for scheduled runs. *By appointment, 8am-midnight.* $$ Around Central Park and Greenwich Village, 212-604-4729, manhattanrickshaw.com

Momenta Art • Williamsburg • Art Gallery

Best Galleries A not-for-profit gallery, Momenta gives up-and-comers unique opportunities to showcase their works in a bigger forum than they might otherwise have access to. Obviously, the competition for such an opportunity is fierce, so those who do get the floor have generally paid their dues, and they tend to greet their big Momenta shows with great ambition and enthusiasm. On more than one occasion, works that debuted here have gone on to the Museum of Modern Art. *Thu-Mon noon-6pm.* 72 Berry St. (N. 9th St.), 718-218-8058, momentaart.org

Museum of Chinese in the Americas • Lower East Side • Museum

MoCA is a tribute to the immigrant artists who left China for New York City. Occupying the second floor of an old school building since 1980, this fascinating museum recognizes the Chinese cultural community's legacy of both beauty and strife. Exhibits like "Mapping Our Heritage" use photos and text to illustrate the changing area within this neighborhood, while others invite locals to submit family recipes and historical essays for posting. Though cash strapped, MoCA only asks for a $3 donation from adults, and $1 from seniors and students. *Tue-Sun noon-6pm except Fri until 7pm.* $- 70 Mulberry St., 2nd Fl. (Bayard St.), 212-619-4785, moca-nyc.org

northside JUNK • Williamsburg • Shop

Oftentimes, the hunt is more exciting than the catch. That's the way most shoppers feel about this Williamsburg furniture store, which stocks everything from retro recliners to old cigarette machines. While a souvenir Tiffany's diamond may sum up a week spent in Midtown, a hula dancer lamp for the den says "I was in Williamsburg." And wouldn't you know, among the vintage ashtrays and leopard-skin pillbox hats, that's just the kind of thing you'll find at northside JUNK. *Thu-Sat 1-7pm and by appointment.* 578 Driggs Ave. (N. 6th St.), 718-302-1045

Realform Girdle Building • Williamsburg • Shop

In order for a mall to take hold in an area that thrives on coffee but won't let Starbucks in the door, it had better be unique. If nothing else, the Realform Girdle Building is unique. This mini-mall without franchises is home to a record store, a couple of designer boutiques, a vintage clothier, a yoga center and spa, a local jewelry designer, and the modern beatnik Verb Café. In other words, there are no teenagers hanging out, and no seniors in sneakers walking laps. *Hours vary with each store; most open around 10am and close around 8pm.* 218 Bedford Ave. (N. 5th St.), 718-302-3007, billbury.com/girdlebuilding

Rock Junket NYC • East Village • Tour

Bust out the leather biker jackets, scuffed-up boots, and ripped jeans for this jaunt through rock 'n' roll New York. See the apartment building depicted on the cover of Led Zeppelin's "Physical Graffiti," the staircase where Mick and Keith loitered in their "Waiting on a Friend" video, and the studio apartment where the entire band Blondie once lived. The tour also stops at venues where greats like Lou Reed and Bob Dylan once graced the stage. Two-hour group tours are $20 per person. Private tours are available, too. *Tours: Sat 11am-1pm.* $$ Tour begins at Bowery and Bleecker St., 212-696-6578, rockjunket.com

St. Mark's Place • East Village • Site

In the '70s and '80s, St. Mark's was the punk rock equivalent of Haight-Ashbury. While there's still a bit of seediness around this long stretch of record, resale, and comic shops, the guy in the green Mohawk bumming cigarettes outside Quiznos is in the minority. There's always a bong or two to be found on the street as well, and those seeking a bag of oregano can find it at Thompkins Square Park, which officially marks the end of St. Mark's Place. St. Mark's Pl. (between Bowery and 2nd Ave.)

Statue of Liberty (Liberty Island) • Tribeca • Site

She's close to 120 years old, has a 35-foot waistline, and never cracks a smile, but Lady Liberty is New York City's most called-after maiden. From 8:30am to 5pm every day but Christmas, tourists come to 12-acre Liberty Island, which has been the monument's home since 1886. Various guided tours of the statue range from 30 to 90 minutes, and they're all free. Ferry trips from Battery Park to Liberty Island run throughout the day, at $8 a ride. Liberty Island's grounds are ideal for picnicking. *Daily 9:30am-5pm.* $ Battery Park Ferry Terminal, 212-269-5755, nps.gov/stli

Tenement Museum • Lower East Side • Museum

Best Unusual Museums The abundant written documents and artifacts at this museum not only tell the story of the families who lived in this house, but of one of this country's first urban neighborhoods as well. Like the neighborhood itself, the Tenement Museum doesn't glamorize a thing—there are no elevators, so large groups will be required to walk through rather tight spaces. Just be grateful you're not carrying groceries. Tickets are $10 apiece and tour reservations are generally required. *Tours: Tue-Fri 1:20-4:45pm, Sat-Sun 11:15am-4:45pm; Store: Mon 11am-5:30pm, Tue-Fri 11am-6pm, Sat-Sun 10:45am-6pm.* $ 108 Orchard St. (Delancey St.), 212-431-0233, tenement.org

Williamsburg Art & Historical Center • Williamsburg • Museum

Way back when Williamsburg was spelled "Williamsburgh," this opulent example of French Second Empire architecture operated as the King's County Savings Institution. Now nearly 150 years old, this landmark at the base of the Williamsburg Bridge serves as a public space where local art, vintage clothing, and the occasional banquet can be found. While film nights and fundraisers are held here on random nights, the space opens every weekend. *Sat-Sun noon-6pm or by appointment.* 135 Broadway (Bedford St.), 718-486-7372, wahcenter.net

Zito Studio Gallery • Lower East Side • Art Gallery

Best Galleries Once Lower East Sider Antony Zito gets his hands on a discarded piece of furniture (or any other paintable and shapable surface), junk is transformed into art. Though at first glance this Lower East Side gallery looks like a junk shop, the trash inside is actually a canvas for Zito's masterful pop icon portraits. When moved, Zito has been known to do on-the-spot portraits, particularly at the nearby Apocalypse Lounge, where his artists' collective finds inspiration and beer. Many items are reasonably priced, and civil haggling can only help. *Sat-Sun noon-5pm, Mon-Fri by appointment.* 122 Ludlow St. (Delancey St.), 646-602-2338, zitogallery.com

ORIGINAL

Classic New York

Whether you first imagine ragged sons of immigrants playing stickball under the Brooklyn Bridge, or fedora-clad and pin-striped knickerbockers strolling down Broadway, New York City has such a vintage vibe, it sometimes seems the days should take place in black and white. Towering over Midtown Manhattan is the classic Empire State Building. Its shadow falls over the busy streets of Times Square, where the whole nation welcomes in the New Year. A block or so east lies the Great White Way, where Mertz and Barrymore became legends, and *Cats'* 20-year run had people believing it might actually be "Now and Forever." Follow Broadway up to 59th Street and you'll find historic Central Park, which is as good a place to be during the day as it is a bad place to be at night. There's a lot of "new" in New York, but it's also a piece of living history.

*Note: Venues in bold are described in detail in the listings that follow the itinerary. Venues followed by an * asterisk are those we recommend as both a restaurant and a destination bar.*

Classic New York:
The Perfect Plan (3 Days and Nights)

Highlights

Thursday

Mid-morning	**Metropolitan Museum**
Lunch	**Café Gray**
Mid-afternoon	**Central Park**
Pre-dinner	**Tavern on the Green*, David Letterman, Washington Sq. Park**
Dinner	**Cru*, Nobu**
Nighttime	**Blue Note, Stonewall**
Late-night	**Chumley's**

Friday

Mid-morning	**NY Stock Exchange, Ground Zero, Empire State Building**
Lunch	**Blue Fin***
Mid-afternoon	**Times Square, Circle Line Cruise**
Pre-theater	**Sardi's**
Nighttime	**Theater**
Dinner	**Joe Allen, Carmine's**
Late-night	**Don't Tell Mama**

Saturday

Breakfast	**Sarabeth's**
Mid-morning	**5th Ave. Shopping**
Lunch	**Morrell Wine Bar***
Mid-afternoon	**Brooklyn Bridge, South Street Seaport**
Pre-dinner	**Harbour Lights, Campbell Apartment, Grand Central Terminal**
Dinner	**Jean-Georges, Aureole**
Nighttime	**Village Vanguard**
Late-night	**Pen-Top Bar**

Hotel: **The Ritz-Carlton New York, Central Park**

Thursday

10am The Upper East Side's **The Metropolitan Museum of Art** (aka "The Met") is one of the wonders of the world, with a vast collection of art, sculpture, textiles, armor, and more. On the opposite side of Central Park is the Upper West Side's **American Museum of Natural History**, which is full of old stuff that smart people have found lying around over the years and that, happily, has washed up quite nicely.

1pm Lunch Your best bet might be relishing a hot dog from a street vendor while sitting on a Central Park bench. For something more substantial, **Café Gray**, in the Time Warner Building at the southwest corner of the park, serves a classic dinner-caliber lunch. You can check out the "mall" en route.

3pm With 800-plus acres, you can easily spend an afternoon in **Central Park**. The sky-high buildings along the southern end of the park can't help but remind you that this is the Big Apple, but the ground-level natural beauty provides a great contrast.

CLASSIC

4pm Were you able to get tickets to watch a taping of *The Late Show with David Letterman* in the storied Ed Sullivan Theater? Two shows are taped on Thursdays, making today your best chance of getting in. Without tickets, you can try hanging around outside—sometimes audience members are chosen off the street. Otherwise, stay in the park and relax with a cocktail at **Tavern on the Green*** (which is also a good place to go if it rains).

7pm Take time before dinner to enjoy Greenwich Village. You may want to start at **Washington Square Park**, and make a long loop either north (up to 12th Street, between Fifth and Sixth Avenues), south, or west. One stop could be **The Strand**, which claims it has 18 miles of books.

8:30pm Dinner Within spitting (as is done for wine-tasting) distance of Washington Square Park, **Cru*** is a modern classic with an awesome wine list. Also nearby is one of New York's most romantic restaurants, **One if by Land, Two if by Sea**, where eclectic Americana cuisine is served in a historic setting (the carriage house once owned by Aaron Burr). Further afield, in the Tribeca/West Village neighborhood, is **Nobu**, where you're likely to see *Goodfella* locals like Robert De Niro and Martin Scorsese enjoying some of the city's best sushi.

10:30pm Southern Greenwich Village is jumping this time of night. For a late-night laugh, check out the up-and-comers at the **Comedy Cellar**. Around the corner, the **Blue Note** jazz club hosts as many big stars as it launches. If you're feeling literary, check out the **White Horse Tavern**, where historic writers like Jack Kerouac passed the time, and Dylan Thomas passed away. Or grab a cocktail at the nearby **Stonewall**, the site of one of the world's most heralded civil rights riots.

1am One for the road is just a short, winding street away at the unmarked former speakeasy, **Chumley's**, where many a playwright has celebrated a success and lamented a failure.

Friday

8:30am To get down to Wall Street, you'll need an early start and a fair amount of time (this might be a good opportunity to try out the subway system), making the hotel breakfast a good choice. Visit Wall Street before the opening bell at 9:30am, when the streets are a flurry of activity. Security policies permitting, take a quick tour of the **New York Stock Exchange**. A short walk west leads to the sobering and profound landmarks at **Ground Zero**, the former site of the World Trade Center. Is this the only landmark in New York that's significant for what's not here?

11am Make your way back uptown to the perennially classic **Empire State Building**, and take a gander at this spectacular city from the observatory on top.

12:30pm Lunch Enjoy seafood at the **Blue Fin*** restaurant, where the windows overlook Times Square, and you feel like you're in the center of the universe. The scene at **Carnegie Deli** is considerably less refined, but you're certain not to leave the place hungry.

2pm Wander through the eye-popping but intensely commercial Times Square, where you'll find Toys R' Us, ESPN Zone, and plenty of police. If you didn't manage to swing tickets to that fabulous, sold-out show, stop by a TKTS booth to check availability (at discount prices).

3:30pm Get a new perspective of the city from one of the **Circle Line Cruise** tours, which depart from both Midtown and Tribeca. If the weather is poor, or plying these not-so-high seas doesn't float your boat, relax like a true blue-blooded New Yorker in the **Oasis Day Spa**.

7:15pm There's no better place for an early evening, preshow drink than **Sardi's**, the official stomping ground of Broadway direc-

tors and stars. The bar area is small, but you won't find a friendlier bartender in the city.

8pm It's showtime. Whether it's a Broadway, Off-Broadway, or Off-Off-Broadway show, the theater scene in New York is one of the things that sets it apart from most anywhere on the planet.

10:30pm Dinner After-theater dinner at the lively **Joe Allen** is, like Sardi's, a Broadway tradition. **Carmine's** also packs 'em in, but occasionally seats the spontaneous. (If you prefer eating before the theater, you'll find reliable food and a terrific view at **Restaurant Above**.)

12:30am Unless you were willing to skip dinner to catch the 11pm cabaret at **Don't Tell Mama**, you'll have to settle for their terrific piano bar. Or stop into **Café Nicole Bar** at the Novotel New York, a popular, upscale watering hole, where amateur critics can be found discussing that night's performances.

Saturday

9am Across from Central Park, have your Goldie Lox—scrambled eggs with smoked salmon and cream cheese—at **Sarabeth's**.

10am Shop and people-watch down Fifth Avenue, America's original

CLASSIC

high-end shopping street. Starting at 59th Street, you'll find a half-mile of retailers, ending with Saks at 49th Street. Perhaps the most opulent landmark in the area, which boasts the world's most expensive retail real estate, is **St. Patrick's Cathedral**. Nothing's for sale, but surely donations are appreciated.

Noon If the season is right, check out **The Rink at Rockefeller Center**, known in the summer as simply "the ground."

1:30pm Lunch You've earned a glass (or two) of wine to accompany a light meal at **Morrell Wine Bar & Café***. For something truly historic way downtown, enjoy lunch in the shadow of the Brooklyn Bridge at the classic **Bridge Café**, which has been serving up seafood for over 200 years.

3pm After leaving the Bridge Café, take a stroll over the **Brooklyn Bridge**, and watch the boats passing below. On the other side is the splendid Brooklyn Promenade, which is worth the wander. If you pass on Brooklyn, absorb the street fair atmosphere at **South Street Seaport**, which also hosts a museum and an operating 19th-century printer, Browne & Co.

5pm Take a load off at South Street's **Harbour Lights** restaurant, where you can sip cocktails and enjoy the panoramic view of the East River. Landlubbers may prefer a pint at the **Heartland Brewery South Street***, at the crossroads of this well-preserved vintage port town. For a different scene, watch the scurrying masses below while unwinding with a late-afternoon cocktail at **The Campbell Apartment**, the upstairs pub located inside that architectural masterpiece, **Grand Central Terminal**.

8pm Dinner End your weekend with a gourmet meal. It would be a crime to leave New York without dining in one of these culinary institutions: the very uptown **Jean-Georges**, Daniel Boulud's **Aureole**, or down in Greenwich Village, **Il Mulino**.

11pm Take a cab over to the **Village Vanguard**, where jazz performers, including Woody Allen, play. Further south in Soho, have a drink at the upscale tavernesque **Onieal's Grand Street***, a former speakeasy rumored to have a tunnel leading to the old police station across the street. If you're dying for a cig with your drink, pop into nearby **Circa Tabac**, one of the only lounges in New York where smoking is still allowed. For those who dined Uptown, you may just want to end your evening with a spectacular view of the city from the **Pen-Top Bar & Terrace** at the Peninsula.

Classic New York:
The Key Neighborhoods

Greenwich Village and **West Village** To its residents, "The Village" is Manhattan. The neighborhood, filled with historic buildings and green spaces, was built before the grid system that defines most of the city, which makes getting lost here easy. The restaurants and nightlife avoid trendiness, opting instead for a sensibility that suits the people who live here.

Midtown The Chrysler Building, Grand Central Terminal, Central Park, Times Square, and Broadway ... this is the New York you'll recognize from television, the New York most visitors have come to expect. In other cities this might be considered touristy—here it is simply "best in show."

Upper East Side and **Upper West Side** These are primarily residential neighborhoods, albeit very exclusive ones, separated by Central Park. The West Side is considered more intellectual and liberal, whereas the East Side is more preppy, fun, and country-clubbish.

Wall Street There's only one Wall Street, and much like Hollywood or Washington, D.C., many people know it more as an idea than a place. Between opening and closing bells, this area of solid old financial institutions still looks a lot like it did around the turn of the 20th century.

Times Square In the Midtown area, where once strip clubs, drug dealers, and boa-wearing pimps ran amok, there is now a plethora of Tokyo-esque neon signage, corporate bars, restaurants, and stores. Whether or not this Disneyfication is a good thing, Times Square is still a must. Broadway, between 46th and 47th Streets.

TKTS

What could be better than getting tickets to a sold-out Broadway show? How about getting those tickets for half-price? Follow the big red lettering on the white backdrops occupying Duffy Square, which is on 47th Street between Broadway and Seventh Avenue. The availability of tickets for same day shows is posted on an electronic board over the booth, which only accepts travelers' checks and cash. *Mon, Tue, Thu, Fri 3-8pm, Wed, Sat 10am-2pm, Sun 11am-7:30pm.*

Classic New York:
The Shopping Blocks

Fifth Avenue (Midtown)

This is the land of luxury, where Trump Tower soars, and rent goes for $850 per square foot. Stiletto-wearing and fur-wrapped heiresses vie for space with the packs of tourists, all fighting for a view of the venerated department store windows as they stroll along Fifth Avenue from 59th Street.

Bergdorf Goodman Ladies really do still lunch at this purveyor of all things status, with an incredible two floors of designer shoes. 754 5th Ave. (58th St.), 212-753-7300

F.A.O. Schwartz Buckets of rainbow-colored candy and other sugar-filled delights await and tempt the kid in all of us. Gawk at stuffed animals that cost more than your first car, and channel your inner Veruca Salt by skipping through Lego Land and Barbie World. Lines require the patience of a saint, but it's worth the wait to bang out chopsticks with your feet on the giant piano—à la Tom Hanks in the movie *Big*. 767 5th Ave. (58th St.), 212-644-9400

Henri Bendel This shop gives Fifth Avenue a kick in the pants, catering more to pop stars than aristocrats. Supertrendy and barely legal are the guiding principles for designer handbags, shoes, clothing, and an entire floor devoted to racy lingerie. 712 5th Ave. (55th St.), 212-247-1100

Louis Vuitton Logos will always be in for Louis Vuitton devotees. The sleek new flagship store, the largest in the world, is white and modern, like an inhabitable iPod, and stocks the ultimate in luxury goods. 1 E. 57th St. (5th Ave.), 212-758-8877

Museum of Modern Art The newly redesigned MoMA, taking a playful approach to minimalism, is not to be missed. All walks of life converge to see the art and eat in the incredibly chic restaurant, the Modern. Poke around the design store for provocative art tomes, art posters, and high-design objects. It's the only way to take the art home. 11 W. 53rd St. (5th Ave.), 212-708-9400

Saks Fifth Avenue The store responsible, in part, for the avenue's cachet still stands tall, dishing out luxurious goods with an old-school sensibility. 611 5th Ave. (Clay St.), 212-753-4000

Tiffany & Co. It's hard not to feel lust for those little blue boxes and the baubles that lurk within. Don't be afraid to go in, the salespeople are very accommodating. 727 5th Ave. (57th St.), 212-755-8000

Classic New York:
The Hotels

The Carlyle • Upper East Side • Timeless (179 rms)
It is one of New York's most luxurious hotels, and though several others have tried to compete for "Carlylian" status, this Upper East Side institution is still one of a kind. Deluxe rooms are spacious, and the higher floors have great Central Park views. Situated on Manhattan's ritziest shopping row, the Carlyle has endless daytime activity options. Of course, this well-preserved classic also captures old-school New York nightlife at its finest. Restaurant Carlyle, the onsite restaurant, offers exquisite French-Continental cuisine in a warm, elegant setting. The Gallery, whose decor and concept were inspired by the Turkish Sultan's dining room, has served the world's richest and most famous for decades. Stop in for afternoon tea, or, better yet, pop in after midnight when top-notch entertainment captivates the crowd at the Carlyle Club, once the venue of choice for such legends as Bobby Short, Eartha Kitt, and Woody Allen. Bemelmans Bar, built in the 1860s, predates the hotel itself. $$$$$ 35 E. 76th St. (Madison Ave.), 212-744-1600 / 888-767-3966, thecarlyle.com

Essex House • Midtown • Timeless (601 rms)
Occupying the 19th through the 36th floors of the historic Essex House building, this luxury hotel finds the balance between boutique-quaint and enormity. With an expansive lobby of marble floors and crystal chandeliers, the Essex House knows how to impress, though even the elegant decor is upstaged by the stunning northward views of Central Park. East-facing rooms tend to be light, yet their views are obscured by neighboring buildings. Executive Queen Park rooms have good views and somewhat updated furnishings. If it's common to find amenities like the spa facilities and fitness center in a New York hotel, not every urban lodging offers horseback riding and a jogging path. There is a considerable difference in room sizes, and it's directly proportionate to cost. Still, everyone is treated like a VIP at Essex House, with freshly cut flowers in every room, Bose CD stereos, and personal butler service. The hotel houses the star-chef restaurant, Alain Ducasse. $$$$$ 160 Central Park S. (6th Ave.), 212-247-0300 / 800-937-8461, essexhouse.com

Hôtel Plaza Athénée • Upper East Side • Timeless (150 rms)
Lush and majestic, this modestly-sized hotel looms large by boutique standards. Swimming in Louis XVI furnishings, opulent chandeliers, and massive floral arrangements worthy of the royal court of Versailles, the Hôtel Plaza Athénée is an international hotel of the highest order. The rooms are designed with European fabrics and furnishings, including Belgian linens and imported terry robes. Plaza Athénée's onsite restaurant, Arabelle, is wildly lauded for its exquisite French-Asian decor, continental cuisine, and popular Sunday brunch. Bar Seine, the hotel's romantic lounge, is exotically designed with African prints, amber lighting, and velvet curtains. The multilingual staff offer a blend of European refinement with a healthy respect for American tipping. Rooms overlooking 64th Street get the best light. $$$$$ 37 E. 64th St. (Madison Ave.), 212-734-9100 / 800-447-8800, plaza-athenee.com

CLASSIC

The Peninsula New York • Midtown • Timeless (239 rms)

Lavish and grand, the Peninsula is the kind of hotel where one could happily check in and never leave—though management may have something to say about that. After a $45 million renovation of this Beaux Arts building in 1998, the Peninsula offers modern comforts with elegant, old-world charm. There are 185 rooms and 54 suites, all of which are flooded with light. Though the Grande Luxe is pricey, it's somewhat larger than the Deluxe, and the city view overlooking Fifth Avenue is guaranteed to take your breath away. The fitness center is new and well-maintained, featuring a spacious, glass-enclosed spa and swimming pool. Those seeking to wet their whistle will love the 23rd floor's Pen-Top Bar and Terrace, where hotel guests and Manhattanites alike converge to sip cocktails under the stars and take in the spectacular view. The Peninsula is geared toward business travelers and a savvy crowd of sophisticates who know their way around the city. $$$$$ 700 5th Ave. (55th St.), 212-956-2888 / 800-262-9467, newyork.peninsula.com

The Ritz-Carlton New York, Battery Park • Tribeca • Timeless (298 rms)

There are New Yorkers who insist on staying Downtown, but can do without a hotel that has a DJ in the lobby. This stunning 39-story beauty was made for them, offering nearly 300 rooms, with those facing the Hudson being the most attractive. Due to its proximity to Wall Street, the Ritz-Carlton Battery Park sees lots of businessmen, but rather than conventioneers with suitcases loaded with gimmicks, they tend to carry alligator-skin briefcases full of high-powered documents with big numbers. Rooms are designed with a contemporary, deco-inspired flair, with unique amenities, like bathroom butlers and telescopes. There are also plenty of creature comforts, like goose down pillows, feather beds, and Ritz-Carlton pajamas. Customer service is excellent, the Rise Bar has harbor views, an outdoor terrace, and the infamous 25-ounce tumbler cocktails. Call to reserve one of the ten tables on the terrace. $$$$$ 2 West St. (West Side Hwy.), 212-344-0800 / 800-241-3333, ritzcarlton.com

The Ritz-Carlton New York, Central Park • Midtown • Timeless (261 rms)

With Central Park South as a front yard, this 1930s-era building houses one of the finest Ritz-Carltons on earth. You can't beat their in-house limo service, considering they aren't your run-of-the-mill Lincolns—they're Bentleys. The lobby alternately provides harpists and pianists, who create a soundtrack for the well-to-do clientele. As a general rule, rooms that overlook the park end in 07, 08, 10, 12, and 14 (the higher the better.) The Park View suite is the one you really want, but you're not alone, which means you should plan ahead. Looking down Sixth Avenue from your window is great, and waking up over a sunny courtyard isn't bad either, but the rooms overlooking Central Park are incomparable. $$$$$ 50 Central Park S. (5th Ave.), 212-308-9100 / 800-241-3333, ritzcarlton.com

The St. Regis • Midtown • Timeless (300 rms)

New York talk-show fans and Notre Dame alumni, take heed—NYC's favorite son, Mr. Philbin, has yet to be canonized. This is New York's other Regis, a posh hotel where the Gilded Age meets Generation Y. The palatial lobby and sumptuous, old-European decor belie a high-tech renovation that has these classic digs wired for the future. With marble-paved hallways and bathrooms, and restored Louis XV furniture, these spacious, high-ceilinged rooms have hosted some of New York's most elite VIPs for the past century. Guests at the St. Regis are treated like royalty, with 24-hour butler service, offering complimentary unpacking and suit-pressing services upon arrival. The two best suites were designed by Christian Dior and Tiffany's, and they maintain a timeless quality. The King Cole Bar, known as the home of the world's first Bloody Mary, sports an 1895 Maxfield Parrish mural of Old King Cole. $$$$$ 2 E. 55th St. (5th Ave.), 212-753-4500 / 877-787-3447, stregis.com

Classic New York:
The Restaurants

Artisanal • Murray Hill • French
When in Manhattan, cheese connoisseurs make a beeline for Chef Terrance Brennan's Artisanal, the Big Cheese of the city's fromageries. The bustling bistro brims with wood tables set closely together family-style, and offers a menu that's a true "homage to fromage." Dip warm hunks of bread into a steaming fondue of Stilton and sauternes; savor a buckwheat crepe oozing Emmenthal; or try the myriad grilled sandwiches *au fromage*, including delectable portobello smothered in melted fontina. Wash it all down with a robust French red and indulge your sweet tooth with, what else?—a creamy wedge of cheesecake. *Mon-Thu 11:45am-11pm, Fri 11:45am-midnight, Sat 11am-midnight, Sun 11am-10pm.* $$ ▤ 2 Park Ave. (32nd St.), 212-775-8585, artisanalcheese.com

Aureole • Upper East Side • New American (G)
Set in an Upper East Side brownstone that's as warm and alluring as restaurateur/chef Charlie Palmer's New American cuisine, Aureole is both comfortable and romantic—even at lunchtime. A regal staircase ascends amid ferns, flowers, and colorful contemporary prints, connecting two floors of white linen–lined tables. The seasonal menu of East Coast entrees, such as Atlantic salmon and Maine lobster salad, can be paired with over 700 wines (including their very own Aureole Cuvée). The wine-happy decor displays choice vintages throughout the restaurant, including a tower of bottles at the central decanting station. *Mon-Fri noon-2:30pm and 5:30-11pm, Sat 5-10pm.* $$$$ ▢ 34 E. 61st St. (Park Ave.), 212-319-1660, charliepalmer.com

Blue Fin* • Midtown • Seafood
Given its location in the heart of Times Square, it's hard to blame Blue Fin for being a little touristy. Occupying two floors of the Times Square W, this seafood restaurant manages to rise above the rest. The upstairs dining area—an elegant space of polished wood, mirrors, and white banquettes—is less harried, with families and couples eating crab cakes and lobster chowder, while downstairs, only two inches of glass separate the cocktail area from one of the busiest sidewalks in the world. The drinks come quickly and with a smile. *Sun-Mon 7-11am, 11:30am-4pm, and 5pm-midnight, Tue-Thu 7-11am, 11:30am-4pm, and 5pm-12:30am, Fri-Sat 7-11am, 11:30am-4pm, and 5pm-1am.* $$$ ⊞⊑▤ W NewYork—Times Square, 1567 Broadway (47th St.), 212-918-1400, brguestrestaurants.com

Blue Mill Tavern • West Village • American
For about 50 years, the historic Grange Hall restaurant occupied this charming corner. Amazingly, Blue Mill Tavern has reached even further into the past, taking the name and style of the locale that preceded Grange Hall. The original oak bar, wooden booths, and well-placed mirrors set a mood of nostalgia, while light jazz plays overhead in the romantic rear dining room. In keeping with the decor, Blue Mill serves sidecars, martinis, and classic American dishes, like crispy duck, prime rib, and succotash. *Daily noon-3:30pm and 5:30-11pm.* $$ �▤ 50 Commerce St. (Barrow St.), 212-352-0009

Bridge Café • Wall Street • Seafood

"Institution" is one of the most overused terms in New York restaurant hype, but in the case of this inveterate 1791 locale, it's undeniable. When the Bridge Café first opened on the cusp of the South Street Seaport, there were no touristy restaurants clustered down the block. Snugly tucked under the Brooklyn Bridge, this onetime hideaway for whiskey-soaked fishermen is now a friendly, even romantic restaurant, with yellow walls, nautical decor, and a well-worn bar. Located directly across the street from the South Street fish market, Bridge Café offers seafood as fresh as it gets without swimming away. *Daily at 11:45am, Sun-Mon closes at 10pm, Tue-Thu at 11pm, Fri-Sat until midnight.* $$ F⬚ 279 Water St. (Dover St.), 212-227-3344, eatgoodinny.com

Café Gray • Upper West Side • New American/French

When the Time Warner Center first opened its food court, featuring restaurants from such culinary giants as Jean-Georges Vongerichten, Thomas Keller, and Gray Kunz, there was plenty of skepticism. Once New Yorkers got over the mall aesthetic outside, Kunz's four-star Café Gray became a huge hit. Modern and moneyed, this otherwise traditional brasserie is lined with dark woods, leather, and mirrors. Small dishes like personal pizzas and crisped lobster tail, and the two signature wines, one from the Hamptons and the other from Austria, are worth sampling. *Call for hours.* $$$ ⬚ 10 Columbus Cir. (58th St.), 212-823-6338, cafegray.com

The Carlyle Restaurant • Upper East Side • French

Carlyle Restaurant is where sophisticated jet-setters and world-class foodies go to dine. Big floral arrangements lighten the otherwise dark mahogany-wood decor, which creates an intimate setting. Attentive waiters whisk around in white shirts, as well-ironed as the linen tablecloths. The menu is French and heavy, with an outstanding Grand Marnier soufflé that takes 20 minutes to prepare (it's well worth the wait), and a luscious filet mignon with foie gras. It's enough to make you go *oui oui oui* all the way home. *Daily 7-10:30am, noon-3pm, and 6-11pm (opens at 8am Sat-Sun).* $$$ ⬚ 35 E. 76th St. (Madison Ave.), 212-744-1600, thecarlyle.com

Carmine's • Midtown • Italian

Everything is big at this Theater District mainstay—the room, the servings, the crowd. Carmine's won't take reservations for groups of less than six after 6pm, which means you should either get there early, or elbow your way into the big bar area with the pretheater crowd. Traditional Italian pasta platters are doused in garlic, and the meat dishes are pretty vampire-proof as well. Happily, the bathrooms have mouthwash dispensers and cups to keep your breath from stealing the show. *Sun 11am-11pm, Mon 11:30am-1pm, Tue-Sat 11:30am-midnight.* $$ ▤ 200 W. 44th St. (Broadway), 212-221-3800, carminesnyc.com

Carnegie Deli • Midtown • Deli

Best Delis Chances are you've seen this Midtown deli in one of its countless TV and film appearances. Many of Carnegie's regulars are famous as well, and they often inspire eponymous sandwich creations. How Bill Cosby becomes a $18.95 turkey, tongue, and corned beef sandwich is hard to explain, though dubbing twin rolls of pastrami and corned beef a "Dolly Parton" is an easier reach. Carnegie Deli is a busy lunchtime destination, so be prepared to wait a few minutes, and don't hesitate to push your way to the counter. *Sun-Sat 6:30am-4am.* $$ ⬚▤ 854 7th Ave. (55th St.), 212-757-2245, carnegiedeli.com

CLASSIC

Corner Bistro* • West Village • American
Despite the burger craze at many steak houses and four-star restaurants, Corner Bistro is the city's staple, with thick burgers and stringy fries soaking right through the paper plates. If you're looking for a sense of community, this is where you want to be (though you don't have to add to the initial-carving in the weathered back booths). This old watering hole works well as an after-work bar, but since the kitchen is open as late as 3:30am, it is more of an after-a-few-bars bar. *Mon-Sat 11:30am-4am, Sun noon-4am.* $- ⓎⒻ▤ 331 W. 4th St. (Jane St.), 212-242-9502, cornerbistro.citysearch.com

Cru* • Greenwich Village • Mediterranean
Plush caramel tones, thick carpeting, and low lighting make Cru a date destination, but more so for foodies than for those who hurry dinner to hit the club scene. Like the clientele, chef Shea Gallante's cuisine is rich in appearance and taste. Lamb and lobster alike are thoughtfully seasoned, and even pastas offer surprises (like frog legs). The wine list is a leather-bound, multivolume tome of 3,400-plus bottles. Because the tables are generously spaced, the best seats are in the middle of the room, away from the high-traffic streets outside. *Mon-Sat 5:30-11pm.* $$$ ⓎⒷⓄ▤ 24 5th Ave. (9th St.), 212-529-1700, cru-nyc.com

Daniel • Upper East Side • French (G)
At this Upper East Side foodie favorite, celebrity chef Daniel Boulud never fails to amaze, with lovingly prepared dishes like the braised short ribs, which marinate for a day and a half before reaching the dining room. And what a dining room it is—limestone columns, sparkling crystal, and a bounty of fresh flowers. The best seating is in the sky-box tables available for groups of four during the week, as long as they agree to the eight-course tasting menu. A deftly handled bar also provides great views of the elegant room. *Mon-Sat 5:45-11pm.* $$$$ ▤ 60 E. 65th St., (Park Ave.), 212-288-0033, danielnyc.com

Delmonico's • Wall Street • Steak House
Best Power Lunches The only thing better aged than this 1837 landmark's interior—a study in elegance, with majestic columns at the entrance and classic chandeliers at the center of the well-appointed room—is its choice beef cuts. Occupied mostly by Wall Street power brokers, the dining room's occupancy could practically tell you the time. From noon until 1pm, the tables are filled with coat-and-tie-clad sharks who return for post-closing-bell gin martinis at 5pm, and then stay for dinner. There is a boys' club aura in effect here, but there's always a place at Delmonico's for carnivorettes who are handy with a steak knife. *Mon-Fri 11:30am-10pm, Sat 5:30-10pm.* $$$ Ⓕ▤ 56 Beaver St. (Pearl St.), 212-509-1144, delmonicosny.com

El Parador Café • Murray Hill • Mexican
This rare Mexican gem is as festive as it is upscale, and its loyal following is both trendy and grown-up. Rosy-cheeked patrons enjoy excellent margaritas and spiced-up steaks amid whitewashed walls and tasteful Mexican ceramics. The shrimp quesadilla is a standout dish, but all entrees are nearly perfect. Inside, El Parador is dark, with candlelit wood and brick. The scene at the colorful tile bar is local and welcoming. *Daily noon-11pm.* $$ Ⓕ▤ 325 E. 34th St. (2nd Ave.), 212-679-6812, elparadorcafe.com

The Four Seasons* • Midtown • New American (G)

Best Power Lunches With beautiful, elegant rooms designed by architectural genius Philip Johnson (who also designed the New York State Theater in Lincoln Center), the Four Seasons is the quintessential place for a special occasion. The Grill Room is famous for financial and publishing industry power lunches, while the shimmering Pool Room is a romantic classic. This timeless venue is the only restaurant in New York City designated a landmark. Chef Christian Albin's classic American cuisine is exquisite, especially the rack of lamb with mashed potatoes. *Mon-Fri noon-2pm and 5-9:30pm, Sat 5-11pm.* $$$$ ⓍⒷ≡ 99 E. 52nd St. (Park Ave.), 212-754-9494, fourseasonsrestaurant.com

Fraunces Tavern* • Wall Street • American

Nothing builds up an appetite like driving the British army off your land, which is why George Washington chose this locale to say farewell to his Revolutionary War troops before pursuing a career in politics. Built in 1719 as a residency, this historic haunt became a tavern in 1762. The wood-paneled walls are lined with old flags, memorabilia, and murals of early American heroes, and the chandeliers and period furniture give it a museum cachet. In fact, an actual in-house museum can be toured for $3. *Mon-Sat 11:30am-9:30pm (bar until 11pm).* $$ ⓍⒻ≡ 54 Pearl St. (Broad St.), 212-968-1776, frauncestavern.com

Grotta Azzurra Restaurant • Soho • Italian

Ring-a-ding-ding! Grotta Azzurra was a favorite of Frank Sinatra, and despite an over-the-top Vatican-esque 2003 makeover, it remains a local favorite for upscale Italian dining. Decked out in gold and marble, and sporting a wall-sized waterfall, the main dining room is less subtle than the tasteful downstairs lounge, located in the middle of the wine cellar (which is available for private parties). The menu is masterfully prepared, especially the pappardelle with braised rabbit. *Daily 10am-midnight.* $$ Ⓕ≡ 177 Mulberry St. (Broome St.), 212-925-8775, grottaazzurrany.com

Il Mulino • Greenwich Village • Italian (G)

Unless you either "know somebody" or made reservations well in advance, you can fuggedabout a weekend dinner in this charmingly tattered, astonishingly dark old-school trattoria. Il Mulino, which looks like it was pulled straight out of a Scorsese film, just may have the best Italian food in New York. Heaping servings of pasta, seafood, and meat come in stages, and it's generally recommended that you let the waiter put something together for you. If you can't make it in for dinner, try stopping in for lunch. *Mon-Fri noon-2:30pm, Mon-Sat 5-11pm.* $$$ ≡ 86 W. 3rd St. (Sullivan St.), 212-673-3783, ilmulinonewyork.com

Jean-Georges • Upper West Side • French (G)

World-renowned French culinary artist Jean-Georges Vongerichten's sparse and airy classic is the barometer by which NYC dining is gauged. The two dining rooms are sunbathed in a minimalist weave of earth tones and light. Entrees are perfectly seasoned without being heavy-handed. The sea scallops, steak frîtes, and frog legs are good, but the seven-course tasting menu is the way to go. Should dinner reservations be a problem, try the three-course lunch menu, which is prepared with equal care. *Mon-Fri noon-3pm and 5:30-11pm, Sat 5:15-11pm.* $$$$ ≡ 1 Central Park W. (60th St.), 212-299-3900, jean-georges.com

CLASSIC

Joe Allen • Midtown • New American
Though Joe Allen is a Theater District mainstay that always receives rave reviews, arriving during the busy times can result in involuntary standing ovations for those who didn't call ahead. Basically a glorified and priced-for-Broadway tavern, Joe Allen surprises with satisfying, serviceable cuisine. The theatrical posters orient the all-ages patrons as to their proximity to the Great White Way, though without a hint of theme-y cheesiness. The crowd can get raucous, but no one goes to Joe's for peace and quiet. *Mon-Fri noon-midnight, Sat-Sun 11:30am-midnight.* $$ ✉ 326 W. 46th St. (8th Ave.), 212-581-6464, joeallenrestaurant.com

Lombardi's • Soho • Pizzeria
Best Pizza Opened in 1897, Lombardi's was the first licensed pizzeria in America, and it's still considered one of the city's best. While many New Yorkers get through lunchtime with a slice from a corner pizza shop, Lombardi's is where those in the know go when they have time to sit down and order an entire pie. Tourists pack the place on weekends and evenings, which is why weekdays for lunch is the time to go. All pies are baked in a coal oven, where the buttery crusts are slightly blackened. *Daily 11:30am, closes Mon-Thu 11pm, Fri-Sat midnight, Sun 10pm.* $ ▣✉ 32 Spring St. (Mott St.), 212-941-7994, lombardispizza.com

Magnolia Bakery • West Village • Bakery
If you can sell cupcakes in a body-conscious neighborhood like the West Village, you're doing something right. When you're selling them so quickly you have to impose a 12 cupcake per person, per day limit, you're Magnolia Bakery. A favorite for tourists, common locals, and neighborhood celebs looking to get their sugar fix, Magnolia has a single table inside and an old park bench outside, though most people just grab their goods and go. *Sex and the City* fans will have seen this spot on several occasions. *Mon noon-11:30pm, Tue-Thu 9am-11:30pm, Fri 9am-12:30am, Sat 10am-12:30am, Sun 10am-11:30pm.* $ ✉ 401 Bleecker St. (11th St.), 212-462-2572

March Restaurant • Midtown • New American (G)
Nothing says "I care" like a flavorful, romantic meal at March Restaurant. It is intimate in every sense of the word—waiters and hosts accommodate marriage proposals and celebrations, and the single room is so tiny that those who opt for the poussin rather than the sweetbreads may have to step outside to change their minds (fortunately, there's a small terrace). Duo tasting menus are so romantic they just may make you weep—in fact, at $200-plus, they may leave you crying like a baby. Cuisine is labeled New American, but Asian spices make frequent appearances. *Daily 5:30-10:45pm.* $$$ ▭ 405 E. 58th St. (1st Ave.), 212-754-6272, marchrestaurant.com

Mas • West Village • French
This beautiful wee restaurant on a sleepy West Village Street specializes in French country cooking, with outstanding results. (How does one shout "yee-haw" in French?) Midsized dishes like lobster bisque, venison in spinach with figs, and tuna in a brown butter sauce are matched with excellent French wines served "country style" in juice glasses. With light wood, lots of windows, and a white ceiling to give the illusion of space, what this little room lacks in size, it makes up for in charm. *Mon-Sat 6-11pm. A smaller late-night menu is served until 4am.* $$$ ▣▭ 39 Downing St. (Bedford St.), 212-255-1790

Murray's Bagels • Greenwich Village/Chelsea • Deli

Best Bagels "Oy. Again with the bagels?" you ask. Yes, you can't throw a handful of sour cream in Manhattan without hitting a bagel shop, but there's nothing run-of-the-mill about Murray's. Here the bagels are thicker and fresher than most people can imagine, which is why this is not only a neighborhood favorite, but a contender for the best in New York. Some complain about Murray's refusal to toast, but as bagel purists will tell you, that's like putting ketchup on prime rib. *Mon-Fri 6am-9pm, Sat 6am-7pm.* $- ▨ 500 6th Ave. (13th St.), 212-462-2830; 242 8th Ave. (22nd St.), 646-638-1335, murraysbagels.com

Nobu • Tribeca • Sushi (G)

Best Sushi No longer the super hotspot it was when Tribeca was "the place to be," Drew Nieporent's masterpiece is now considered one of the city's top informal restaurants. A favorite among visiting celebs, Nobu still sees frequent visits from glamorous residents like Robert De Niro and Harvey Keitel. The ultrachic Japanese confines give off a surprisingly casual vibe, where expensive suits are often worn with tee shirts. For the ultimate experience of interior hipness and Tribeca charm, request one of the tables overlooking Hudson Street (which is generally where the VIPs sit). *Mon-Fri 11:45am-2:15pm and 5:45-10:15pm, Sat-Sun 5:45-10:15pm.* $$$ ▣▬ 105 Hudson St. (Franklin St.), 212-219-0500, myriadrestaurantgroup.com

North Square Restaurant • Greenwich Village • New American

Dining in this old-school restaurant is a voyeuristic affair, with windows overlooking an endless current of humanity en route to Washington Square Park. North Square is a sit-down, dinerlike throwback to the days when fedora-wearing gentlemen removed their hats once inside. The cuisine is farther reaching, with Mexican chef Yoel Cruz serving an eclectic menu that ranges from fresh corn tamales with oyster mushrooms to Australian rack of lamb. *Call for hours. Lounge: daily 4pm-midnight.* $$ Ⓑ▬ Washington Square Hotel, 103 Waverly Pl. (W. 7th St.), 212-254-1200, northsquareny.com

One if by Land, Two if by Sea • West Village • New American

Aaron Burr's former coach house has come a long way. Widely regarded as one of the city's most romantic restaurants, One if by Land, Two if by Sea leaves a lantern on for couples looking to celebrate something special. A fireplace roars in the dimly lit room, as a pianist plays ambient tunes (creating the perfect soundtrack for many a wedding proposal). Though the menu is billed as New American, the French influences are hard to miss, such as the signature buttery beef Wellington with foie gras. *Daily 4-11pm.* $$$ ▣▬ 17 Barrow St. (W. 4th St.), 212-255-8649, oneifbyland.com

The Palm • Midtown • Steak House

Best Power Lunches Bronwyn Birn, whose caricatures have lined these weathered walls since the 1920s, still draws visitors' portraits in this old-school New York restaurant. Portions are generous, and though the dry-aged cuts may come off as bland to some, this is how traditional steak lovers like it best. The jumbo lobster is a house specialty, and could easily feed a small family. Across the street, the Palm Too has the same menu and caricatures on the walls, but lacks the "classic" air of the original. *Mon-Fri noon-11:30pm, Sat 5-11:30pm.* $$$ ▨ 837 2nd Ave. (45th St.), 212-687-2953, thepalm.com

CLASSIC

The Patio* • Midtown • American

This New Orleans–inspired eatery, which sports a mural of Bourbon Street and tin bucket lampshades, is filled with intimate nooks hidden among its shabby-chic green booths. The fountains and heat lamps on the Patio's outdoor terrace are a lovely urban oasis, attracting high-profile locals like Harrison Ford, Derek Jeter, and Kurt Vonnegut, to name a few. Menu items include deli sandwiches, light appetizers, and lots of wine. Live jazz bands play on warm summer nights from 5pm to 8pm. *Mon-Fri 8am-10pm, Sat-Sun 9am-9pm.* $$$ ⏰🍷≡ 47th St. (1st Ave.), 917-446-0018, thepationyc.com

Rainbow Room* • Midtown • New American

Huge windows line the perimeter of this storied ballroom restaurant, which represents corporate New York at its most luxurious. Major power brokers from the NBC studios below come here to buy and sell souls over excellent, though extremely pricey, cocktails and New American fare. It isn't hard to imagine a young Johnny Carson dining somewhere between the thick drapes and the rotating dance floor, while a 12-piece big band plays. Don't forget to dress the part— show up in casual wear and the cane may pull you right off the stage. *Sun-Sat 5pm-1am. (The ballroom opens on most Fridays and Saturdays 7pm-1am.)* $$$$ ⏰🍷≡ 30 Rockefeller Plz. (49th St.), 212-632-5100, rainbowroom.com

Restaurant Above • Midtown • New American

Up in the sky, it's a bird, it's a plane, it's Restaurant Above, saving the city from overpriced mediocrity. Located on the 21st floor of the Times Square Hilton, this sophisticated, well-appointed restaurant is one of the best deals in town. Restaurant Above's master chef, Brad Barnes, defends the American way of cooking, making even the most seemingly conventional veal dishes interesting. With creative menu items like cinnamon-seared duck breast, and an interesting array of Asian-inspired fare, the fabulous view is like the cherry on top. *Mon-Fri 6:30am-10pm, Sat-Sun 7am-10pm.* $$ 🅱≡ Hilton Times Square, 234 W. 42nd St., 21st Fl. (8th Ave.), 212-642-2626, hilton.com

Sarabeth's • Midtown • American

Sarabeth's restaurants have popped up everywhere over the past couple of years, but the best is here at the base of Central Park. Decked out in wood, wicker, and zebra prints, the Sarabeth's vibe is casual, and celebrity sightings aren't unheard of. Porridge, omelets, pumpkin waffles, standard baked goods, and "Goldie Lox" round out the excellent brunch menu. Though there's always a wait for brunch tables, patrons don't think twice about perusing the Sunday *Times* after eating. Sarabeth's takes the same easy-breezy approach to its seasonally changing dinner. *Mon-Fri 8am-11pm, Sat-Sun 8am-4pm and 5:30-11pm.* $$ ≡ 40 Central Park S. (5th Ave.), 212-826-5959, sarabethscps.com

Soup Kitchen International • Midtown • International

Seinfeld fans know of this tightly run take-out joint, where lobster bisque is in high demand, and the infamous "Soup Nazi" rules with an iron ladle. Al "The Soupman" Yeganeh may serve goulash under Gulag conditions, but wow, is it good. You know the drill: know what you want, have your money ready, ask no questions, and move to the left once you've been served (they really can be mean). Arrive before 6pm, or "no soup for you!" *Mon-Sat noon-6pm, Sun: Nein!* $ ≡ 259 W. 55th St. (Broadway), 212-757-7730, therealsoupman.com

Sylvia's Restaurant • Upper East Side • Soul Food

If the Apollo theater is the best-known building in Harlem, Sylvia's is probably number two. Known for its down-home soul food, this busy restaurant is especially popular for the Sunday Gospel Brunch. Hallelujah! Side dishes are heavy and sweet, and there's no skimping on brown sugar, barbecue, or honey when it comes to saucing up their famous chicken, ribs, and pork chops. The tourist-to-local mix here is good-spirited and harmonious. *Mon-Sat 8am-10:30pm, Sun 11am-8pm.* $ B≡ 328 Lenox Ave. (126th St.), 212-996-0660, sylviassoulfood.com

Umberto's Clam House • Soho • Italian

Originally located about two blocks from its current location, this Little Italy staple is infamous for being the place where gangster Crazy Joe Gallo was whacked. But don't worry, Umberto's is now a friendly joint, which hosts more conventional "families" who get a kick out of the kitsch nautical decor—exposed brick walls covered in ocean prints, boat oars, and life preservers. The menu boasts traditional trattoria selections, like linguini with red sauce, as well as more exotic old-country fare, like calamari risotto. Of course, the clams are, shall we say, too good to refuse. And while Luca Brasi sleeps with the fishes, you should feast on the lobster—it's one of their specialties. *Sun-Sat 11am-4am.* $$ B≡ 178 Mulberry St. (Broome St.), 212-431-7545, umbertosclamhouse.com

Union Square Cafe* • Flatiron • New American (G)

This cherished Tuscan restaurant is a city landmark in its own right. Amid the country-club design, awash in hunter greens, creams, and mahogany, power brokers and publishers impress tourists with their air of importance as they seal deals over lunch. Foodies come for the inspired Italian menu, filled with fresh produce from the local green market. The pastas are prepared to perfection, though the osso buco and grilled lamb chops scotta dita are best for hearty appetites. The top-notch staff is attentive, and well versed in the seasonally changing menu. *Sun-Thu noon-2:15pm, 5:30-9:45pm, Fri-Sat noon-2:15pm, 5:30-10:45pm.* $$$ TF≡ 21 E. 16th St. (Union Square W.), 212-243-4020, unionsquarecafe.com

Veritas • Gramercy • American (G)

There very well may be as many sommeliers as waiters here on a given night, but that's completely understandable. The New American cuisine, including generous helpings of short ribs, lamb, and rib-eye steak, is subtly complimented by Asian dishes like hamachi tartare. French touches figure most prominently in the dessert menu. The midsized room is one of minimal decor, which isn't to say it wasn't well planned—brick walls and bare floors gladly take second billing to food and wine. *Mon-Sat 5:30-10:30pm, Sun 5-10pm.* $$$ ≡ 43 E. 20th St. (Broadway), 212-353-3700, veritas-nyc.com

Wollensky Grill • Midtown • Steak House

For lunching on the Flintstones-esque sirloin burger and irresistible fries at this rustic eatery, you might want to wear your loosest pants. A masculine setting of wood floors and black-and-white photos mark Wollensky Grill, where patrons can sample prime cuts without forking over dinner prices. This is also a good place for a late lunch, though don't expect to be hungry for dinner. Salads and fresh seafood are available for lightweights. *Daily 11:30am-2am.* $$ F≡ 201 E. 49th St. (3rd Ave.), 212-753-0444, smithandwollensky.com

CLASSIC

Classic New York:
The Nightlife

The Apollo Theater • Harlem • Performance
Ella Fitzgerald, James Brown, and Michael Jackson are among the legends who started at the Apollo Theater, where late-night Saturdays offer amateur perform-ances. In these famed showdowns between artist and audience, there is no mys-tery as to whether an act succeeded or failed. Despite its recent gentrification, and although Harlem is another New York casualty of television, where a bad reputation exceeds reality, evenings in Harlem are still for the adventuresome. Know where you're going and, when in doubt, cab it. *Shows begin around 8pm and tours start at 11am.* C≣ 253 W. 125th St. (Amsterdam Ave.), 212-531-5305, apollotheater.com

Bemelmans Bar • Upper East Side • Lounge
Best Cocktail Mixologists A huge mural by *Madeleine* author Ludwig Bemelman (who lived in the hotel) graces the drinking and dining area of this storied hotel, just steps off Central Park. This posh, dimly lit bar has been serving specialty cocktails to the well-heeled, pinky-in-the-air crowd since 1929. It's still a great place to whisper sweet nothings over the live piano while sipping a creative cocktail. The menu is French, the digs are chichi, and prices are *assez coûteux. Mon-Sat noon-12:30am, Sun noon-11:30pm.* ⊞_ The Carlyle Hotel, 35 E. 76th St. (Madison Ave.), 212-744-1600, thecarlyle.com

Blue Note • West Village • Jazz Club
Best Jazz Clubs Though it's only been open about 20 years, the Blue Note is a jazz venue of historic proportions. The sound system is great, the lines are long, and the booking is as good as it gets. Performers like Chick Corea, Arturo Sandoval, and Ron Carter are regulars here, but occasional surprises like Danny Aiello and Sergio Mendez keep things interesting. Ticket prices for bigger acts go for up to $45 for table seating and $30 to stand at the bar. *Sun-Thu 7pm-2am, Fri-Sat 7pm-4am.* C F≣ 131 W. 3rd St. (6th Ave.), 212-475-8592, bluenotejazz.com

Brandy's Piano Bar • Upper East Side • Piano Bar
Best Piano Bars At this colorful addition to an otherwise white-bread neighbor-hood, the servers are as likely to burst into song as they are to take your order. Brandy's gay following could rival that of Liza Minnelli, and though everyone's always welcome, it's not the place to try out your rendition of "Mack the Knife." The bartenders, servers, and pianists who perform are all veterans of the Great White Way. If anyone does get pulled out of the crowd to sing, it's usually a Broadway star stopping by on his or her night off. *Daily 4pm-4am.* ≣ 235 E. 84th St. (3rd Ave.), 212-744-4949, brandyspianobarnyc.com

Café Nicole Bar • Midtown • Hotel Bar
After a Broadway show or a night on Times Square, a little comfort goes a long way. Club chairs and sofas are spread throughout the generous space, luring hotel guests and passersby alike into its oasislike calm. Another draw here is the big terrace that provides a sweeping view of the bustling Midtown streets. *Sun-Sat noon-2am.* F≣ Novotel New York, 226 W. 52nd St. (8th Ave.), 212-315-0100, novotel.com

The Campbell Apartment • Midtown • Lounge

Located in the middle of Grand Central Terminal, this posh room of high ceilings and roaring '20s charm was once the office of industrialist John W. Campbell. While one needn't dress to the nines for entry here, they do preserve an old-fashioned sophistication by prohibiting jeans and sneakers. Theme drinks range from Manhattans and sidecars to champagne concoctions, like the Flapper Dress. Campbell heats up after the workday ends, and a crowd of well-dressed 9-to-5ers pours in from local offices to blow off steam before heading to the Connecticut-bound trains below. *Mon-Sat 3pm-1am, Sun 3-11pm.* ≡ 15 Vanderbilt Ave. (Grand Central Terminal), 212-953-0409, hospitalityholdings.com

Cherry Lane Theater • West Village • Performance

Best Off-Broadway Theaters Located within one of the West Village's most scenic enclaves, the Cherry Lane Theater is geographically Off-Broadway, but the undiscovered talent inside is top-notch. Built in 1817 as a silo on the Gomez farm, Cherry Lane didn't establish the theater until 1924. The original seats remain, as does the charmingly rustic vibe. Many big names have performed at this modest house on their way to the big time, including Gene Hackman, James Earl Jones, Harvey Keitel, Gary Sinise, John Malkovich, and Peter Falk. *Shows typically Tue-Sat at 7pm, with Sat 3pm matinee.* ©⊒ 38 Commerce St. (Barrow St.), 212-989-2020, cherrylanetheatre.org

Chumley's • West Village • Bar

Al Capone aside, few benefited more from Prohibition than this former speakeasy, whose front was once an unmarked and out-of-the-way blacksmith shop. The ale continues to flow at Chumley's, now an informal tavern where neighborhood dogs sleep by the fireplace, and locals drink pints with pub food. Woody Allen chose this classic joint as the setting for several scenes in his film *Sweet and Lowdown.* On the walls are the photographs of other celebs who've shown their faces here over the years. *Sun-Thu 5pm-midnight, Fri-Sat 5pm-2am.* F⊒ 86 Bedford St. (Grove St.), 212-675-4449

Circa Tabac • Soho • Cigar Bar

A certified cigar lounge with grandfather status, a cigar humidor, and dozens of imported cigarettes, Circa Tabac combines New York's knickerbocker past with its hip here and now. Cigar-chomping Wall Streeters and nicotine-craving Europeans come together to celebrate one of the city's last remaining legal smoking venues. (Though the state passed a smoking ban in 2002, a handful of places have legal loopholes.) Technically, Circa Tabac considers itself a "cigarette bar," but the 1930s vibe pervades, even when the bass-heavy soundtrack kicks in late at night. *Mon-Tue 4pm-2am, Wed-Fri 4pm-4am, Sat noon-4pm, Sun noon-1am.* ≡ 32 Watts St. (W. Broadway), 212-941-1781, circatabac.com

City Hall* • Wall Street • Restaurant Lounge

This classic bar, reminiscent of the hotel lounge from *The Shining,* hosts a scene of Wall Street high rollers and politicos from nearby City Hall. With vaulted ceilings, masculine oak decor, leather seating, and towering floral arrangements, it's not hard to picture Al Capone in one corner and Clark Gable in another. The upstairs Rose Room is where you want to be, but should that be full, the downstairs Granite Room will more than suffice. *Call for hours. Everyone knows that City Hall is closed on Sunday.* B⊒ 131 Duane St. (Church St.), 212-227-7777, cityhallnewyork.com

CLASSIC

Comedy Cellar • Greenwich Village • Comedy Club
This is New York's quintessential comedy venue. Its intimate confines with a brick wall and spotlight decor are where comedians like Jerry Seinfeld, Colin Quinn, Dave Attell, and Janeane Garofalo come to workshop their material. Don't think you've been beamed into the Twilight Zone if you see William Shatner, David Lee Roth, or "Mr. Kotter" on stage—it happens. The Comedy Cellar's kitchen serves marked-up bar food, which works in a pinch, but is worth skipping in this restaurant-saturated neighborhood. *Sun-Thu 9pm and 11pm, Fri 8pm, 9:45pm, and 11:30pm, Sat 7:30, 9:15, and 11pm, and 12:45am.* ©F⊟ 117 MacDougal St. (Minetta Ln.), 212-254-3480, comedycellar.com

Don't Tell Mama • Midtown • Piano Bar
Best Piano Bars Somewhere over the rainbow, and just outside of the Theater District, lies this cabaret lounge where drag queens, tourists, and Broadway performers fill three rooms with raucous fun. The cabaret shows run about $20 a piece while the main room can be yours for a song—and a two-drink minimum during performances. If you've always wanted to sing on Broadway, ask the pianist if you can sit in for a tune. Just be sure you're on your game; the regulars here have high standards. ▤ 343 W. 46th St. (8th Ave.), 212-757-0788, donttellmama.com

Harbour Lights • Wall Street • Lounge
Though Harbour Lights is unmistakably touristy, these well-heeled ramblers wouldn't be caught dead in a Planet Hollywood. Huge windows and outdoor seating provide a great view of the East River Seaport, with its retired vintage fishing ships, active passenger liners, and illuminated bridges. The seafood may not be the city's best, but the vibe is wonderfully romantic. This is the place to come for a relaxing nightcap after a hectic day of shopping and taking in the sights. *Daily 10am-late.* F⊟ Pier 17, 3rd Fl. (South Street Seaport), 212-227-2800, harbourlightsrestaurant.com

Heartland Brewery South Street* • Wall Street • Brewery
Throughout the city there are several links on the microbrewery chain, and they're all strategically placed to attract both after-workers and tourists. While that may reek of Bennigan's, it isn't the case on South Street, where the seafood standards are New York City high. Heartland Brewery is an upscale woodsy tavern with sidewalk seating set up along the cobblestone street outside. The seasonally changing signature beers, like chocolate and pumpkin blends, draw a lively, casual crowd, more interested in beautifully crafted ales and conversation than chronic hipness. *Sun-Sat 11:30am-11:30pm.* F▤ 93 South St. (Fulton St.), 646-572-2337, heartlandbrewery.com

The Late Show with David Letterman • Midtown • Performance
Best Live Tapings Given its historical significance, the Ed Sullivan Theater would be a worthwhile attraction in its own right (after all, it's where America met the Beatles for the first time, not to mention countless other bands and comedians). Throw in a taping of late-night king David Letterman, and a visit to this landmark becomes a priority. Tickets are tough to come by, so plan in advance by calling 212-975-5853. True fans may want to stop at Hello Deli around the corner and say hello to Rupert after the show. *Tapings: Mon-Wed 5:30pm, Thu 4:30 and 7pm.* ⊟ The Ed Sullivan Theater, 1697 Broadway (W. 53rd St.), 212-975-6644, cbs.com

Lincoln Center • Upper East Side • Performance

Seven buildings occupy an entire city block, combining to form the pinnacle of high culture—even if monkeys and clowns do take it over in November and December. The rest of the year (when the Big Apple circus isn't in town), opera greats fill the Metropolitan Pavilion, orchestras play Avery Fisher Hall, and Walter Reade Theater screens fine films. The world's best jazz musicians perform in Frederick P. Rose Hall overlooking Central Park and the Manhattan skyline, and salsa and swing bands liven summer nights on the Josie Robertson Plaza. *Event times vary.* C⬜ 62nd St. (Columbus Ave.), 212-875-5456, lincolncenter.org

Morrell Wine Bar & Café* • Midtown • Wine Bar

Best Wine Bars With two floors of tables and a world of wine, Morrell's pulls in a large crowd of underdressed tourists and overdressed Rockefeller Center employees, all vying for space both inside and out. Operated by the eponymous family that also owns one of Manhattan's best wine retail operations, Morrell offers 2,000-plus vintages for sale, among the best in town. After-work hours are by far the busiest. To ensure that your night is about *wining* rather than *whining*, call ahead to reserve a table. To satisfy evening cravings, small Mediterranean-infused New American dishes are available. *Mon-Sat 11:30am-midnight, Sun noon-6pm. (The kitchen closes an hour before the bar.)* F⬜ 1 Rockefeller Plz. (49th St.), 212-262-7700, morrellwinebar.com

Oak Room • Midtown • Hotel Lounge

Best Hotel Lounges Forget the pace of the world outside. In the Oak Room, it's still 1930s Manhattan. This perennial lounge in the lobby of the Algonquin Hotel is awash in burgundy and oak, with old fashion white linen on the tables and attentive, career waiters all but clicking their heels. A formally clad clientele sip sidecars and martinis, while top notch crooners sing jazz standards. Harry Conick, Jr. and Nancy La Mott have played here. Be sure to make a reservation. *Tue-Sat 7-11:30pm. (Show is at 9pm, Fri-Sat: 2nd show at 11:30pm).* F⬜ Algonquin Hotel, 59 W. 44th St. (5th Ave.), 212-840-6800, algonquinhotel.com

Onieal's Grand Street* • Soho • Lounge

Look up information on Onieal's and you'll probably get a hundred different spellings of the place. Though this romantic Little Italy hideaway is another Prohibition-era speakeasy, it has never lost its sophisticated air. The ornate ceilings imported from Venice, wooden shutters, and antique mahogany bar are lush environs for the clubby lounge. There's even a secret tunnel-cum–wine cellar alleged to lead to the former police headquarters across the street. For those whose sense of history doesn't predate 2002, this was the *Sex and the City* watering hole, Scout. *Kitchen daily 6pm-1am, the bar's often open later.* F⬛ 174 Grand St. (Lafayette St.), 212-941-9119, onieals.com

Pen-Top Bar & Terrace • Midtown • Hotel Lounge

A priceless Fifth Avenue view draws tourists and Uptowners to the 23rd floor of the Peninsula Hotel. Despite the high altitude, Pen-Top's air gets a little thick with conservative visitors who are more into the view than the vibe. That said, this is still the place to make bedroom eyes at someone over cocktails. Come by around sunset, grab a piece of lawn furniture, and watch the daylight disappear over the Hudson. *Mon-Thu 5pm-midnight, Fri-Sat 5pm-1am.* B⬛ Peninsula Hotel, 700 5th Ave. (55th St.), 212-956-2888, newyork.peninsula.com

CLASSIC

Pete's Tavern • Gramercy • Pub/Tavern

The pub where O. Henry wrote "The Gift of the Magi" in 1904 may no longer offer literary inspiration, but this postcollegiate haunt is still a good place to swill beers. Rumored to be the oldest continuously operating bar and restaurant in New York City, Pete's is a popular spot for concertgoers awaiting the opening of nearby Irving Park. Tables line the wall across from the long bar, where patrons drink and feed on greasy, but reliable, pub fare. *Sun-Tue 11:30am-2am, Wed-Sat 11:30am-3am.* F≣ 129 E. 18th St. (Irving Pl.), 212-473-7676, petestavern.com

PJ Clarke's • Midtown • Pub/Tavern

Though its age is only an estimate (ranging from 120 to 140 years old), this stalwart restaurant pub is like a living museum of New York history. The men's room still uses old-school urinals, the back staircase is lined with black-and-white photos, and the pay phone and cigarette machine are rumored to have been broken since WWII. Once a magnet for icons like Jackie O., Frank Sinatra, and Babe Ruth, recently renovated, PJ Clarke's now draws a crowd of bankers, salesmen, and tourists. *Daily 11:30am-3am.* F≣ 915 3rd Ave. (55th St.), 212-317-1616, pjclarkes.com

Radio City Music Hall • Midtown • Performance

Everyone knows about Radio City Music Hall's legendary Christmas Spectacular, which features the Rockettes and the *Nutcracker* ballet, but not everyone knows about the great rock concerts as well. Bands including the White Stripes, Alicia Keys, Jill Scott, and the Strokes have recently played this vintage setting, where carpeted floors and a steep shimmering balcony make this one of the loveliest venues in town. The 5,900-plus original seats have all been refurbished since their installation in 1932, and they still offer a great view from every corner. C⌐ 1260 6th Ave. (W. 50th St.), 212-307-7171, radiocity.com

Sardi's • Midtown • Lounge

Sardi's has long been the post–opening night place to be for Broadway directors and their stars, who sip cocktails and nervously await reviews. Caricatures of celebrated performers cover the walls, while waiters in burgundy jackets rush about. Underdressed tourists with shorts and fanny packs also fill the tables, though anyone with savoir faire is dressed for a night at the theater. A nightcap among big-time theater players is the Great White Way to go. *Tue-Sat 11:30am-11:30pm, Sun noon-7pm.* F⌐ 234 W. 44th St. (Broadway), 212-221-8440, sardis.com

Stonewall • West Village • Pub/Tavern

Best Gay/Lesbian Bars When the winds of change in the West Village started blowing, Stonewall was at the eye of the storm. This was once a hidden dive that, like every other same-sex bar in New York, suffered police harassment. In 1969, when police staged a thinly veiled stop-being-gay raid, riots broke out at the Stonewall, which rallied the movement for gay rights. Throughout Stonewall remains a friendly bar for locals and tourists alike. If you're feeling lucky, come by on Tuesday for bingo night. *Daily 3pm-4am.* ≣ 53 Christopher St. (7th Ave. S.), 212-463-0950, stonewall-place.com

Tavern on the Green* • Upper West Side • Restaurant Lounge

The name might imply a country-club cantina, but ... actually, despite its notoriety, that's pretty much what this New York institution is. Crested blazer-wearing bluebloods and socialites mix with wide-eyed tourists in the theatrical setting highlighted by twinkling chandeliers. A classic American menu is available, but given its location in the heart of Central Park, the best time to visit is in the summer, when a lively crowd gathers for alfresco cocktails. Live jazz plays in the lush, private garden, sensually lit with Chinese lanterns. *Sun 10am-3pm and 5-10pm, Mon-Thu 11:30am-3pm and 5-10pm, Fri 11:30am-3pm and 5-10:30pm, Sat 10am-3pm and 5-10:30pm.* F⊜ Central Park W. (W. 67th St.), 212-873-3200, tavernonthegreen.com

21 Club* • Midtown • Restaurant Lounge

Even back when it was a speakeasy, the 21 Club had high standards, requiring that all gents wore a jacket and tie. Thanks to Sammy Davis Jr. who came in wearing a turtleneck and blazer, the rules have relaxed ... but only slightly. With a polished oak bar, red leather banquettes, and a bizarre collection of model trucks and planes dangling overhead, this landmark lounge attracts a formidable scene of power players and media heavyweights. Those who stay for American fare at lunch or dinner pay dearly for the privilege. *Main rooms: Mon-Fri noon-2:30pm and 5:30-10pm (Fri-Sat until 11pm). 21 Upstairs: Tue-Sat 5:30-10pm.* F⊜ 21 W. 52nd St. (5th Ave.), 212-582-7200, 21club.com

Village Vanguard • West Village • Jazz Club

Best Jazz Clubs Whenever a jazz musician would brag about a big gig in New York City, he or she generally meant the Village Vanguard. Opened in 1935, the Vanguard may be less refined than its contemporaries, but you can't touch its historical lineup, which includes Miles, 'Trane, Thelonious Monk, and Hank Mobley, among many others. Tickets here often sell out, so call in advance, and hope for the best. Even if it's an act you've never heard of, it's almost certain that if they're here, they're good. *Nightly 8pm-2am, sets begin at 9 and 11pm.* C⊜ 178 7th Ave. S. (Greenwich Ave.), 212-255-4037, villagevanguard.com

White Horse Tavern* • West Village • Pub/Tavern

"This I believe is the record," was said to have been legendary poet Dylan Thomas's final words before downing his last shot at the White Horse Tavern, and collapsing. (That record is said to be 18, and there's no free tee shirt for matching it.) Over the years, many literary legends sought inspiration at the Horse, including Norman Mailer, James Baldwin, Anaïs Nin, and Jack Kerouac. Today, the no-frills, plain wood, English-style pub fills to the hilt with both literary types and the everyman, especially on the weekend. *Sun-Thu 11am-2am, Fri-Sat 11am-4am.* ⅨF⊜ 567 Hudson St. (11th St.), 212-243-9260

CLASSIC

Classic New York:
The Attractions

American Museum of Natural History • Upper West Side • Museum
The Natural History Museum, as it's often called, is the city's most physically imposing museum. The huge, glass-enclosed Rose Center for Earth and Space alone practically occupies its own solar system. Mammal Hall, which gives painstaking attention to the accuracy of its dioramas depicting various animal habitats, may look familiar to "Friends" fans as the workplace of obsessive pale-ontologist Ross Gellar. The first Monday of every month at the museum sees live jazz performances from 6-7pm and 7:30-8:30pm. *Daily 10am-5:45pm; Rose Center open on the first Friday of every month.* $ 175 Central Park W. (61st St.), 212-769-5000, amnh.org

Bite of the Big Apple Tour • Midtown • Tour
You don't have to be an athlete to pedal around the city. These leisurely, enthu-siastically guided bike tours are only an hour long, so they won't leave partici-pants too weary and sore to dance the night away. Groups ranging from 10 to 25 pay $35 per person to ride from 59th Street to 110th Street and back, using Fifth Avenue and Central Park West. Tours start at 10am, 1pm, and 4pm daily. (Additional tours are sometimes added in the summer.) Sites include Strawberry Fields, Belvedere Castle, and Shakespeare Garden. $$$ *Daily 10am, 1pm, 4pm.* 2 Columbus Cir. (59th St.), 212-541-8759, centralparkbiketour.com

Brooklyn Bridge • South Street Seaport • Site
If someone offers to sell you this property, you may want to rethink what you're wearing. It took 14 years to build this stone-and-steel extension bridge, which stretches just short of 6,000 feet. With a foundation that runs 78 feet under water, the structure's as sound as its Gothic columns imply. Street traffic tends to move quickly here, which makes driving over less than scenic. Try the wide pedestrian pass that doubles as a workout trail for weekend joggers, cyclists, and strollers. South Street Seaport

Central Park • Upper East Side/Upper West Side • Park
Best Outdoor People-Watching In a city where an 800-square-foot apartment is considered luxurious, this 843-acre park is beyond comparison. There are over 26,000 trees to choose to sit under with a picnic and a bottle of wine (which you should hide when the cops ride by on horseback.) Possibly the most famous park in the world, Central Park has plenty of little treasures you won't want to miss, including a concert space, numerous gardens, a zoo, a much-lauded restaurant, and a historic carousel. Maps can be purchased for $4 at the Arsenal (64th St. & 5th Ave.), Room 222, 2nd Fl. Between 58th & 110th Sts., and 5th & 8th Aves., centralparknyc.com

Central Park Conservatory Gardens • Upper East Side • Gardens
Practically anyone can give you directions to Central Park, which will generally result in a "Where are you folks from?" or "Give me your wallet." Though it takes up six acres, it's a little harder to find the Conservatory Gardens. The Park's only formal gardens feature Italian, French, and English landscapes, which have

provided the backdrop for many a wedding photo. The best way to enter is through the Vanderbilt Gate at 105th Street and Fifth Avenue. Don't bother trying to find the conservatory—it was taken down in 1934. *Daily 8am-sunset.* 5th Ave. (between 104th & 106th Sts.), centralparknyc.com

Circle Line Cruise • Midtown • Tour
Best City Tours Circle Line offers three-hour all-island tours that circle Manhattan, and two-hour mini trips that circle the Statue of Liberty, with the Magellan-esque long ones costing $28 for adults, and the Columbus-like shortcuts costing $5 less. Both trips run year-round, though Tuesdays and Wednesdays are black through January and February. (The crew also takes Tuesdays off in March.) The crowd is family-oriented on the morning tours; the predinner "Harbor Lights" tour provides a more "Love Boat" atmosphere. Hours change seasonally. *Three-hour tours run three times a day in the warmer months, 9:30am-4:30pm. In the cold months, there's only a single 12:30pm cruise. The two-hour Harbor Lights tour ends with a sunset, so it starts around 6pm in the winter and 7pm in the summer.* $$ Pier 83, W. 42nd St. (12th Ave.), 212-563-3200, circleline.com

Empire State Building • Gramercy • Site
There was a time when the Empire State Building was the world's tallest building. After the World Trade Center collapse in 2001, it once again became the tallest skyscraper in New York City. Located 1,050 feet above street level, the 86th floor's Observation Deck welcomes 3.5 million visitors a year. At night, you can see the strobelike camera flashes coming from the Deck even from miles away. The building was immortalized in the original *King Kong,* when the giant ape was shot down from the tower. *Daily 8am-midnight (last elevator goes up at 11:15pm).* $ 350 5th Ave. (Broadway), 212-736-3100, esbnyc.com

Grand Central Terminal • Midtown • Site
Look at all these people! What is this, Grand Central Station? Technically, it's Grand Central Terminal, which is the correct term for a "station" where trips terminate. Thanks to the 13-foot clock in the center of the main concourse, the 150,000-plus daily commuters know just how late they are. For a sweeping view, grab a bite at Michael Jordan's Steakhouse, or check out the southwest balcony where John Campbell's office has become a popular after-work lounge. At 12:30pm every Wednesday, a free tour is given, starting at the information booth. *Daily 5:30am-1:30am.* 42nd St. (Park Ave.), 212-532-4900, grandcentralterminal.com

Ground Zero • Tribeca • Site
This hallowed ground tells the tale of two cities. On the one hand, standing on the observatory that overlooks a sobering 10 million square feet of space brings to mind the horrific images of the September 11 tragedies that killed 2,752 people. On the other hand, plans to rebuild (if the powers-that-be reach agreement) demonstrate the city's resiliency. Should the observation deck be crowded, wander over to the World Financial Center where the North Bridge, a 400-foot pedestrian pass, also provides a view of the site, not to mention a food court. Broadway and Liberty Sts., groundzero.nyc.ny-us

CLASSIC

Intrepid Sea, Air & Space Museum • Midtown • Museum

Seeing an aircraft carrier off the coast can be disconcerting, but luckily for Midtown, the Intrepid comes in peace. This old battle-ax has paid her dues; during WWII she survived seven bomb attacks, five kamikaze strikes, and a torpedo hit. Now, decommissioned aircrafts find their final resting place on this floating museum, which also has screening rooms, cafeterias, and various air and sea exhibits. *Spring and summer: Mon-Fri 10am-5pm, Sat-Sun 10am-6pm; fall and winter: Tue-Sun 10am-5pm.* $ Pier 86 (12th Ave. & 46th St.), 212-245-0072, intrepidmuseum.org

Manhattan Carriage Company • Midtown • Tour

Is there anything more romantic than seeing Central Park from a horse-drawn buggy? That's a rhetorical question—the answer is no. Rides can be booked in advance, but more often than not, empty carriages can be flagged down at the south end of the park, generally around 59th Street and Fifth Avenue. A one-hour ride is $40 and that's for a maximum of four people. A four-mile, 80-minute ride can be booked, but be warned: these jockeys will apply charges for no-shows or late arrivals. *Reservations Mon-Sat 10am-3pm and 6-8pm, the last rides begin at midnight.* $$$$ 59th St. (7th Ave.), 914-374-3893, ajnfineart.com/mcc.html

The Metropolitan Museum of Art • Upper East Side • Art Museum

Founded in 1870, the Met set out to be a place where average people could view and learn about art. After having become the first public museum to accept work by Matisse, forming a cache of Impressionist works starting with a 1907 Renoir, and acquiring 5 of the fewer than 40 known Vermeers on the planet, this collection rose to the ranks of the world's most revered. Today, if it's "art," it's probably represented here—arms and armor, musical instruments, furniture, costume, Egyptian, medieval and modern art. Even the casual art lover could easily spend a full day here. *Tue-Thu and Sun 9:30am-5:30pm, Fri-Sat 9:30am-9pm.* $ 1000 5th Ave. (82nd St.), 212-535-7710, metmuseum.org

Museum of Jewish Heritage • Tribeca • Museum

Though the 2,000 photographs and 800 artifacts that make up this collection can barely begin to tell the story of 20th-century Judaism, the Museum of Jewish Heritage is a fascinating and educational experience. Six different wings, symbolic representations of the points on the Star of David, make up this modern 30,000-square-foot museum, which was erected in 1997. As this is a living memorial to the Jews who perished in the Holocaust, the mood is generally somber, though there is also plenty here to inspire. *Sun-Tue and Thu 10am-5:45pm, Wed 10am-8pm, Fri and the eve of Jewish holidays 10am-5pm.* $ 36 Battery Pl. (West St.), 646-437-4200, mjhnyc.org

New York Stock Exchange • Wall Street • Site

While September 11 may have closed down the trading-floor tours, walking around Wall Street to check out the hectic scene and powerful exterior of the NYSE and financial buildings is truly a surreal experience. Men in $5,000 suits breeze past National Guardsmen with trained dogs and automatic weapons, and frazzled floor traders march down the sidewalk two-fisting coffee. The ban is reportedly indefinite, though not permanent, and there's no telling when tours may resume. It doesn't hurt to check in and see if tickets are available. *Mon-Fri 9am-4:30pm.* 11 Wall St. (New St.), 212-656-3000, nyse.com

Oasis Day Spa • Murray Hill/Gramercy • Spa

Best Spas Oasis is so conscious of your busy schedule, they've opened one of their top-notch spas at the JFK Jet Blue terminal. Too busy? Oasis has massage therapists that travel to Manhattan hotels to give 60-minute massages for $135. Hour-long, side-by-side massages are available for couples. For those who are having a hard time adjusting their sleep schedule to Eastern time, Oasis suggests a 75-minute Aromayoga course, which combines healing incenses and a workout (by appointment). *Mon-Fri 10am-10:15pm, Sat-Sun 9am-9:15pm.* $$$$ 1 Park Ave. (E. 32nd St.), 212-254-7722; 108 E. 16th St. (Irving Pl.), 212-254-7722, oasisdayspanyc.com

Oscar Wilde Memorial Bookshop • West Village • Shop

Opened in 1967, this quaint bookstore was a treasured touchstone in the West Village's Stonewall-era gay movement. Today, an enthusiastic staff guides visitors through an extensive collection of gay literature, stopping occasionally to show off autographed and first-edition copies from neighborhood legends like Allen Ginsberg and Walt Whitman, among many others. As expected, the great point of pride is the bookstore's framed and signed pages from beloved, and less earnest than important, Oscar Wilde. *Mon-Sat 11am-7pm, Sun noon-7pm.* 15 Christopher St. (W. 9th St.), 212-255-8097, oscarwildebooks.com

The Rink at Rockefeller Center • Midtown • Activity

There's no better place to fall on your keister than right here. Beneath Rockefeller Center's enormous, twinkling Christmas tree, this well-lit, seasonal rink opens from October to April. For $10, rinkside photographers snap shots of you gliding blissfully over ice, and put them into Christmas cards that make great keepsakes. The line here can be intimidating, but it moves quickly. To avoid waiting, show up while everyone else is at dinner, and let them fight for post-10pm ice time. *Mon-Thu 9am-10:30pm, Fri-Sat 8:30am-midnight, Sun 8:30am-10pm.* $ 601 5th Ave. (50th St.), 212-332-7654, therinkatrockcenter.com

South Street Seaport • Wall Street • Museum

Once the country's busiest port, the South Street Seaport now beckons endless fleets of tourists to her polished shores for drinking, dining, and shopping. The cobblestone roads of Schermerhorn Street define this mini neighborhood, where the South Street Seaport Museum resides—worth a short visit if you love boats. Next door is the charming Browne & Company Stationers, which is both a museum and an operating 19th-century printing shop. Many locals still come to this vintage printer for custom-made wedding invitations and stationery. 19 Fulton St. (Water St.), 212-732-8257, southstreetseaport.com

St. Patrick's Cathedral • Midtown • Religous Site

Now in its 140-something year of construction, St. Patrick's Cathedral is Manhattan's Notre Dame, minus the Hunchback. Archbishop Edward Egan holds court in this Gothic-style structure, which is dwarfed by Midtown's skyscrapers and upscale retailers. The cathedral can hold up to 2,200 worshippers for mass, beneath the spectacular 300-foot spiral. More than 3 million visitors make a stop at these fashionable digs each year, where the St. Michael and St. Louis altars were designed in true New York style—by Tiffany & Co. *Daily 6:30am-8:45pm. Call for service hours.* 14 E. 51st St. (5th Ave.), 212-753-2261, saintpatrickscathedral.org

The Strand • Greenwich Village • Shop
Bookstores don't get much bigger than this. Claiming 18 miles of new and used books, the Strand's multilevel shop includes a collector's paradise on the third floor, stocked with hard-to-find art books, autographed first editions, and the city's largest collection of rare books. Cheap paperbacks and hard covers are sold for $2 to $5 out front to make room for new stocks. The Strand also has satellite locations near Wall Street and Midtown. *Mon-Sat 9:30am-10:30pm, Sun 11am-10:30pm.* 828 Broadway (12th St.), 212-473-1452, strandbooks.com

Trinity Church • Tribeca • Religous Site
At one point, Trinity Church was Downtown Manhattan's tallest structure. Sailors would see the cross atop its ornate steeple from a distance, and seek out the church for shelter. After September 11, many people flocked here for sanctuary and, of course, many a funeral service. Incredibly, this 160-year-old Neo-Gothic structure withstood those attacks, while the giants fell around it. To this day, Trinity Church is Manhattan's only active cemetery. *Daily 7am-6pm.* Broadway (Wall St.), 212-602-0800, trinitywallstreet.org

Van Cortlandt Park Golf Course • Bronx • Golf Course
The nation's oldest municipal course, Van Cortlandt was built in 1885 as a nine-hole design, which was helpful in keeping scores low, but left serious golfers wanting more. Though the course has long since added a back nine, scores remain low, thanks to an abundance of tree-free straightaways. A day at Van Cortlandt makes for some serious exercise, as there are many par fives, including hole number two, which is 620 yards from tee to cup. Plaid pants aren't required, but tank tops and cutoffs are forbidden. *Sun-Sat sunrise-sunset.* $$$$ Van Cortlandt Park S. (Bailey Ave.), 718-543-4595, nycgovparks.org

Washington Square Park • Greenwich Village • Park
Best Outdoor People-Watching Though not as grand (or as central) as Central Park, Washington Square Park is still the quintessential urban square. Its entrance boasts a giant faux Parisian archway leading to the central fountain where acrobatic street artists perform. It was here that Henry James found inspiration for his novel, *Washington Square*. Also historic (and creepy) is the large tree in the northeast corner where public hangings took place. Once sketchy, this park is now well monitored and secure. Between 5th Ave. and Thompson St., nycgovparks.org

PRIME TIME
NEW YORK

Everything in life is timing (with a dash of serendipity thrown in). Would you want to arrive in Pamplona, Spain, the day *after* the Running of the Bulls? Not if you have a choice and you relish being a part of life's peak experiences. With our month-by-month calendar of events, there's no excuse to miss out on any of New York's greatest moments. From the classic to the quirky, the sophisticated to the outrageous, you'll find all you need to know about the city's best events right here.

Prime Time Basics

Eating and Drinking

Aside from Midtown, where everyone works the New York 9-to-5 (which is actually 10-to-6), there's really no consistent breakfast or lunch time, other than the usual noon to 1pm. Weekend brunches get busy around 11:30am, so getting there by 11:15am will save time waiting in line. Since late nights and late mornings are part of the norm here, few people eat dinner before 8pm, with weekend dining often starting around 9pm to 10pm. Those who can't get reservations at top restaurants should ask about 7pm or 11pm seatings. In Midtown and the Financial District, after-work drinking goes from about 5pm to 9pm. Nightclubs generally open their doors around 11pm, but arriving before midnight is only slightly less gauche than coming barefoot.

Weather and Tourism

Dec.–Feb.: It's said that everybody talks about the weather, but no one does anything about it. In New York, the motto is "shut up and deal with it." These are tough months in New York, though the tall buildings tend to cut off some of the stiff wind. December temperatures average about 37 degrees Fahrenheit, and January drops several degrees until things "warm up" to a smoldering 34 degrees in February. Snow isn't uncommon, but blizzards can make for an interesting little adventure, when Broadway becomes a winter wonderland.

Mar.–May: It's also said that if you don't like the weather in spring, wait five minutes. It isn't uncommon to see a 70-degree Tuesday turn into a snowy 20-degree

Seasonal Changes

Month	Fahrenheit High	Low	Celsius High	Low	Hotel Rates
Jan.	39	26	4	-3	S
Feb.	40	27	4	-3	S
Mar.	48	34	9	1	S
Apr.	61	44	16	7	S
May	71	53	21	12	S
June	81	63	27	17	S
July	85	68	29	20	L
Aug.	83	66	28	19	L
Sept.	77	60	25	15	H
Oct.	67	51	19	10	H
Nov.	54	41	12	5	H
Dec.	41	30	5	-1	H

H-High Season; S-Shoulder; L-Low

Wednesday in New York. April temperatures hover around 52 degrees, and when 63-degree May weather arrives, the most hardened New Yorker will throw around a "How ya doin'." Flash floods often threaten weekend retreats.

June–Aug.: The thrill of spring turns into the dog days of summer, with Manhattan temperatures averaging a comfortable 71 degrees, rising as the day progresses to a sizzling 90-plus. Humidity is high, and the hotter the days, the grittier the city feels. New York parks are packed, and people-watching becomes an outdoor activity. This is high tourist season, when patio cafes and rooftop bars are buzzing.

Sept.–Nov.: The Big Apple is ripe with relief when summer has passed, and fall temperatures drift down to a pleasant 68 degrees. Five minutes later, everyone's complaining about the cold, but what joy those five minutes bring. September is an active month, as the last of the tourists are still bustling about, and the local out-and-about crowd enjoys the end of their Hamptons leases. October brings things down to around 58 degrees, while November's warm days and chilly nights usher in the flu season.

National Holidays

New Year's Day	January 1
Martin Luther King Day	Third Monday in January
Valentine's Day	February 14
President's Day	Third Monday in February
Memorial Day	Last Monday in May
Independence Day	July 4
Labor Day	First Monday in September
Columbus Day	Second Monday in October
Halloween	October 31
Veterans' Day	November 11
Thanksgiving Day	Fourth Thursday in November
Christmas Day	December 25
New Year's Eve	December 31

Listings in blue are major celebrations but not official holidays.

The Best Events Calendar

January
- Restaurant Week

February
- Tax Free Week
- Chinese New Year
- Westminster Kennel Club Annual Dog Show
- Fall Fashion Week

March
- St. Patrick's Day Parade

April
- Tribeca Film Festival

May
- Fleet Week

June
- Belmont Stakes
- Film Festival at Bryant Park
- Gay Pride Parade

July
- 4th of July Macy's Fireworks

August
- U.S. Open

September
- The Feast of San Gennaro
- Spring Fashion Week
- Broadway on Broadway

October
- World Series
- CMJ Music Marathon
- New York City Marathon
- Halloween Parade
- Big Apple Circus

November
- Macy's Thanksgiving Day Parade

December
- Radio City Music Hall Christmas Spectacular
- New Year's Eve Ball Drop

Night+Day's Top Three Events are in blue.
High season is from September-December, represented by blue banner.

The Best Events

January

Restaurant Week
Participating restaurants, nycvisit.com

> The Lowdown: Founded as a way of luring politicos to the city's restaurants during the 2002 Democratic National Convention, this popular week is an opportunity for average locals to indulge in some of the city's finest (and often most exclusive) cuisine. *The last week of January.* $24.07-$35

February

Tax Free Week
New York citywide

> The Lowdown: Throughout this week, the city waives its 8.5% sales tax on all clothing items under $110, and stores often run simultaneous sales. The Broadway strip of Soho and Fifth Avenue near Central Park are especially busy on the final weekend. *First week of February; generally begins on a Monday.*

Chinese New Year
Chinatown

> The Lowdown: Each year the streets of Chinatown come alive with bursting firecrackers and dancers dressed as lions and dragons. (Mayor Bloomberg banned fireworks in 1997, but their crackles and pops are still prevalent on the side streets off the "official" route.) *The Chinese New Year starts with Bing-Yin, the Chinese calendar's first New Moon, which will be February 2 for the next four decades or so. The celebrations end with the full moon that arrives 15 days later, called Gui-Chou.* Free.

Westminster Kennel Club Annual Dog Show
Madison Square Garden, 212-213-3165, westminsterkennelclub.org

> The Lowdown: When it comes to pooch pageants, the Westminster Kennel Club's annual competition is easily the best in show. This is a pretty hard ticket to fetch, but those who know a few tricks (like calling in advance, or showing up at the Garden and waiting patiently) should make it in. *Mid-February.* $40-$90.

Fall Fashion Week
Bryant Park (42nd St. & 6th Ave.), olympusfashionweek.com

> The Lowdown: Models and designers from all over the world literally pitch their tents in Bryant Park, where a multitude of runway shows creates a press frenzy. Giselle, Naomi, Ralph, Giorgio ... *everyone* is here. While tickets are scarce, there's a buzz around the park where fashionistas gather to gawk at the glamorous

tall girls and their rock-star boyfriends. For every fashion show there's at least one after-party, so the city's clubs become more "fabulous" than ever. *Mid-late February (the clothing preview is for the following season's fashions).*

March

St. Patrick's Day Parade
5th Ave. (44th to 86th Sts.), ny.com/holiday/stpatricks/parade.html

The Lowdown: New York City's St. Patrick's Day parade attracts roughly 150,000 people annually when it starts at 11am. Lightweight drinkers, beware; everybody is Irish when St. Paddy's Day comes around. The bars open their doors early and the action spills onto the streets, especially in the Upper East Side's Second and Third Avenues, and around Midtown. *March 17.* Free.

April

Tribeca Film Festival
Various venues, 212-321-7400 (box office), tribecafilmfestival.com

The Lowdown: New York City's answer to Sundance or Cannes, the two-week Tribeca Film Festival is the brainchild of Robert De Niro and Jane Rosenthal, and is often attended by Tribeca locals Martin Scorsese, Harvey Keitel, and the Weinstein brothers. Each night, the stars shine brightly and press tents abound. But buying advance tickets is highly recommended. *Late April–early May.*

May

Fleet Week
Midtown, fleetweek.com

The Lowdown: Once a year, military personnel on leave flock to the Big Apple en masse. Ships dock near the Intrepid Museum in Hell's Kitchen, and while the servicemen are exploring New York, civilians are allowed to tour their ships. *Last week of May.*

June

Belmont Stakes
Belmont Park Race Track, 2150 Hempstead Turnpike, Belmont, NY, 718-641-4700, nyra.com/belmont

The Lowdown: This is the third leg of horse racing's storied Triple Crown, often called "the most exciting 2 $\frac{1}{2}$ minutes of sports." While the pony show is the main attraction, the pre- and postrace cocktailing is half the fun. *Early–mid June, usually the second Saturday of the month.*

Film Festival at Bryant Park

42nd St. (6th Ave.), 212-512-5700, bryantpark.org/calendar/film-festival.php

The Lowdown: Depending on the weather, upward of 10,000 people attend this free outdoor theater every Monday in summer (Tuesday being the backup day in case of rain). The event is sponsored by HBO. *Mid June–Late August.* Free.

Gay Pride Parade

From 5th Ave. and 52nd St. (Christopher and Greenwich Sts.), hopinc.org

The Lowdown: Everyone from leather daddies to the boy and girl next door marches in this celebration of diversity, which ends at the site of the landmark Stonewall riots in the West Village. Cheering crowds and rainbow flags abound in this feel-good event, which culminates in the sardine-packed gay clubs, where the boa count is high.

To volunteer along the parade route, contact the Heritage of Pride Volunteers at 212-807-7433. *Last Sunday in June.* Free.

July

4th of July Macy's Fireworks

34th St. at the East River, FDR Expy. and South St., and over the Statue of Liberty, ny.com/holiday/july4

The Lowdown: Manhattan's skies are always awash in light, but never so much as on American Independence Day. There are several hotel rooftops where firework viewing can be paired with cocktails and dinner. Rare View at the Shelbourne Hotel, Rise Bar atop the Battery Park Waldorf Astoria Hotel, and Harbour Lights Restaurant in Pier 17 of the Seaport are among the better viewing eateries. *July 4.*

August

U.S. Open

USTA National Tennis Center, Flushing, Queens, 718-760-6200, usopen.org

The Lowdown: Sitting courtside to watch the Williams sisters grunting and swatting their way to glory may cost up to $2,995 a seat. If that's too rich for your blood, there are three "show courts" that host most of the action, and though it doesn't include entrance to the Arthur Ashe stadium (the main area), a "grounds pass" allows visitors to visit the restaurants, practice courts, and souvenir stands, as well as have access to first-come tickets at the field courts (not including Arthur Ashe.) *Late August–mid September. The women's tournament ends on the final Saturday, the men's on the following Sunday.*

PRIME TIME

September

The Feast of San Gennaro
Mulberry St. (Canal to Houston St.), littleitalynyc.com/sg_page1.asp

The Lowdown: The Little Italy neighborhood's gotten smaller, but the San Gennaro Fest is as big as ever. More than 300 vendors set up for the Feast of San Gennaro's 11-day run, raising money for local charities and businesses by selling sausages, tee shirts, pastries, and all things related to the patron saint of Naples. *Mid–late September.*

Spring Fashion Week
Bryant Park, olympusfashionweek.com

The Lowdown: There are two Fashion Weeks in New York, and both of them draw the world's most famous models and designers to Bryant Park for runway shows, press junkets, and general fabulousness. Many of the city's hotels and show-rooms also host big fashion shows, where amateur fashionistas can sneak a peek at next season's trends in the making. *Mid-September.*

Broadway on Broadway
Times Square, broadwayonbroadway.com

The Lowdown: Broadway on Broadway is an opportunity to preview all of the upcoming shows at once. The city literally closes down the strip of Broadway that runs through Times Square for this concert, which attracts a crowd of 50,000-plus. A couple of days after the performance, a scaled-down one-hour version screens on prime-time television. *Around 11:30am, Sunday morning, second or third Sunday of September.* Free.

October

World Series
Yankee Stadium, 161st St. (Riverside Ave.), 718-293-4300, yankees.com

The Lowdown: OK, so there's no guarantee that the Fall Classic will take place at Yankee Stadium, but the Bronx Bombers have played in 39 World Series since 1913, winning 26 of them. Those who are in New York City during the fall very well may find themselves at a victory parade. *Mid–late October.*

CMJ Music Marathon
Lincoln Center, Columbus Ave. (65th St.), Upper West Side, 917-606-1908, cmj.com/marathon/showcase.php. Organizers—151 W. 25th St., 12th Fl.

The Lowdown: Comparable to the South by Southwest music festival in Austin, Texas, the CMJ Marathon can all but promise a band in every bar. It's not uncommon to see established rock stars popping into unassuming venues for a visit. All schedules and venues are likely to change, and generally last minute, so weekly free papers prove very useful. One four-day weekend in mid or late October.

New York City Marathon

From the Verrazano Bridge through Manhattan and Brooklyn, 212-423-2249, nyrrc.org

> The Lowdown: The city starts hyping this big event a week in advance, news stations advertise the marathon route, and 36,000-plus runners meet at the Verrazano Bridge to begin a 26-mile-and-385-yard run through city streets, where scores of spectators line the entire raceway to cheer them on and hand out cups of water. Those wishing to take part in the race should make a reservation as early as possible. Afterward, well-wishers like to converse with the athletes, hitting them up with questions about training, sneaker types, and post-marathon parties. *First Sunday in November.* Free to watch.

Halloween Parade

6th Ave. (Spring to 23rd St.), halloween-nyc.com

> The Lowdown: Attended by over 2 million people annually, this is the nation's largest public Halloween celebration and only major nighttime parade. The parade starts its procession around 8:30pm. Undercover judges abound, rewarding their "best costume" selections with prizes like Broadway show tickets. Those wishing to march should show up on Sixth Avenue and Spring Street by 6:30pm. *The Sunday night nearest Halloween.* Free.

Big Apple Circus

Damrosch Park, Lincoln Center—62nd St. (between Columbus and Amsterdam Aves.), bigapplecircus.org

> The Lowdown: Lions, tigers, human oddities ... they're all here, and there's nothing like sharing the tent with this coterie of bizarre entertainers. You may not be a kid anymore, but the grandeur of this spectacle serves as a psychological fountain of youth. *Late October–early January.* Tickets range $18-$74.

November

Macy's Thanksgiving Day Parade

77th St. (Central Park W. to W. 34th St.), macysparade.com

> The Lowdown: Viewed by millions via television every year, the Macy's parade attracts hundreds of thousands of spectators from Central Park to Macy's Herald Square store. Founded in 1924, this parade has become an American tradition. Waving politicians roll by on floats, while above their heads (and filled with just as much hot air), massive, awe-inspiring balloons of Spiderman, Underdog, and Bullwinkle drift below towering skyscrapers. *Thanksgiving Day.* Free.

PRIME TIME

December

Radio City Music Hall Christmas Spectacular
Radio City Music Hall, 1260 Ave. of the Americas, 800-451-9930, radiocity.com

The Lowdown: A historic event in a historic venue, Radio City Music Hall's *Christmas Spectacular* features the Rockettes, the *Nutcracker* ballet, and live camels that pose for a manger scene on center stage. *Early November–early January.* Tickets range $87-$458.

New Year's Eve Ball Drop
Times Square, 1560 Broadway, Ste. 800, 212-768-1560, timessquarenyc.org

The Lowdown: Organized by the Times Square Alliance, the dropping of the half-ton Waterford Crystal Ball can be seen on Broadway, between 34th and 53rd Streets, and on Seventh Avenue between 43rd and 59th Streets. Half a million people (85% of them tourists) start lining up for this event around sunrise on New Year's Eve. *December 31.* Free.

HIT the GROUND RUNNING

There will be moments that test your "I'm not a tourist" credentials. Every city has a "right look"—*how do you avoid being cited by the fashion police?* You go to the city for business—*what do you bring home for your spouse?* You arrive at JFK early and the security lines are short—*where are the airport's best restaurants?* Here are the *City Essentials* and *Cheat Sheet* facts that will practically put your picture on a New York driver's license.

City Essentials

Getting to New York: By Air

John F. Kennedy International Airport (JFK)
718-244-4444, kennedyairport.com

JFK airport is located 15 miles east of Midtown Manhattan, near Queens' eastern shore.

JFK has nine terminals for both arrivals and departures, serviced by 75 airlines. While airports everywhere have stepped up security over the past few years, early arrivals are especially encouraged here, for reasons that extend beyond heavy traffic volume. Under no circumstances should bag checks and body searches be taken lightly.

Three times larger than LaGuardia, JFK is a functional airport, serving more airlines, but less high-quality

Flying Times to New York	
From	Time (hr.)
Chicago	2
Las Vegas	5½
London	6½
Los Angeles	6
Mexico City	5
Montreal	1½
San Francisco	6
Seattle	5
Toronto	1½
Washington, D.C.	1½

food and drink. Still, this is New York, and travelers looking to fill up on more than peanut snack packs will find more than your typical airport scene. Terminal One offers a serviceable little hangout called Anton's Napa Valley Wine Bar, with great Chardonnay and West Coast–inspired bites. For those who'd rather tap the keg than smell the cork, the A concourse of Terminal Four hosts the Brooklyn Brew Pub, offering hearty fare and brewskis. For a different kind of buzz, the ubiquitous Starbucks occupies Terminals Three and Nine. Only in an airport does a $4 espresso seem like a bargain. Another nice little spot is Sylvia's Grill in Terminal One, which is an offshoot of Harlem's most famous restaurant. Those who don't go for soul food can hit Terminal Seven's Seventh Ave. Deli, where knishes, corned beef, and bagels are on the ready. The poshest of JFK restaurants is Terminal Seven's Latitudes, which is a surf-and-turf eatery offering California fusion cuisine and several dozen wines by the half bottle.

Major Airlines Serving New York Airports

Airlines	Website	800 Number	JFK	LaGuardia	Newark
Aero Mexico	aeromexico.com	800-237-6639	1		
Air Canada	aircanada.ca	888-247-2262	7	A	A
Air China	airchina.com.cn	800-982-8802	1		
Air France	airfrance.us	800-237-2747	1		B
AirTran Airways	airtran.com	800-247-8726		B	A
Alaskan Airlines	alaskaair.com	800-426-0333			A
America West	americawest.com	800-235-9292	7		A
American (Dom.)	aa.com	800-433-7300	9	D	A
American (Int'l)	aa.com	800-433-7300	8		A
ANA (All Nippon)	fly-ana.com	800-235-9262	7		
Asiana	us.flyasiana.com	800-227-4262	4		
ATA	ata.com	800-435-9282	4	B	A
Austrian Airlines	austrianair.com	800-843-0002	1		
British Airways	britishairways.com	800-247-9297	7		B
BWIA	bwee.com	800-538-2942	4		
Cathay Pacific	cathaypacific.com	800-233-2742	7		
China Airlines	china-airlines.com	800-227-5118	3		
Continental	continental.com	800-523-3273	2	A	C
Delta	delta.com	800-221-1212	3	Delta	B
Iberia	iberia.com	800-772-4642	7		
Japan Airlines	japanair.com	800-525-3663	1		
JetBlue	jetblue.com	800-538-2583	6	AB	
KLM	klm.com	800-374-7747	4		B
Korean Air	koreanair.com	800-438-5000	1		
Lufthansa	lufthansa.com	800-645-3880	1		B
Mexicana	mexicana.com	800-531-7921	4		B
Midwest	midwestairlines.com	800-452-2022		B	
Northwest	nwa.com	800-225-2525	4	Delta	B
Qantas	qantas.com	800-227-4603	7		A
Singapore Airlines	singaporeair.com	800-742-3333	4		B
Song	flysong.com	800-359-7664	2	Delta	B
Southwest	southwest.com	800-435-9792			
Spirit	spiritair.com	800-772-7117		B	
TACA International	grupotaca.com	800-535-8780	4		
United Airlines	united.com	800-241-6522	7	C	A
US Airways	usairways.com	800-428-4322		US Airways	A
Virgin Atlantic	virgin-atlantic.com	800-862-8621	4		B

HIT THE GROUND

Shopping at JFK isn't just duty-free cigarettes and liquor (two things that will cost you a bundle in Manhattan). Terminal Four's retail hall hosts retailers including DKNY and Sephora in its 10,000-square-foot confines, which are said to span four city blocks. Not impressed? Hit Terminal One and tax your credit card at duty-free boutiques like Ferragamo and Hermès.

JFK is located 15 miles from Midtown, and takes 45 minutes to get to by car. We repeat that driving in New York City is not pleasant, but people do it. Start at the Van Wyck Expressway (airport exit), aka I-678, into Grand Central Parkway West. Cross the Triborough Bridge to FDR Drive South. There are exits roughly every mile from Midtown to Downtown.

Into Town by Taxi: As mandated by the city's Taxi & Limousine Commission (dial 311), the flat rate between Manhattan and JFK is $45 plus tolls.

Into Town by Airport Shuttle: While the Port Authority runs both New York City airports, the New York Airport Service (718-875-8200) is the only bus company authorized to provide door-to-door service from JFK and LaGuardia to various points in Manhattan, and back.

The $15 Manhattan-bound JFK shuttle makes stops at Grand Central and Port Authority before arriving at Penn Station 1 hour and 45 minutes after starting its route. (Reverse the routes back to the airport.) This shuttle's runs into the city start at 6:15am, and it makes the last pickup at 11:10pm. The first reverse run from Penn Station starts at 7:40am, and the last one departs at 8:40pm. These shuttles run every 20-30 minutes. Those wanting to get off to an earlier start can climb aboard the bus as early as 5:10am at Grand Central, or 5:20am at Port Authority.

Taking a Taxi from the Airport

All cabs have strict four-passenger maximums, and while a tip isn't required, a 15% to 20% gratuity is the norm. (Drivers can't charge for helping with or transporting luggage.) Often found at the airports are "gypsy cabs," unlicensed drivers in unofficial taxis who offer rides into the city for a discounted rate. Ignore them. Designated cabstands are set up outside the airports, and certified cabbies are always lined up and waiting. Legitimate drivers will never solicit inside the building. Getting back to the airports can sometimes be a bit more complicated. Despite city laws requiring that drivers take passengers wherever they ask to go, many cabbies don't want to leave the city, especially during busy times. (The driver either ends up spending prime time at the airport-operated cab line or coming back to the city without a fare.) Stand blocking your luggage when hailing a taxi to the airport, and don't tell the driver where you're going until you've opened the back door.

Into Town by Public Transit: The New York State Metropolitan Transportation Authority (MTA) nonemergency number is 212-878-1001. The MTA subway ride to and from JFK is simple and inexpensive. For $5, those arriving in New York can catch the AirTrain that takes passengers to the Howard Beach A train, or to the Jamaica E, J, or Z stop. The brown-coded J and Z runs through the Lower East Side and Chinatown before emptying out near Wall Street. Besides being much cleaner and more reliable than the J and Z, the blue-coded A and E lines go through downtown Manhattan near Wall Street, cutting under Soho, through the West Village, under Penn Station, then continuing up the city's near West Side. Just short of Central Park, the E breaks across Midtown under 51st Street and heads into Queens. The A stays on course, heading along the western fringe of the park, up the west side, and ending near the top of the island at 207th Street. The subways run all night. For the reverse commute, just make sure you're on the A train marked Far Rockaway or Rockaway Park, and not Lefferts Boulevard.

LaGuardia Airport (LGA)
718-533-3400, laguardiaairport.com

LaGuardia Airport sits eight miles from Midtown Manhattan, near Queens' northmost point.

Its four terminals only accommodate domestic flights, and they're spread out. US Airways has the only independent (unshared) terminal. La Guardia can't compete with JFK for size, but it wins hands-down in culinary charm, namely because it hosts celebrity chef Todd English's restaurant/lounge, Fig's. At this stylish space, which would be a top-notch restaurant in most cities, let alone an airport eatery, diners enjoy individual pizzas and English-Mediterranean fusion, much like that found in Manhattan's Olives (also featuring a Todd English menu).

Stressed-out travelers flying JetBlue will love the Oasis Day Spa, where those in a pinch can stop in for a 10-minute chair massage, and those with time to kill can enjoy a full hour-long rubdown.

Shopping at LaGuardia is nothing special. Of course, if you're heading to Boston, stop into Lids for a Yankees cap and make an impression the minute you step off the plane—then duck!

The 25-minute, 10-mile drive from LaGuardia to Manhattan is easy—take Grand Central Parkway West to the Triborough Bridge. Cross over to FDR Drive South.

HIT THE GROUND

Into Town by Taxi: Most cabs and limos wait outside the central terminal, as well as the US Airways terminal. The meter is in effect to and from LaGuardia, and will cost $24 to $28 to Manhattan, before tax and tip.

Into Town by Airport Shuttle: From LaGuardia to Manhattan, the $10 to $12 shuttles pick up every 20 to 30 minutes as well, and they do so between 7:20am and 11pm. The reverse commute runs from 7:40am to 7:10pm. The LaGuardia shuttle's first stop is at Grand Central. Ten minutes later it arrives at Port Authority, and 20 minutes later it finishes its run at Penn Station.

Into Town by Public Transit: Coming from LaGuardia, the M60 bus runs to all airport terminals and leads through Queens to the N and W trains at Astoria Boulevard. This is very much a city bus, where luggage doesn't store easily and stops are made in neighborhoods where many travelers would rather not "stop." Both the N and the W run through the middle of Manhattan, but just below Chinatown at Chambers Street, the W breaks toward Wall Street, and the N heads to Southern Brooklyn. Buy your MTA card at one of LaGuardia's vending machines, or have singles on hand, because you can't get MTA cards on the bus. (You can get transfers.) This bus runs from 5am to 1am, but if you're new in town, avoiding it at night isn't a bad idea.

Rental Cars: There are surprisingly few reputable rental car agencies in Manhattan. Each of these selections has offices in New York's airports as well as in the city.

Agency	Website	800 Number	Local Number
Avis	avis.com	800-230-4898	212-677-1411
Budget	budget.com	800-527-0700	
Enterprise	enterprise.com	800-261-7331	800-736-8222
Hertz	hertz.com	800-654-3131	212-486-5900

Luxury Car Rentals:

- Prestige Car Rental   prestigecarrental.com   888-310-9211
- Image Exotic Car Rentals   imagerentacar.com   888-718-0001

Limos: There are countless limo companies that run from Newark, JFK, and LaGuardia to Manhattan. On average, rides to or from Newark are $75, JFK is $65, and LaGuardia is $50. These costs don't include tips or tolls. A limo ride from MacArthur (Islip) to Manhattan will start at $100.
- Manhattan Limo   212-777-7799

An equally unpleasant experience, the Q48 bus also picks up at all terminals, and it runs to the Main Street 7 train, where a Manhattan-bound transfer will deliver weary travelers to Midtown Manhattan ... eventually. If you're not staying in Midtown, get ready for another transfer. Catching the 6 train at Grand Central will take visitors Uptown or Downtown via the East Side. Staying on the 7 for about four more minutes will lead to Times Square, where the 1 and 9 trains run uptown and downtown along the West Side. If the gods of the subway transfer are with you, the Midtown portion of this trip should take about an hour and cost $2. Allow more time for the transfer and journey uptown or downtown, and hope that your two-hour transfer hasn't expired. It's important to note that transfers work from bus to bus and from bus to train, but not from subways to buses.

Newark Liberty International Airport (EWR)
973-961-6000, newarkairport.com

Though more difficult to reach by car, Newark is only 16 miles from Midtown, and 12 miles from Wall Street. It accommodates less conventional carriers, like Hooters Air. Newark has three terminals: A, B, and C. In A and B, the upper levels, are for tickets and departures. The lower levels are for arrivals, baggage claim, and ground transportation. The ground level is used for operational purposes. Terminal C's upper and mid levels are for departures, and the lower level accommodates arrivals.

Into Town by Taxi: The long haul between Manhattan and Newark Airport costs between $69 and $75, plus a $15 out-of-state surcharge.

Into Town By Airport Shuttle: From Newark, the $11 Olympia Express Bus runs in order from the airport to the Port Authority, Grand Central, and Penn Station and it does so every 15-minutes, from 7am–10pm, every half hour from 10pm–1am, and then takes a break until 4am, at which time it runs every half hour until resuming its 7am schedule. These buses run a downtown route that goes from Newark to Lafayette Sts., continues south to Church and Barclay Sts., then heads back to the airport. This run is made every half hour from 7am–2pm, slows to every 40-minutes from 2:40–6:40pm, then calls it an early night, thus proving Newark's a city that does indeed sleep. The reverse commute starts at 7:30am, and maintains roughly the same pattern until 7:20pm.

HIT THE GROUND

Long Island MacArthur Airport (ISP)

631-467-3210, macarthurairport.com

MacArthur is a godsend for Long Island, but not for the city itself. It is 50 miles from Manhattan, and with no direct public transportation, the journey can be tricky. The 50-mile ride from MacArthur Airport to Manhattan is a road trip indeed. Start on Johnson Avenue and go to Route 454 leading to I-495. Then put the entire *Beatles Anthology* in the CD player and enjoy the ride.

Getting to New York: By Land

By Car: Though driving in New York City is not very pleasant, plenty of people brave the asphalt battlefields every day. Not all roads lead to Manhattan, but a lot of them do. The Brooklyn Queens Expressway (BQE), also know as Interstate 278, runs along the east side of the East River in the boroughs for which it's named, and has exits onto the Williamsburg, Brooklyn, and Manhattan Bridges, all of which lead into Manhattan. Interstate 78 is the Holland Tunnel approach. The Holland Tunnel essentially connects Jersey City to Lower Manhattan's Tribeca neighborhood. The Lincoln Tunnel, on the other hand, connects Northern New Jersey's 495 to Queens via Midtown Manhattan.

Driving Distance to New York

From	Miles	Hours
Albany, NY	150	3
Atlanta, GA	370	14
Atlantic City, NJ	100	2½
Baltimore, MD	180	3½
Boston, MA	420	4
Chicago, IL	800	14
Hartford, CT	120	2½
Niagara Falls, NY	300	5½
Philadelphia, PA	80	1½
Providence, RI	180	3½
Toronto	350	6½
Washington, DC	220	4½

New York: Lay of the Land

Since there are more exceptions than rules to New York City address-es, it's easier to use cross streets than street addresses. A cab driver will not know where 58 East First Street is; he will know First Street between First and Second Avenues. Remember: STAVE—as in Street-Avenue. If someone says, "It's at 11th and Fourth," they mean 11th Street and Fourth Avenue. What's the difference? While 11th and Fourth overlooks the East River, Fourth and 11th would be on the Hudson, which is the opposite side of the island. So close, yet so far.

Getting Around New York

By Car: If ever there were a city where you neither want nor need a car, it's this one. Rentals can be upward of $100 a day, and getting the car is just the beginning of your expenses. Street parking is hard to come by, and more often than not, a neighborhood permit is required. If the police don't ticket you for reasons you'll probably never know, there's always the chance of a dent, scrape, or broken window. Unfortunately, using a garage will cost you roughly $40 a day while only slightly reduc-ing the possibilities of the aforementioned problems. If you insist on driving, remember that most drivers use horns and accelerators rather than turn signals and brakes, and right turns on red are not permitted.

By Taxi: New Yorkers have a love-hate relationship with cabdrivers, and the feeling seems to be mutual. Thanks to there being more than 12,000 licensed taxis in the city, vacant ones are as likely to run you over as they are to stop when you wave. Generally less expensive than cabs in most cities, a New York City taxi ride starts at $2.50 upon entry, with a 40-cent charge for every 1/5 mile at 6 mph or more, or every 120 sec-onds when moving slower or idling. There's a 50-cent evening surcharge between 8pm and 6am, and a peak-hour surcharge of $1 between 4pm and 8pm on weekdays. There is no additional per-passenger charge.

Many cabbies speak on barely visible cellular headphone sets while working, so don't worry if it appears your driver is talking to himself. That said, don't assume he's sane, either. Just because you're not accountable doesn't mean a cab ride is safe. Though all things consid-ered there are remarkably few cab accidents on the streets, wearing a seatbelt is recommended. Many less scrupulous cabbies will claim not to have change for $20 bills, but nine out of ten times they'll somehow find an extra single or two if you deny them their excessive tip request. Should you be looking for change of a bill larger than $20, ask the driver before entering his car. Cabs seem to be toughest to come by around 4pm when some shifts change for the new rush hour.

NYC's taxis are city regulated, and are flagged down (available when light on roof is lit), not called. If you have issues or questions, call the Taxi and Limousine Commission, 212-692-8294.

By Public Transit: The often (and often wrongfully) vilified New York City subway system is an entire city under the city, and even millionaire mayor Michael Bloomberg uses it. Free maps can be found at any station, and they can also be studied online at mta.nyc.ny.us/. One-way passes cost $2, and discounts come with purchasing higher-value cards, starting with the $10 pass, which includes a $2 bonus, and the seven-day pass, which offers unlimited rides for $21. Short-term visitors may prefer the $7 one-day unlimited pass, which is the only option that entails buying a card through a station vending machine, rather than from a subway attendant, currency exchange, or the occasional deli.

By Metro and Bus: These cards are good for buses and trains, and the in-station vending machines take credit cards. New York City's buses and bus drivers are less helpful. Bus machines don't take coins, the drivers don't sell cards, and you have a better chance of driving the vehicle than of getting a "thank you" or "sorry." The buses provide better scenery than the subways, but they're slowed by the same traffic that slows down everyone else.

Parking: Driving in New York City is a bad idea. There are tons of cabs, public transportation is good, and you're rarely more than two miles away from your destination. Plus, car rentals and insurance are highly inflated, and that's without adding on parking, the inevitable tickets that come with parking in unmarked no-parking zones, and various nicks and dings, which are all but guaranteed, whether you use a ridiculously priced garage or 25-cents-per-15-minutes meters; most of which have two-hour limits.

Garage rates range from $6 to $15 for the first hour, and about $40 a day, with $20 a day for Sundays sometimes available. A tip of $2 to $5 is standard. Remember not to leave valuables in the car—more often than not, they'll be accepted as gifts.

Other Practical Information

Money Matters (Currency, Taxes, Tipping and Service Charges): It's dollars ($) and cents (100 to the dollar). For currency conversion rates, go to xe.com/ucc/. There is no national sales (value-added) tax. However, the sales tax within the city limits (includes both state and city taxes) is 8.62% for NYC and 4.25% for state, and they're added onto the bill (not included in price). Hotels add 14% for taxes to their prices. Service charges are not included in prices, but, depending on the venue, may be added to the bill. Tipping for restaurants and bars is expected to be in the 20% range, with 15% being "punishment." For cabs, 15% is fine for higher fares and 20% on the lower end. (If the total is $5.80, leave $7 and call the cabby's bluff if he claims to have no change.) Leaving $3 per day for the hotel housekeeper is becoming standard practice.

Metric Conversion

From	To	Multiply by
Inches	Centimeters	2.54
Yards	Meters	0.91
Miles	Kilometers	1.60
Gallons	Liters	3.79
Ounces	Grams	28.35
Pounds	Kilograms	0.45

Safety: The good news is that New York City is considerably safer than Hollywood would have you believe, and that's especially true in the case of the subways. The bad news is that there will be crime anywhere 8 million-plus people live together. Most crimes are nonviolent, and will come in the form of pickpocketing or general scams. Keep wallets in jacket or front pant pockets, always stay near your bags and packages, and don't take out your pocketbook if a situation feels uncomfortable. Largely because of the outrageous realty costs throughout Manhattan, the "bad neighborhoods" are generally far from where visitors have any reason to be. The outer boroughs tend to be more sparsely concentrated than the city, so the farther you go from Manhattan, the more rundown things become. Though "rundown" doesn't necessarily mean dangerous in this old city, be extra cautious on the lower fringes of the Lower East Side, and borderline neighborhoods that start atop the Upper East and Upper West Sides. Locals here can generally spot a visitor rather quickly, so if you start feeling out of place, you probably are. Regardless of how assertive their approach, most panhandlers are just asking, and overreacting to them can create a problem where there needn't be one. Trust the inner voice that tells you when a situation seems uncomfortable, and don't worry about being polite or politically correct; no one here does.

Gay and Lesbian Travel: The West Village is one of gay New York's best-known areas, and right above it to the north is the often younger and hipper Chelsea neighborhood. Christopher Street runs right by the site of the famous Stone Wall riots, and the neighborhood is awash in piano bars, neighborhood "bear" joints, and outdoor patio bars. Despite the abundance of tourists who come through here, rarely does a same-sex couple get a double-take. Above 23rd Street, the clubbier, more singles-driven Chelsea area begins. Overall, New Yorkers are among the most liberal Americans you'll ever meet, but the conservative frat-bar neighborhoods of the Upper East Side and Upper West Side are best avoided at night by overtly gay and lesbian travelers. Despite the high-fiving, butt-slapping, and wrestling that happens in these areas' male-dominated haunts, some of the younger locals are still struggling with their own identities, and tequila shots don't help.

Traveling with Disabilities: Most public places offer facilities for disabled visitors, including wheelchair access. For a good resource, go to access-able.com or disabilitytravel.com.

Radio: This is a big pedestrian town, where not many people own cars, and the tall buildings wreak havoc with radio signals. While a lot of stations broadcast from NYC, many of them are as well known outside the city as they are here. Howard Stern is a favorite son in this city, where nothing is considered shocking. Largely due to the self-proclaimed "King of All Media" and his much-anticipated switch from transmitters to satellites, Sirius Satellite Radio has close to 1 million subscribers, many of whom reside in the shock jock's hometown. Also popular with slacking office workers are Internet stations like NPR (also on conventional radio), Air America, and East Village Radio—a hip downtown outfit that had been a pirate station for years.

Radio Stations (a Selection)

FM Stations

88.3	WGBO	Jazz
89.1	WNYU	College Radio
92.3	WXRK	aka "K-Rock" (Howard Stern/Rock)
93.9	WNYC	NPR/News/Talk
96.7	WKHL	Oldies
98.7	WRKS	Soul/Hip-Hop
104.3	WAXQ	Classic Rock

AM Stations

660	WFAN	Sports
710	WOR	Talk
770	WABC	News/Sports
820	WNYC	NPR/News/Public Affairs
880	WCBS	News/Yankees
1010	WINS	Traffic/News/Weather/Sports

Print Media: *The Old Grey Lady*, or *New York Times* as you may know it, is arguably America's best known-paper. Its reviews of art, performance art, and restaurants are widely respected, but not easily accessible on a daily basis. When it comes to trends, the internationally read *Times* Sunday Style section creates as many as it reports.

For day-to-day coverage of the city's happenings, the local papers do it best, as they're both more likely to report on fashion and nightclubs than population shifts in Novosibirsk. Rupert Murdoch's racy *New York Post* is probably its most infamous. New York City's third major daily is the *Daily News*, which rivals the *Post* when it comes to attention-grabbing headlines.

There are several free papers in the city and a new one is born just about every week. *The Village Voice* however is the strongest and it can be found on almost every street corners and subway car floor. (Or, if you're wearing a fanny pack, a homeless person might sell you one for a price to be negotiated.) Considering the price, "The Voice" is pretty well written and though its top-notch entertainment listings skew "insider," non-New Yorkers who know their way around DJs, bands, and theater will find it helpful.

New York Magazine and *Time Out New York* compete for best magazine for trend-spotting and taste making.

Shopping Hours: The trend is increasingly for stores to open later in the morning, at 10am rather than 9am, and to stay open later, until 9pm on weekdays and 6pm on weekends. Obviously store hours vary, and boutiques with skeleton staffs are likely to work 11am to 7pm.

Attire: Despite its intense pace, the New York "look" is surprisingly laid-back. However, this brand of "casual" tends to be more European than Midwestern. Carpenter-style and stonewashed jeans, sweatshirts, white sneakers, pleats, and khakis scream, "I'm not from around here!" For men, many of the city's nicer restaurants and clubs will forgive a form-fitting or boot-cut pair of jeans, so long as they're paired with a dress shirt, blazer, or both. Women may find that less is more in this deceptively heady fashion capital. Leave the hair unsprayed and keep makeup subtle, or fear being labeled "Jersey." This city is about attitude—if you think you can pull it off, go for it. That said, there's nothing worse than waiting for an hour in a velvet-rope line only to be turned away at the door. A lot of nightclubs will welcome unshaven guys in hats and tee shirts, and women in next to nothing, but it's always a gamble. With all of the model types here (not to mention the high population of actual models), "the body beautiful" is defined by

HIT THE GROUND

Size Conversion

Dress Sizes

US	6	8	10	12	14	16
UK	8	10	12	14	16	18
France	36	38	40	42	44	46
Italy	38	40	42	44	46	48
Europe	34	36	38	40	42	44

Women's Shoes

US	6	6½	7	7½	8	8½
UK	4½	5	5½	6	6½	7
Europe	38	38	39	39	40	41

Men's Suits

US	36	38	40	42	44	46
UK	36	38	40	42	44	46
Europe	46	48	50	52	54	56

Men's Shirts

US	14½	15	15½	16	16½	17
UK	14½	15	15½	16	16½	17
Europe	38	39	39-40	41	42	43

Men's Shoes

US	8	8½	9½	10½	11½	12
UK	7	7½	8½	9½	10½	11
Europe	41	42	43	44	45	46

an entirely unrealistic standard. Thin is in, which may be why everyone in New York walks everywhere and belongs to a health club.

When Drinking Is Legal: The drinking age in New York City is 21, and most bars and clubs check IDs. Don't expect any breaks. Mega clubs like Spirit and Crobar, both in West Chelsea, sometimes have 18-plus events, in which legal drinkers are given wristbands. These clubs might stay open until 6am on weekends, but *nobody* serves liquor after 4am.

Smoking: Like it or not, smoking is not allowed in New York City bars or restaurants. (A couple of cigar bars have grandfathered-in permits, but they're extremely rare.) A lot of watering holes have designated smoking areas, and they're always outdoors.

Drugs: Most people in New York use delivery services if they want drugs. This may seem odd to most people, but it's as easy as getting a pizza if you know someone. "Dealers" selling in parks or on the street are more often than not scammers out looking for tourists and suckers. Asking around in bars and clubs can pay off, but it can also get you thrown out. While police would generally rather ignore pot smokers, they will act if users flaunt their stash.

Time Zone: New York City runs on Eastern time (EST), which means it's five hours behind Greenwich mean time (the Greenwich in England, that is). The East Coast gets the new day, like everything else, before any other place in the country. When it's noon in LA, it's 3pm here. When it's noon in Chicago, it's 2pm here. When it's 1958 in Kansas, it's 2006 here. A note on daylight savings time: Clocks are set ahead one hour at 2am on the first Sunday in April and set back one hour at 2am on the last Sunday in October.

Area Codes: There's still a premium on 212 numbers, though 917 and 646 are still Manhattan (mostly cell phones, though some residential). The outer boroughs are most associated with 718, but use 374 also.

Additional Resources for Visitors

New York City Convention & Visitors Bureau Pick up brochures, maps, and tour tickets, *Mon-Fri 8:30am-6pm, Sat-Sun 9am-5pm.* 810 7th Ave., 212-484-1200, nycvisit.com

Foreign Visitors
Foreign Embassies in the United States: state.gov/misc/10125.htm
Passport requirements: travel.state.gov/travel/tips/brochures/brochures_1229.html
Cell phones: North America operate on the 1,900MHz frequency. Cell phones may be used while driving. For buying or renting a phone, go to telestial.com/instructions.htm.
Toll-free numbers in the United States: 800, 866, 877, and 888.
Telephone directory assistance in the United States: 411
Electrical: U.S. standard is AC, 110 volts/60 cycles, with a plug of two flat pins set parallel to one another.

The Latest-Info Websites
Go to NYC & Company, nycvisit.com
And of course, **pulseguides.com**

HIT THE GROUND

Numbers to Know (Hotlines)

As in all American cities, 911 is the number for emergency police, ambulance, and fire services. For less-urgent complaints of a nuisance and quality-of-life variety, the city's 311 number can be helpful. Think of 311 as a compromise between 911 and 411.

Most of New York City's hospitals are excellent, but they often require a wait for non–life-threatening matters. Mt. Sinai is located uptown at 1190 5th Ave. at 100th Street, and their general information number is 212-241-6500.

The only 24-hour emergency room below 11th Avenue is the NYU Downtown Hospital at 170 William St., near Wall Street. The number for emergency room admitting is 212-312-5063.

Not far from the Meatpacking District and West Chelsea's nightlife, St. Vincent's emergency room is always busy. The entrance is on Seventh Avenue at West 11th Street, and the number is 212-604-7000.

Not open 24 hours, but still useful, is the New York Eye & Ear Infirmary at 310 East 14th St., 212-979-4000.

On the East Side of Manhattan is Cabrini Medical Center and Emergency Room, which is at 227 East 19th St., between Second and Third Avenues, and can be reached at 212-995-6000.

There are about 30 24-hour pharmacies in lower Manhattan, and your concierge will surely know the nearest one. If not, the CVS pharmacy chain will direct you to one if you dial 800-746-7287. Duane Reade is another reliable chain, and their most uptown location can be reached at 212-799-3172; their most centrally located Midtown branch can be reached at 212-682-5338. The ubiquitous Rite Aid chain has a downtown 24-hour locale at 212-213-9887.

Hotlines: Here's a listing of other numbers we hope you won't be using:

Hospital Patient Location Information	718-416-7000
Drug Abuse	800-395-3400
Physicians on Call (licensed doctors come to you, usually within two hours)	718-238-2100
Animal Bites	212-676-2483
Poison Control	212-340-4494
Dental Emergencies	212-677-2510

The Cheat Sheet
(The Very Least You Ought to Know
About New York)

Everything in New York moves very quickly. This countdown will get you looking like a local fast.

 ## Streets

Bleecker Street Bleecker Street has a modest east-side strip of residences and neighborhood bars, but the Greenwich Village and West Village stretch is considerably livelier. College bars and brunch-leaning eateries abound, along with a smattering of knickknack and clothing shops.

The Bowery At one time, the Bowery was a seedy stretch of the Lower East Side and East Village, where sailors on leave looked for various ways to spend their paychecks. In the late '70s, it became a hangout for punk rock bands, and though it maintains a slightly dirty vibe today, it's filled with worthwhile late-night spots and odd characters.

Broadway This is the granddaddy of all Manhattan streets. Stretching from one end of Manhattan to the other, Broadway runs through Uptown's West Side neighborhoods, cuts through the neon heart of Times Square, past the Theater District that bears its name, and continues Downtown, where Soho and Greenwich Village's shopping districts line its path.

Fifth Avenue Running from Central Park to Washington Square Park, Fifth Avenue divides the city between east and west, briefly veering east at Central Park, where it's forced to take sides. Some of the most expensive retail space on the planet can be found on upper Fifth Avenue, with retailers like Bergdorf Goodman, Tiffany's, and Saks.

42nd Street When most people think of 42nd Street, they think of the famous Broadway musical. While it's worth a look, Midtown's lower starting point is a circus of Broadway performers, beggars, tourists, transvestites, and commuters, who are all minding their own business.

Ludlow Street The unofficial capital of Hipsterville, Ludlow Street itself is little more than a pedestrian-cluttered slab of concrete that provides a bit of breathing room between popular rock bars. Very recently, Uptown investment bankers have clashed with LES bohemians in a land battle that has seen divey music venues sharing walls with upscale restaurants. The only thing you can't get here is bored.

Madison Avenue This famous New York street travels through several high-end worlds as the cross streets ascend in numbers. Between 42nd and 59th Streets, Madison Avenue is the advertising world's Vatican City, which gives way to upscale jewelers and chichi boutiques as it approaches 72nd. From

72nd to 86th is Museum Row, which includes world-class cultural institutions like the Whitney, among others. As it climbs Carnegie Hill, the top-flight shops, spas, and cafes give Madison Avenue the look of a shining city atop a hill.

Mulberry Street All that's really left of Manhattan's Little Italy is this tacky but charming street of restaurants and souvenir shops. In the summer, Mulberry Street is often closed to traffic so that visitors can enjoy their Italian ice cups and cappuccinos in peace.

Park Avenue One of the world's most prestigious mailing addresses, Park Avenue was designed with beauty in mind. Though the street itself technically starts above Grand Central, its sister, Park Avenue South, resumes below the mighty train depot as a tree-lined boulevard, rolling as far as the eye can see.

65th Street Not even afraid to pass through Central Park at night, the unstoppable 65th Street cuts across the middle of Manhattan, connecting east to west, and providing a scenic but fast-moving tour of the zoo, the carousel, and Tavern on the Green.

9 Neighborhoods

Chelsea A long-running late-night area for gay clubbers, the Chelsea scene now has a little something for everyone. The once desolate far west side now hosts the city's hottest nightspots, which include household names like Bungalow 8 and Marquee, as well as some of Manhattan's most innovative and cutting-edge art galleries.

Financial District Way, way downtown, the Financial District is home to Wall Street and some of the world's most affluent financial companies. With narrow winding roads and tall, imposing buildings, the Financial District is reminiscent of Batman's Gotham City—especially at night when it's dark and relatively empty. On the eastern edge of the Financial District lies South Street Seaport, full of pricey tourist restaurants overlooking the East River. This part of town is early to rise and early to bed, so cabs are tough to come by after sunset.

The Flatiron District The Flatiron District is centrally located between Midtown and Downtown, and, fittingly, it walks the line between hip and corporate. New restaurants and lounges open constantly, drawing a combination of khaki-clad professionals and scraggly bohemians. This area really peaked in the Internet boom, when startups couldn't afford Midtown office prices.

Gramercy/Murray Hill The two neighborhoods that fill the east side gap between the East Village and Midtown are very similar. Heavily residential Gramercy and Murray Hill are largely occupied by 9-to-5 Midtown middle-management types. Park Avenue South runs down the middle of these neighborhoods, and on its perimeters are several worthwhile restaurants. Both Second and Third Avenue are lined with sports bars and average pubs that are reminiscent of all things Middle America.

Midtown In terms of financial, commercial, and scenic visibility, this neighborhood is the heart of Manhattan. All trains and buses lead to Midtown, which is chock-full of office buildings, skyscrapers, restaurants, and high-priced condos and hotels. Stretching from 42nd Street to Central Park, and reaching from river to river, this area hosts the UN, Rockefeller Center, and the NBC studios, not to mention the Theater District known as the Great White Way.

Soho Named for its coordinates (South of Houston), Soho may be New York City's most popular neighborhood. In the '80s, many local artists moved into this otherwise abandoned manufacturing area and established residencies in large, inexpensive spaces not legally zoned for occupancy. Now this very expensive area is home to scores of actors, models, and musicians, and its streets buzz with tourists who come for the galleries, boutiques, restaurants, and bars.

Tribeca In the mid-1990s, Tribeca (an abbreviation for "triangle below Canal Street"), made the leap from warehouse and factory district to one of the city's hottest neighborhoods, thanks to the JFK Junior–led jet-set invasion. Being the residential neighborhood nearest the World Trade Center, Tribeca's popularity suffered after September 11. But recently, the hot restaurants have returned, and the annual Tribeca Film Festival draws local cinema elite, like neighborhood residents Robert De Niro and Harvey Keitel.

The Upper East Side The Upper East Side is largely conservative, preppy, and family oriented, making it the antithesis of Downtown. By day, people from all walks of life flock to famed museums like the Whitney and the Frick, which are steps from the Central Park border. Beautiful old-money estates line the western border of the Upper East Side, but by night, the inland noisy bar scene takes on a more postcollegiate feel.

The Upper West Side Also wealthy, museum heavy, and family oriented, the Upper West Side is considerably more appealing by day than it is by night. Though the show was shot in a Hollywood studio, *Seinfeld* fans may recognize many of this area's diners, stores, and apartment building exteriors.

8 New York Movies

Annie Hall This is one of Woody Allen's finest films, which pits the beautiful authenticity of Allen's beloved city against a vapid, narcissistic California culture.

Arthur This film takes a kooky look at the uptown lifestyles of the rich and the famous, and what happens when you get caught between the moon and New York City.

Bringing Out the Dead This movie's high-speed ambulance ride through the entire city shows more of Manhattan than anyone could dream of seeing in two hours while obeying the speed limit.

Manhattan Shot in black-and-white and boasting an all-Gershwin score, this is Woody Allen's cinematic love letter to New York City.

The Pope of Greenwich Village A then-sane Mickey Rourke and Eric Roberts play small-time hoods who claim Greenwich Village and Little Italy as their stomping grounds.

HIT THE GROUND

Taxi Driver Sure, it's disturbing, but this Martin Scorsese masterpiece effectively captures the spirit and look of an angry and desperate late '70s Manhattan.

Spiderman Although a scene featuring the World Trade Center was removed from this film after September 11, there are still several classic NYC shots in this blockbuster, with the web-slinger and Green Goblin's first confrontation happening at the 34th Street parade.

When Harry Met Sally There are a lot of single people looking for romance in this sometimes lonely city, and this movie tells the story of two of them. Thanks to the film, Katz's Delicatessen will never be the same.

7 Pro-Sports Teams

New York has more major professional sports franchises than any other city:

Giants National Football League, 201-935-8111, giants.com

Jets National Football League, 516-560-8200, newyorkjets.com

Knicks National Basketball League, 212-465-5867, nba.com/knicks

Liberty Woman's National Basketball League, 212-465-6073, wnba.com/liberty

Mets Major League Baseball, 718-507-8499, mets.com

Rangers National Hockey League, 212-465-6073, newyorkrangers.com

Yankees Major League Baseball, 718-293-6000, yankees.com

6 Shopping Areas

Bleecker Street The city's newest strip of upscale shopping, where you can find everything from a shiny new Polo store to the classic Bleecker Street Records.

Canal Street Lined with shops and outdoor vendors selling original paintings; here you'll find the best imitation designer handbags this side of Bangkok.

Fifth Avenue From 42nd Street to Central Park, it's lined with high-end retailers including Saks Fifth Avenue, which obviously realizes the value of the three lanes of traffic outside.

Madison Avenue Uptown shopping in every definition of the word. Spas and salons are part of the package.

Soho Along Broadway you'll find boutiques and franchises like Giorgio Armani, Levi's, and Arden B.

St. Mark's Old-school New York souvenir shopping. While there are probably still snow globes to be found here, comic books, hard-to-find videos, and tee shirts are the main draw today.

Historic Neighborhoods

Chinatown/Little Italy New York City's ever-expanding Chinatown is a true immigrant stronghold. Many of its residents speak very little English, despite having lived here for many years. Though the streets are largely unclean and foul smells abound, this neighborhood has tons of character and plenty of authentic Chinese cuisine. Sandwiched between Chinatown and Soho is what's left of Martin Scorsese's old 'hood, Little Italy. Still, the central and largely commercialized area around the intersection of Mulberry and Mott Streets offers the sites and scents of the neighborhood where "fuggedaboudit" was coined.

East Village A little seedy and very hip, the East Village is where the American punk rock scene was born, and its influences can still be felt. Dive bars and music venues abound, starting with the famed CBGB, which launched acts including Blondie, the Talking Heads, and the Ramones (the nearby section of Third Street was recently named for the latter). Jeans and tee shirts make up this neighborhood's shabby-chic aesthetic.

Greenwich Village Standing at the corner of Fifth Avenue and Tenth Street, where writers Mark Twain, Dawn Powell, Sinclair Lewis, and Dorothy Thompson all lived, one can see the Empire State Building to the north and Washington Park's magnificent arch to the south. (This inspiring neighborhood is also where Henry James's *Washington Square* was set.) Wander up the street to the Cedar Tavern and gain further inspiration imbibing where Jack Kerouac, Allen Ginsberg, Bob Dylan, and Jackson Pollock reveled in their younger days.

Lower East Side In the past, the Lower East Side was a seedy melting pot comprised largely of low-income immigrants and families. In the '90s, popular dive bars and music venues began popping up at the sites of former tenements, attracting local rockers from bands like the Strokes, the Yeah Yeah Yeahs, and Interpol. After a series of posh new hotels and condos popped up, locals braced themselves for an inevitable gentrification, which is already under way.

West Village With its winding, narrow, tree-lined streets, the West Village has gotten popular and pricey. Still, there's a certain coziness that harkens back to the days when legends like Allen Ginsberg, Bob Dylan, and Dylan Thomas called it home. In the northwest corner of the West Village is the painfully popular Meatpacking District, the zeitgeist of the *Sex and the City* craze. Once filled with butcher shops, this neighborhood's cobblestone streets are now home to a carnivalesque frenzy of nightclubs and restaurants.

HIT THE GROUND

4   New York Eats

Bagels Since New York City has the nation's largest Jewish population, the bagels here have to be good, and they are.

Burgers Where else do top-notch restaurants offer $25 to $100 gourmet patties?

Falafel Cheap, ubiquitous, and authentic, this Middle Eastern fast food is easy to come by anytime of the day.

Pizza Generally served by the slice with only cheese as a topping, New York pizza can be found at all hours, in almost every neighborhood.

3   Skyscrapers

American International Building At 952 feet, this limestone art deco masterpiece is the city's 3rd (and nation's 14th) tallest. 70 Pine St. (Pearl St.), Wall Street

The Chrysler Building In the year prior to the Empire State Building's completion, this was the world's tallest building. 405 Lexington Ave. (42nd St.), Midtown, 212-682-3070

The Empire State Building King Kong fell 1,454 feet from the top of this monstrous building, which was the world's tallest from 1931 to 1972. 350 5th Ave. (Broadway), Gramercy, 212-736-3100

2   Parks

Central Park As far as parks are concerned, they don't get much bigger than this one. Smack dab in the middle of Manhattan, these 843 acres are a sight to see, preferably during the day.

Washington Square Park In the days of public executions, people would gather in the northwest corner of this park to watch criminals swing from Washington Square Park's hanging tree. Now, this warm and busy park hosts protests, vigils, book fairs, and more.

1   Singular Sensation

Madison Square Garden "The World's Most Famous Arena" sits atop Pennsylvania Station, hosting everything from rock concerts to Knicks games to the Ringling Brothers Circus.

Coffee (quick stops for a java jolt)

Big Cup Coffee may not be as sexy as cocktails, but this place sustains a popular gay scene. 228 8th Ave. (21st St.), Chelsea, 212-206-0059

Café Gitane Though it's regarded more as a restaurant, Café Gitane has a coffee selection not to be overlooked. The Soho setting is also oh so hip. 242 Mott St. (Spring St.), Soho, 212-334-9552

Cafe Pick Me Up Parisian aesthetic complete with Café de Flore vibe, this is the kind of place where philosophy majors, English professors, and wannabes with a laptop drop by to drink java from mugs and fix the world's problems ... or at least talk about them. 145 Ave. A (9th St.), East Village, 212-673-7231

Café Sabarsky This isn't a coffeehouse—it's a Kaffeehause. The difference? Coffeehouses can be found in Ohio, Kaffeehausen are genuine Viennese cafes where they take coffee, spaetzle, and chocolate cake seriously. 1048 5th Ave. (86th St.), Upper East Side, 212-288-0665

Coffee Shop A coffee "scene" just off Union Square Park, this place is especially hot in the summer when sidewalk seating wraps around its corner locale. 29 Union Square W. (16th St.), Flatiron, 212-243-7969

Dean & Deluca Rockefeller Center The chain is reliable, if not enjoyable, and this locale overlooks an ice-skating rink in the winter and provides good loitering space in the summer. 1 Rockefeller Plz. (50th St.), Midtown, 212-664-1363

DT·UT Free Internet service until 8pm is a big plus at this *straight-out-of-Friends* cafe, though most customers are getting wired on their cappuccino. The Rice Crispy treats aren't bad either. 1626 2nd Ave. (84th St.), Upper East Side, 212-327-1327

Joe The folksy, tree-lined West Village was made for sipping coffee. There's nowhere better to do it than this hip but laid-back java house. 141 Waverly Pl., (Gay St.), West Village, 212-924-6750

Porto Rico Importing Company There's no seating here, which is fine since the imported coffees make customers want to get up and go. 40½ St. Mark's Pl. (1st Ave.), East Village, 212-533-1982

The Verb Williamsburg is the new Bohemia, and this is its coolest coffeehouse. Come here any given afternoon and try to figure out what all these 20-somethings do for a living. In their defense, the boiled coffee beans are addictive. 218 Bedford Ave., (N. 5th St.), Williamsburg, 718-599-0977

HIT THE GROUND

Just for Business and Conventions

What better place to "write it off" than in the country's most expensive city? Unlike many towns where the convention centers are located across the street from the airport, New York's biggest trade centers require a drive right through the middle of Manhattan, and the hotels are a far cry from the Dayton Ramada. Leave the whoopee cushion and handshake buzzer behind, because conventioneering in NYC is a different ball game. Here are some tips to make the most of it.

Business and Convention Hotels

These hotel selections are for those placing a premium on proximity to the Meadowlands, the Javits Center, or Madison Square Garden.

Affinia Manhattan This "all suites" hotel often hosts athletes who wander across the street to beat the Knicks. $$$$ 371 7th Ave. (31st St.), Midtown, 212-563-1800

Embassy Suites Hotel The best hotel within walking distance of the Meadowlands Expo Center. $$ Secaucus-Meadowlands, 455 Plaza Dr. (Harmon Meadow Blvd.), Secaucus, NJ, 201-864-7300

Hotel Pennsylvania Immortalized by a Glenn Miller song when it was the Statler. Business travelers love this hotel's location, across the street from MSG and half a mile from the Javits Center. $$ 401 7th Ave. (32nd St.), Midtown, 212-736-5000

Sheraton Meadowlands Hotel and Conference Center Typical high-end business hotel across the highway and parking lot from the Meadowlands Stadium. $$ 2 Meadowlands Plz. (S. Service Rd.), East Rutherford, NJ, 201-896-0500

Towers at the New Yorker Right across the street from Madison Square Garden and quite posh on floors 38 to 40. The lobby is an atmospheric place for morning coffee and strategizing. $$ 481 8th Ave. (34th St.), Midtown, 866-800-3088

Business Entertaining

Here are a few good choices for sealing a deal that don't appear in our Black Book:

Brandy Library Bar A well-appointed, modern-classic cognac, and whiskey bar loved by Wall Streeters. 25 N. Moore St., (W. Broadway), Tribeca, 212-226-5545

Michael's California cuisine is served to power brokers of all stripes, as long as they're media connected. 24 W. 55th St. (5th Ave.), Midtown, 212-767-0555

Regency Still, after all these years, this is power-broker central, especially at breakfast (might as well get the deals done early). Regency Hotel, 540 Park Ave. (61st St.), Upper East Side, 212-339-4050

Stone Rose Rande "W" Gerber's most posh lounge to date, just a West Side Highway crawl from the Javits Center. 10 Columbus Cir. (8th Ave.), Upper West Side, 212-823-9769

Also see: **Best Cocktail Mixologists,** (p.23)
                   Best Power Lunches, (p.39)
                   Best Steak Houses, (p.44)
                   Best Wine Bars, (p.48)

Ducking Out for a Half Day

These places, close to either Javits or MSG, are ideal for stretching your legs.

Chelsea Piers This is where working folks decompress by bowling or hitting balls on the driving range. (p.106) 23rd St. (Hudson River), Chelsea, 212-336-6666

Hudson River Park Walk a stretch of the scenic 32-mile round-island course, which includes a pier-side jaunt along the Hudson River. Battery (59th St.)

Intrepid Sea, Air & Space Museum After its honorable discharge, this aircraft carrier became a museum. $$ (p.160) Pier 86 (12th Ave. & 46th St.), 212-245-0072

Also see: **Best Outdoor People-Watching,** (p.36)
                   Best Spas, (p.43)
                   Best Unusual Museums, (p.47)

Gifts to Bring Home

You won't find "I Love New York" tee shirts at these places:

Barneys New York If we were to pick one store that captures the essence of New York, this is it. (p.56) 660 Madison Ave. (61st St.), 212-826-8900

Cooper-Hewitt, National Design Museum As one might expect from a design museum, this shop has interesting tech-oriented trinkets and books. (p.76) 2 E. 91st St. (5th Ave.), Upper East Side, 212-849-8400

Museum of Modern Art (Store) Cutting-edge products in addition to the usual books and prints. (In case you're wondering, it's here.) (p.140) 11 W. 53 St. (5th Ave.), 212-708-9700

Also see: **Unique Shopping Index,** (p.237)

HIT THE GROUND

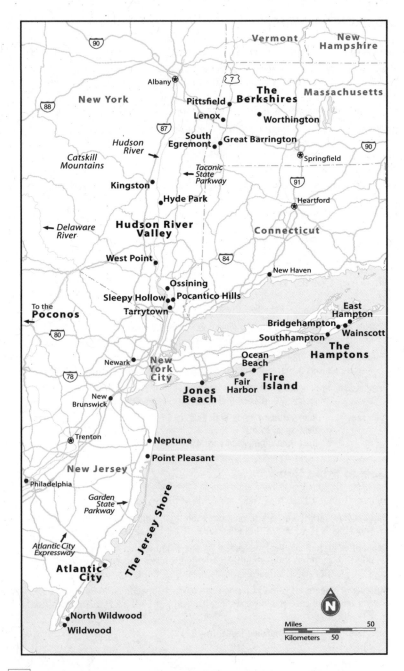

Vermont

New Hampshire

90

Albany

7

New York

Pittsfield

The Berkshires

Massachusetts

88

Lenox

Worthington

87

South Egremont

Great Barrington

90

Hudson River

Springfield

Catskill Mountains

Taconic State Parkway

91

Kingston

Hyde Park

Heartford

Delaware River

Hudson River Valley

Connecticut

West Point

84

New Haven

Ossining

Sleepy Hollow

Pocantico Hills

East Hampton

To the Poconos

Tarrytown

Bridgehampton

Wainscott

80

Southhampton

The Hamptons

Newark

New York City

Ocean Beach

78

Fair Harbor

Fire Island

New Brunswick

Jones Beach

Trenton

Neptune

Point Pleasant

New Jersey

Philadelphia

Garden State Parkway

The Jersey Shore

Atlantic City Expressway

Atlantic City

N

North Wildwood

Miles 50

Wildwood

Kilometers 50

LEAVING NEW YORK

Because New York City's dizzying pace can be as exhausting as it is exciting, its residents place a premium on weekend retreats. Whether you're looking for a scenic New England countryside, a majestic mountain resort, or boardwalks and beachfronts, they're all a short jaunt beyond the bright lights.

Atlantic City

Hot Tip: Atlantic City is at its best in the late summer months, once the ocean has heated up and walks along the Boardwalk are more comfortable. Try August or September.

The Lowdown: This famous resort town, with its festive Boardwalk and grand hotels, was once the paragon of American glamour and excess, and the inspiration for the board game Monopoly. It may no longer be the playground of icons like Frank Sinatra and Marilyn Monroe, but "A.C." is still a fun place to attend a convention or, historically, a Miss America pageant. And, if you enjoy gambling or Tom Jones shows, it is well worth the easy trip down the Garden State parkway from New York City. But those looking for a Las Vegas–style experience will be disappointed. The closest A.C. comes to that is the sleek and upscale Borgata Hotel, which also hosts the majority of this city's best restaurants. The Borgata, however, is not located on the boardwalk or in the convention center area where purists still believe the "real" Atlantic City is found. No matter— that's what taxis are for.

Best Attractions

Absecon Lighthouse An ordinary lighthouse with extraordinary views over Atlantic City and the Jersey coast. 31 S. Rhode Island Ave. (Atlantic Ave.), 609-449-1360

The Atlantic City Boardwalk Four miles of tee-shirt shops, amusement park rides, wax museums, video arcades, and cheap bars sandwiched between the beach and A.C.'s old-school casino hotels.

The Quarter at the Tropicana Hotel and Casino The most sophisticated spa and shopping locales off the boardwalk are in this new glitzy complex attached to the Tropicana. The "Old Havana" theme comes off more like Morocco. 2831 Pacific Ave. (S. Iowa Ave.), 800-843-8767, tropicana.net/thequarter

Wild West Casino Bally's Atlantic City's best themed casino has a Western decor and diverse people-watching that might also appeal to nongamblers. 1133 Boardwalk, 609-340-2000

Best Hotels

Atlantic City Tropicana After renovations in 2005, this Tropicana is now more sophisticated and modern than its Las Vegas counterpart, which still isn't saying much. The best rooms are the suites with a view of the beach. S. Brighton Ave. (on the Boardwalk), 609-340-4020 / 800-843-8767, theborgata.com

Borgata Hotel Casino & Spa The only hotel/casino comparable to those on the Vegas strip. This is the hotel of choice for high rollers, which, in A.C., means those wearing the nicest track suits. 1 Borgata Way (Huron Ave.), 609-317-1000, theborgata.com

Caesars Atlantic City Though the accommodations can't hold a Roman candle to those at the Vegas Caesars, the bar scene is active. 2100 Pacific Ave. (Columbia Pl.), 609-348-4411, caesars.com

Hilton Casino Resort Probably the best hotel option directly off the boardwalk, featuring large rooms and a private beach area. Boston Ave. (on the Boardwalk), 609-347-7111, hiltonac.com

Best Restaurants and Nightlife

The Bacchanal A foodie favorite that offers an "authentic Roman feast" in an elaborate, if conservative, atmosphere. Caesar's Atlantic City, 2100 Pacific Ave. (S. Arkansas Ave.), 609-348-4411

Capriccio An elegant Italian bistro with outdoor seating during the summer. Resorts Atlantic City Casino & Hotel, 1133 Boardwalk (North Carolina Ave.), 609-340-6789, resortsac.com

Deja Vu A good-looking 20-something crowd from New York dances to laser lights and DJ-spun tunes. New York Ave. (on the boardwalk), 609-348-4313

Forum Lounge A quiet glass-enclosed lounge with a grand piano. Caesars Atlantic City, 2100 Pacific Ave. (Columbia Pl.), 609-348-4411, caesars.com

Lefty's 1200 A throwback from the supper club era that feels like Bugsy Segal's Vegas. 1200 Atlantic Ave. (N. North Carolina Ave.), 609-348-5677

OPA Bar & Grille A leaning-toward-hip international diner with great afternoon martinis and windows for people-watching on the boardwalk. 1700 Boardwalk (MLK Blvd.), 609-344-0094, opa1.com

Suilan Chinese-French fusion in lush surroundings with an upscale clientele. Borgata Hotel, Casino & Spa, 1 Borgata Way (Huron Ave.), 609-317-7725, theborgata.com

Temple Bar and Grill Hip sushi restaurant with palm trees, tuna, and celebs. Connected to Caesars. 2100 Pacific Ave. (S. Arkansas Ave.), 609-441-2345

Contacts

Atlantic City Convention and Visitors Authority 2314 Pacific Ave. (Mississippi Ave.), 609-348-7100, atlanticcitynj.com

Getting There: By Car: Take I-95 south to the Garden State Parkway south. Exit 38 will take you to downtown Atlantic City.
By Bus: From Penn Station, buses leave every half-hour between 6:30am and midnight (3:30am on the weekends). "Lucky Streak" tickets can be purchased directly at Port Authority's gates 79 and 80. Call 800-229-9424 for more information.

LEAVING

The Berkshires

Hot Tip: New England autumns are stunning, but winters get very cold. Late September through early December is ideal.

The Lowdown: About halfway between Boston and New York City are the woodsy and mountainous Berkshires. A popular get-out-of-town destination for many Manhattan weekenders, this series of scenic mountain communities is the antithesis of the beach-and-nightlife-driven Hamptons. Winters up here get very cold, which explains the wool, angora, and down coats that abound in these parts. Towns like South Egremont offer prime skiing and shopping to visitors who use verbs like "antiquing." Rustic downtown Great Barrington is lined with arts and crafts stores and cozy New England bed and breakfasts that book up quickly. While semiposh lodges like the Egremont Inn are charming and cozy, smaller operations like the Weathervane Inn are just as friendly ... and cheaper. Because these locals are quite used to the year-round vacationers who "discover" their towns every weekend, there aren't a lot of bargains to be found. Still, many of the bookstores and record shops along the way are well worth a look. For the adventurous, Worthington Ballooning offers a bird's-eye view of the Berkshires' scenic landscape. There is also a thriving theater scene here that's well worth checking out. Actors, including Chris Noth, have been known to make the rounds.

Best Attractions

Barrington Stage Company Top-notch theater company that draws a lot of Manhattan talent and spectators. (At the Consolati Performing Arts Center), 491 Berkshire School Rd., South Barrington, MA, 413-528-8888

Berkshire Opera Company This 20-year-old theater has sent more than one performer to the Met, and the *New York Times* has sent its share of reporters here as well. Small venue, big talent. 297 North St., Pittsfield, MA, 413-442-0099

Butternut Basin Well-maintained mountainous ski trails, beautiful setting. Route 23, Great Barrington, MA, 413-528-2000, skibutternut.com

Charles L. Flint Antiques Charming county gallery of folk art, occasional Rockwells, and other rarities. 52 Housatonic St., Lenox, MA, 413-637-1634

The Mahaiwe Performing Arts Center A century-old pre-talkies theater that reopened as a performing arts center in 2005, the Mahaiwe is under review for National Register of Historic Places status. 14 Castle St., Great Barrington, MA, 413-528-0100

Worthington Ballooning Field launches and landings, and flight over miles of mountains and greenery. 159 Buffington Hill Rd., Worthington, MA, 413-238-5514

Best Hotels

Canyon Ranch Luxury resort and health spa in 1897 mansion based on Louis XV's Versailles chateau, with manicured gardens, health center, and dining room. 165 Kemble St., Lenox, MA, 800-742-9000, canyonranch.com

Cranwell Resort and Golf Club A castlelike property with stunning views, 18-hole golf course, tennis courts, heated pool, and 380 acres of rolling hills. 55 Lee Rd., Rte. 183, Lenox & Tanglewood, MA, 413-637-1364 / 800-272-6935, cranwell.com

Egremont Inn Slightly less isolated, somewhat larger inn with shops in walking distance. 10 Old Sheffield Rd., South Egremont, MA, 413-528-2111, egremontinn.com

Weathervane Inn Quiet bed and breakfast with great stable houses in the woods. Route 23, South Egremont, MA, 413-528-9580, weathervaneinn.com

Best Restaurants and Nightlife

Bistro Zinc Classic French fare in a cheerful setting. The bar is lively, and generally the place to be at night in Lenox. 56 Church St., Lenox, MA, 413-637-8800

Club Helsinki An intimate club featuring live jazz, blues, soul, rock, and folk. 284 Main St., Great Barrington, MA, 413-528-3394

John Andrews Restaurant Excellent New American fusion cuisine that's Manhattan worthy. Route 23, South Egremont, MA, 413-528-3469, jarestaurant.com

Old Mill 1790s blacksmith shop now serves thoughtfully prepared outdoorsman-friendly entrees. Route 23, South Egremont, MA, 413-528-1421

Swiss Hutte Restaurant and Motel Swiss cuisine in a woodsy inn with spectacular mountain views. Route 23, Hillsdale, NY, 413-528-6200, swisshutte.com

Union Bar Excellent New American cuisine in a hip, cosmopolitan-feeling locale. 293 Main St., Great Barrington, MA, 413-528-6228

Contacts

Berkshire Visitors Bureau berkshires.org
Berkshire Eagle online berkshiresweek.com
The Berkshire Web berkshireweb.com

LEAVING

Getting There: Take Saw Mill River Parkway to Taconic Parkway to Route 23 Exit East. Turn right on Route 23. Follow Route 23 to South Egremont.

90
miles
E

The Hamptons

Hot Tip: Townies live here year round, but "the scene" runs from July 4 to Labor Day.

The Lowdown: The fortune-seeking immigrants who founded the Hamptons' oldest town, Southampton, in 1640, were drawn to the sumptuous grasslands of Long Island's easternmost point, deemed perfect for raising cattle. Today, this collection of interlocked beach communities has become a seasonal stomping ground for Manhattan's wild glitterati. Every summer, the rich and famous flock to the Hamptons, where celebrities, including Howard Stern, Martha Stewart, and Jerry Seinfeld, own multimillion-dollar estates. Many of the city's most prominent nightclub owners also operate hotspots here. Not even in New York can you get more glam than the Hampton's Jet East and the Star Room, which pass the summer months jammed to the hilt with vacationing models and Hollywood celebrities. The Playstation Two House is the home of P. Diddy's annual White Party, the toughest (and most overrated) ticket in town. Because nightlife can get crazy (as in July 2001 when socialite Lizzie Grubman mowed down a crowd of clubbers with her SUV), the days are good for downtime. The Hampton's chronically cute towns offer refuge for shopaholics, who will find plenty of flashy boutiques and antique shops to work out their credit cards. If you have a sundress or a seersucker suit, there's often a polo match to be found in Bridgehampton, where $20 will buy you a bleacher seat (unless you can schmooze your way into one of the invite-only VIP tents). Those without a local beach permit will find accessible sand and water along Montauk's Kirk Park Beach, Southampton's Fowler Beach, and Wainscott's Beach Lane seafront.

Best Attractions

Bridgehampton Polo Club The nation's quintessential polo grounds, hosting some of the world's most prestigious players. 849 Hayground Rd., Bridgehampton, Long Island, 203-661-3344

Fowler Beach Beautiful nonpermit beach with upbeat scene. Site of Gordon Gecko's beach house in the movie *Wall Street*.

Best Hotels

Hunting Inn Quaint 300-year-old inn with comfortable rooms and a romantic country ambience. 94 Main St., East Hampton, 631-324-0410

J. Harper Poor Cottage Bed & Breakfast More elegant mansion than cottage; the best rooms overlook the lovely garden. Room 11 has a two-person whirlpool. 181 Main St., East Hampton, 631-324-4081

The Mill House Inn 18th-century colonial house with gorgeous rooms and a breakfast to die for. 31 North Main St., East Hampton, 631-324-9766, millhouseinn.com

Southampton Bays Hotel located on five acres of landscaped grounds within walking distance of Shinnecock Bay. Includes a private pool and tennis courts. 240 Montauk Hwy., Southampton, 631-283-2406

Best Restaurants and Nightlife

Cabana A Manhattan-like club for the A-plus list. 281 County Rd. 39, Southampton, 631-287-9888

Cain Southampton Club The beachfront outpost to one of Manhattan's chicest nightclubs. This spot's in very high demand—phone first! 1181 N. Sea Rd., Southampton, 631-283-0808

Della Femina Italian fusion hotspot where seeing and being seen is as important as the food itself. 99 N. Main St., East Hampton, 631-329-6666

Jean-Luc A posh and stylish extension to a popular but more traditional Manhattan-based French restaurant. East 103 Montauk Hwy., East Hampton, 631-324-1100

Nick and Toni's A popular celebrity hangout with heavy Americana fare. 136 N. Main St., East Hampton, 631-324-3550

Publick House Widely regarded as one of the country's best beer bars. 40 Bowden Square, Southampton, 631-283-2800

red/bar French-inspired American brasserie with a lively, Manhattan-inspired scene. 210 Hampton Rd., Southampton, 631-283-0704

Star Room A celebrity-driven supper club, with an emphasis on "club." 378 Montauk Hwy., Wainscott, 631-537-3332

Contacts

East Hampton Chamber of Commerce Main St., 631-324-0362
Sag Harbor Chamber of Commerce 631-725-0011

Getting There: With only one road leading to the Hamptons, express trains and buses are the fastest option. However, properties here are all about wide lawns and seclusion, so being here without transportation can be lonely. While car services are available, they're both pricey and in high demand.
By Car: Long Island Expressway (Route 495) east to Exit 70. Make a left onto Route 27, which leads through Southampton and virtually turns into a parking lot on summer Friday afternoons.
By Bus: The Hampton Jitney departs from multiple Third Avenue stops in Manhattan. $47 round trip. 631-283-4600
By Rail: From Penn Station one-way tickets cost $19 during peak hours, $13 otherwise.

LEAVING

Hudson River Valley

Hot Tip: This area's at its best in full bloom. Fall and spring are prime.

The Lowdown: The Hudson River was named after the English seaman Henry Hudson, who'd been hired by a Dutch trading company to find a passage to China. Though it wasn't the shortcut Hudson had hoped for, his "discovery" was responsible for the region's earliest Dutch settlements. During the Revolution, George Washington fought many a battle along the Hudson. A bridge now stands where the great general was forced to cross the river, losing Forts Washington and Lee to the British (fortunately his luck would change). Today, history buffs can visit the sites of these battles and catch blow-by-blow accounts at West Point's renowned military museums. The stretch of the Hudson that once carried prisoners "up the river" to Sing Sing is now the route of comfortable cruisers filled with wine connoisseurs and museumgoers. NY Waterway cruises launch from Pier 78 in Manhattan, at 38th Street and the Hudson River. While the river itself extends 315 miles, it's the 100 miles north of the city that make up the valley. The roadways through the River Valley start at the Statue of Liberty, run the length of Manhattan, past the Cloisters museum, past the Hudson River Museum in Yonkers, beyond *The Legend of Sleepy Hollow* author Washington Irving's Sunnyside estate, and through Ossining, home to Sing Sing prison. (The nearby Caputo Community Center is a museum dedicated to Sing Sing.) There are more than a dozen vineyards along these fertile shores, and many of them offer tours.

Best Attractions

Kykuit the Rockefeller Estate Comprehensive tours are given of this great estate and its stellar art collection. 1 Phillipsburg Manor Visitors Center (off of Route 9), Sleepy Hollow, NY, 914-631-9491

Sunnyside This was the estate of Washington Irving, who penned *The Legend of Sleepy Hollow* and *Rip Van Winkle*. 1 W. Sunnyside Ln. (off Rte. 9), Tarrytown, NY, 914-591-8763

Vanderbilt Mansion A 54-room mansion that typifies the aristocratic lifestyle of one of America's wealthiest families. 519 Albany Post Rd., Hyde Park, NY, 914-229-9115, nps.gov/vama

West Point America's most prestigious military institution offers tours and has a museum. Garrison Commander Bldg. 681, U.S. Military Academy, West Point, NY, 845-938-2638

Best Hotels

The Castle on the Hudson This sprawling, regal resort overlooking the Hudson is a favorite of dignitaries and celebrities. 400 Benedict Ave., Tarrytown, NY, 914-631-1980, castleattarrytown.com

Renaissance Westchester Hotel A modern Mariott hotel on 30 acres of countryside. 80 W. Red Oak Ln., White Plains, NY, 914-694-5400, marriott.com

The Thayer Hotel A luxury hotel located on the grounds of West Point U.S. Military Academy. 674 Thayer Rd., West Point, 845-446-4731, thethayerhotel.com

Best Restaurants

Blue Hill at Stone Barns Owned by successful Manhattan restaurateurs, Blue Hill's country cuisine comes from regional farms and dairies. 630 Bedford Rd., Pocantico Hills, NY, 914-366-9600

Buffet de la Gare Wildly popular eatery that is as fashionable as it is foodie. 155 Southside Ave., Hastings-on-Hudson, NY, 914-478-1671

Le Canard-Enchainé Classic French restaurant thought by many to be the best this side of Manhattan. 276 Fair St., Kingston, NY, 845-339-2003

Crabtree's Kittle House A top destination restaurant in the area, with live blues and jazz on weekends. 11 Kittle Rd., Chappaqua, NY, 914-666-8044, kittlehouse.com

Guida's Upscale Italian eatery literally on Main Street. Near Sleepy Hollow and Sing Sing. 199 Main St. (Rte. 9), Ossining, NY, 914-941-2662

Harvest-on-Hudson Italian nouvelle cuisine with views overlooking lovely private gardens and the river. 1 River St., Hastings, NY, 914-478-2800

Horsefeathers Cozy townie eatery with outdoor dining. 94 N. Broadway, Tarrytown, NY, 914-631-6606

Xaviar's at Piermont Prix fixe menu of fusion cuisine that has garnered top food ratings five years in a row. 673 Croton Heights Rd., Yorktown, NY, 914-962-4090, prattsinn.com

Contacts

Historic Hudson Valley 150 White Plains Rd., Tarrytown, NY, 914-631-8200, hudsonvalley.org

Getting There: Take Henry Hudson Parkway North into Saw Mill River Parkway. Take Exit 21 West onto Route 119, which runs through most of the valley.

The Jersey Shore

Hot Tip: The ocean takes a while to heat up, but it does hold the warmth well. July and August are best for swimming and crowd-watching.

The Lowdown: As much as Manhattanites complain about the weekend influx of New Jersey residents, they don't seem to feel any guilt about flooding the Jersey Shore when summer rolls around. Rock 'n' rollers will want to make a stop in Asbury Park to catch a band or two at the Stone Pony, aka the house that "Bruce" built. For a more relaxing time, beachgoers find sun and surf on the coasts of Matawan—the beach town where a series of 1916 great white shark attacks inspired Peter Benchley's *Jaws*. Like the rest of the Jersey shore, Matawan's waters are very safe and the fish stories are simply folklore. Starting just below Atlantic City in a suburban town called Margate, the Jersey Shore spans roughly 100 miles down to the Victorian-era resort town of Cape May. With its bustling nightclubs and amusement parks, Wildwood might be the most exciting town along the Jersey shore. In addition to the 35 rides in Wildwood's Mariner's Landing is the East Coast's largest Ferris wheel, and slightly south at Morey's Adventure Pier is the country's only wooden roller coaster built on a pier. How's that for terrifying? Those who'd prefer to control their own destiny can find peace and tranquility at Cape May—the shore's southernmost point.

Best Attractions

Aqua Trails Kayak nature tours of the saltland marshes inland from Cape May. "Mainstream" tours from May to September. Also offers sunset and full moon tours. 956 Ocean Dr., Cape May, NJ, 609-884-5600, aquatrails.com

Morey's Adventure Huge seaside amusement park chain, 90 rides, two water parks, and more. Mariner's Landing is probably the most exciting of the bunch. Pier 3501, Boardwalk, Mariner's Landing, Wildwood, NJ, 609-522-3900, moreyspiers.com

Stone Pony Jersey's most storied rock venue—the house that "Bruce" built. 913 Ocean Ave., Asbury Park, NJ, 732-502-0600, stoneponyonline.com

Best Hotels

Harbor Mist Across Jersey's Ninth Street bridge, on the dry island of Wildwood (no alcohol), this hotel is just off the 5-mile exercise course that surrounds the mini land mass. 511 E. 11th Ave., North Wildwood, 877-517-2022, harbormistmotel.com

Ocean Place Resort & Spa European-style luxury spa overlooking the Jersey shore. 1 Ocean Blvd., Long Branch, 800-411-6493, oceanplaceresort.com

The Queen Victoria Bed and Breakfast Beautiful Victorian-style Cape May B&B near the ocean. Tea in the afternoon. 102 Ocean St., Cape May, 609-884-8702, queenvictoria.com

The Virginia Hotel Newly renovated 1879 boutique hotel in Cape May's historic district. 25 Jackson St., Cape May, 800-732-4236, virginiahotel.com

Best Restaurants and Nightlife

The Ark Pub & Eatery A friendly wood-on-wood-on-wood seaside pub with a few TVs, lots of locals, and mature tourists. 401 Sea Ave. (Rte. 35 N.), Point Pleasant, 732-295-1122

Buona Sera Ristorante World-class Venetian cuisine in an elegant setting with open kitchen and antique bar. 50 Maple Ave., Red Bank, NJ, 732-530-5858, buona-sera.com

Headliner For better or worse, this is Jersey Shore nightlife at its most postcollegiate. Think Jimmy Buffet meets Bon Jovi, with a sports-bar edge—that is, volleyball and margaritas. 1401 Hwy. 35, Neptune, 732-775-6200, theheadliner.com

Joe & Maggie's Bistro on Broadway Popular and fun eatery with creative international fare. 591 Broadway, Long Branch, 732-571-8848, joeandmaggiesbistro.com

Lobster House Restaurant & Bar Slightly touristy, but comfortable seafood restaurant with excellent lobster. Fishermans' Wharf, Cape May, 609-884-8296, thelobsterhouse.com

Neil's Steak & Chowder House Fresh seafood and well-prepared cuts in an informal beachfront setting. Neighborhood favorite. 222 E. Schellenger Ave., Wildwood, 609-522-5226

Contacts

Chamber of Commerce of Greater Cape May 609-884-5508
Margate City Hall 609-822-5438
Matawan Chamber of Commerce 732-290-1125
Wildwood Chamber of Commerce 609-729-4000

Getting There: Take the I-95 south. Merge onto the New Jersey Turnpike and follow to exit 11, the Garden State Parkway. Exit Lafayette Street/Cr-633 south to Ocean Street in Cape May, NJ.

Fire Island

Hot Tip: Get a jump on the summer crowd by coming in June, as the hordes here aim for July and August. Most of the island closes down in the winter.

The Lowdown: Accessible only by boat, this spirited island is almost completely automobile-free, which means centralized activities for partygoers and serene escapes for tranquility seekers. Extremely informal, few of Fire Island's restaurants have a shoes-or-shirt policy, and the laid-back approach to service has a Caribbean feel (no doormen). On weekends, an upscale collection of Manhattanites packs Ocean Beach's restaurants and nightclubs, creating the perfect amalgamation of cosmopolitan savoir faire and island ease. Fire Island is largely about eating and drinking, but it's also a popular recreational spot for water jocks and nature buffs. The Sunken Forest's 40 acres of dunes, swamps, marshlands, and twisted overhead canopies make for rewarding hikes and exceptional bird watching—there are more than 300 species on the island.

Best Attractions

Atlantique, Point O' Woods, Smith Point, and Cherry Grove Surfing and sunning are great in these coastal areas. 877-386-6654, funonli.com

Sailor's Haven Visitor's center with 1/2-mile boardwalk that cuts through the 40-acre maritime forest. (Sunken Forest) Middle of the Island, 631-597-6183

Best Restaurants

The Dock Good, creative seafood restaurant for watching the sunset before dancing on the seashore. 60 Bay Walk, Fair Harbor, NY, 631-583-5200

The Hideaway American beach cuisine served indoors and outdoors to a relatively sedate crowd. Houser Hotel, 785 Evergreen Walk, Ocean Beach, NY, 631-583-8900

Maguire's Bay Front Restaurant Big on burgers, fun, and square footage, Maguire's is one of Fire Island's more popular meeting places. The nightlife scene takes place outdoors. 1 Bay Walk, Ocean Beach, NY, 631-583-8800

Contacts

Fire Island Chamber Association 631-583-5069
Fire Island Ferries 631-666-3600

Getting There: The total trip takes about two hours, and that includes the 25-minute ferry ride. From Manhattan, take the Long Island Expressway to Exit 53 (Bay Shore) and park near the harbor.
By Train: The Long Island Rail Road runs from Penn Station to Bay Shore, Sayville, and Patchogue, the three harbors that run ferries to Fire Island. The trains start running at 6:36am during the week and 7:15am on weekends.

33 miles E

Jones Beach

Hot Tip: July and August are best for beach-going. June to September are the prime concert months.

The Lowdown: "Water, water everywhere but not a place to swim." Yes, Manhattan is an island, but due to pollution and general ickiness, you'd need a machete to part its murky waters. Happily, Jones Beach, New York City's answer to *Baywatch*, is just a short trip away. Sun-seeking urbanites flock to the sand and waves in droves during the sweatiest summer months, where swimmers can choose between two pools, a mellow bay, and 6.5 miles of ocean beach. If that's not reason enough to make the quick 33-mile jaunt down the Meadowbrook Parkway, Jones Beach State Park is also host to one of the best music venues in New York, an oceanside amphitheater that seats 15,200 fans. It's a great place to catch the Blue Angels in May, but the Tommy Hilfiger Jones Beach Theater is best known for its summer-night music shows. Not only do artists such as David Bowie, Cheap Trick, Snoop Dogg, and No Doubt regularly rock the place out, it's the home of Ozzfest, Kid Rock's "Dysfunctional Family Picnic," Lollapalooza, and other big festivals that should never breach city limits. Beachgoers can pack picnics, eat in the Boardwalk restaurant, or pig out at the many fast-food options. The paid parking lots closest to the beach go fast in the summer, so get there early or be prepared to hoof it.

Best Attractions

Tommy Hilfiger Jones Beach Theater One of the area's biggest concert venues. 516-221-1000

Contacts

Jones Beach State Park 516-785-1600, jonesbeach.com

Getting There: Take the Brooklyn Bridge to the Brooklyn-Queens Expressway and continue east to the Meadowbrook Parkway South. The Meadowbrook Parkway leads straight to the beach.

LEAVING

The Poconos

Hot Tip: Campers should come in June and July, while skiers will prefer December-February.

The Lowdown: Just 90-miles from New York City lies western Pennsylvania's historic Poconos. Over 2,400 square miles of rock, woods, rivers, and waterfalls surround the towns along this mountain range, once occupied by the native Iroquois, Shawne, Minisink, Lenape and Paupack nations. The Pocono mountain natives were first joined by Dutch settlers who pitched camp here in 1659, and later by the English who "discovered" the area in 1664. Within the Poconos' 72,000 acres of state forests lie 7 state parks where visiting landlubbers will run out of daylight long before they run out of real estate. For water-seekers, the Poconos has 150 lakes, the main attraction being Lake Wallenpaupack, with 52-miles of shoreline to offer swimmers, paddlers, and fishermen. Whitewater adventurers will keep busy with the 170 river miles running through these parts. The Poconos are in full operation year-round, with winter temperatures generally hovering around the freezing mark, and the summer climate around 80 degrees.

Best Attractions

CamelBack Ski Area The Poconos largest skiing area, with 33 slopes, 13 lifts, and wait times rarely exceeding 20 minutes. There's a water park here in the summer. Tannersville, PA, 570-629-1661

Glen Brook Golf Club Designed in 1924 by first-ever PGA president, Robert White, Glen Brook's 6,500 yards are hilly, woodsy, and as good for a game as they are for a leisurely stroll. Glen Brook Rd., Stroudsburg, PA, 570-421-3680

Best Restaurants and Nightlife

The Crescent Lodge Combines a woodsy cabin aesthetic with Jacuzzis and a central locale. Also holds one of the area's better restaurants and pubs, complete with piano player. Paradise Valley, Cresco, PA, 570-595-7486

The Inn at Jim Thorpe A quaint town just outside the primary resort area, this town was dubbed "America's Little Switzerland" by the Swiss Tourist Board. This 1840s era lodge has hosted its share of Americans, including Ulysses S. Grant, President William Taft, Thomas Edison, and John. D. Rockefeller. 24 Broadway, Jim Thorpe, PA, 800-329-2599

Contacts

Poconos Mountains Vacation Bureau 1004 Main St., Stroudsburg, PA, 570-476-8959

Getting There: From the New Jersey City Turnpike merge onto I-280 west. Exit onto I-80 and go west to PA-191/Broad Street. Turn left onto Main St..

NEW YORK BLACK BOOK

You're solo in the city–where's a singles-friendly place to eat? Is there a good lunch spot near the museum? Will the bar be too loud for easy conversation? Get the answers fast in the *Black Book*, a condensed version of every listing in our guide that puts all the essential information at your fingertips.

A quick glance down the page and you'll find the type of food, nightlife, or attractions you are looking for, the phone numbers, and which pages to turn to for more detailed information. How did you ever survive without this?

New York Black Book By Neighborhood

Code: H-Hotels; R-Restaurants; N-Nightlife; A-Attractions
Blue page numbers denote listings in 99 Best, black denotes listings in Experience section.
Venues followed by an * are those we recommend as both a restaurant and a destination bar.

BLACK BOOK

Notes

New York Black Book

Hotels

NAME TYPE (ROOMS)	ADDRESS (CROSS STREET) WEBSITE	AREA PRICE	PHONE 800 NUMBER	EXPERIENCE	PAGE
Blue Moon Hotel Timeless (22)	100 Orchard St. (Broome St.) bluemoon-nyc.com	LE $$$$	212-533-9080	Original	117
Bryant Park Hotel Trendy (130)	40 W. 40th St. (5th Ave.) bryantparkhotel.com	MT $$$	212-869-0100	Cool	88
The Carlyle Timeless (179)	35 E. 76th St. (Madison Ave.) thecarlyle.com	UE $$$$$	212-744-1600 888-767-3966	Classic	141
Chambers—A Hotel Modern (77)	15 W. 56th St. (5th Ave.) chambershotel.com	MT $$$	212-974-5656 866-613-9330	Hot	57
Dream Hotel Trendy (220)	210 W. 55th St. (7th Ave.) dreamny.com	MT $$$$	212-247-2000	Cool	88
Dylan Hotel Trendy (107)	52 E. 41st St. (Madison Ave.) dylanhotel.com	MH $$$	212-338-0500	Original	117
Essex House Timeless (601)	160 Central Park S. (6th Ave.) essexhouse.com	MT $$$$$	212-247-0300 800-937-8461	Classic	141
Four Seasons Hotel NY Timeless (368)	57 E. 57th St. (5th Ave.) fourseasons.com	MT $$$$$	212-758-5700 800-819-5053	Hot	57
Hotel Gansevoort Trendy (187)	18 9th Ave. (13th St.) hotelgansevoort.com	MP $$$$	212-206-6700 877-426-7386	Hot	57
Hotel on Rivington Trendy (110)	107 Rivington St. (Ludlow St.) hotelonrivington.com	LE $$$$	212-475-2600 800-915-1537	Original	117
Hôtel Plaza Athénée Timeless (150)	37 E. 64th St. (Madison Ave.) plaza-athenee.com	UE $$$$$	212-734-9100 800-447-8800	Classic	141
Hotel QT Modern (140)	125 W. 45th St. (Broadway) hotelqt.com	MT $$$	212-354-2323	Original	118
Hotel Roger Williams Trendy (191)	131 Madison Ave. (31st St.) hotelrogerwilliams.com	MH $$$	212-448-7000	Original	118
Hudson Hotel Trendy (1000)	356 W. 58th St. (9th Ave.) hudsonhotel.com	MT $$$	212-554-6000 800-606-6090	Cool	88
The Lowell Timeless (70)	28 E. 63rd St. (Madison Ave.) lowellhotel.com	UE $$$$$	212-838-1400 800-221-4444	Cool	89
Mandarin Oriental Modern (251)	80 Columbus Cir. (W. 60th St.) mandarinoriental.com	UW $$$$$	212-805-8800 866-801-8880	Hot	58

Neighborhood (Area) Key

CH = Chelsea	MH = Murray Hill	UW = Upper West Side
EV = East Village	MP = Meatpacking District	WM = Williamsburg
FL = Flatiron	MT = Midtown	WS = Wall Street
GR = Gramercy	SH = Soho	WV = West Village
GV = Greenwich Village	TR = Tribeca	VA = Various
LE = Lower East Side	UE = Upper East Side	

BLACK BOOK

Hotels (cont.)

NAME TYPE (ROOMS)	ADDRESS (CROSS STREET) WEBSITE	AREA PRICE	PHONE 800 NUMBER	EXPERIENCE	PAGE
The Maritime Hotel Trendy (125)	363 W. 16th St. (9th Ave.) themaritimehotel.com	CH $$$	212-242-4300	Cool	89
The Mercer Hotel Trendy (75)	147 Mercer St. (Prince St.) mercerhotel.com	SH $$$$	212-966-6060	Hot	58
The Muse Hotel Modern (200)	130 W. 46th St. (Broadway) themusehotel.com	MT $$$	212-485-2400 877-692-6873	Original	118
Paramount Hotel NY Trendy (592)	235 W. 46th St. (7th Ave.) paramountnewyork.solmelia.com	MT $$	212-764-5500 888-956-3542	Cool	89
The Peninsula New York Timeless (239)	700 5th Ave. (55th St.) newyork.peninsula.com	MT $$$$$	212-956-2888 800-262-9467	Classic	142
The Ritz-Carlton NY, BP Timeless (298)	2 West St. (West Side Hwy.) ritzcarlton.com	TR $$$$$	212-344-0800 800-241-3333	Classic	142
The Ritz-Carlton NY, CP Timeless (261)	50 Central Park S. (5th Ave.) ritzcarlton.com	MT $$$$$	212-308-9100 800-241-3333	Classic	142
Royalton Hotel Trendy (205)	44 W. 44th St. (6th Ave.) royaltonhotel.com	MT $$$	212-869-4400 800-697-1791	Cool	90
60 Thompson Trendy (98)	60 Thompson St. (Broome St.) 60thompson.com	SH $$$$	212-431-0400 877-431-0400	Hot	58
Soho Grand Trendy (363)	310 W. Broadway (Grand St.) sohogrand.com	SH $$$$$	212-965-3000	Hot	59
Soho House Trendy (24)	29-35 9th Ave. (13th St.) sohohouseny.com	SH $$$$	212-627-9800	Cool	90
The St. Regis Timeless (300)	2 E. 55th St. (5th Ave.) stregis.com	MT $$$$$	212-753-4500	Classic	143
Tribeca Grand Hotel Trendy (203)	2 6th Ave. (White St.) tribecagrand.com	TR $$$	212-519-6600 877-519-6600	Hot	59
W New York Modern (688)	541 Lexington Ave. (49th St.) whotels.com	MT $$$$	212-755-1200 888-625-5144	Cool	90
W New York—Union Square Modern (270)	201 Park Ave. S (E. 17th St.) whotels.com	GR $$$$	212-253-9119 888-625-5144	Hot	59

Restaurant and Nightlife Symbols

Restaurants
Singles Friendly (eat and/or meet)
▯ = Communal table
Ⓧ = Bar scene
▯ = Limited bar menu
Ⓕ = Full menu served at bar
(G) = Gourmet Destination

Nightlife
Price Warning
Ⓒ = Cover or ticket charge
Food served at bar or club
▯ = Limited bar menu
Ⓕ = Full menu served at bar

Restaurant + Nightlife
Prime time noise levels
— = Quiet
= = A buzz, but still conversational
≡ = Loud

Venues followed by an * are those we recommend as both a restaurant and a destination bar.

Note regarding page numbers: *Italic* = itinerary listing; Roman = description in Experience section listing.

Restaurants

NAME / TYPE	ADDRESS (CROSS STREET) / WEBSITE	AREA / PRICE	PHONE / SINGLES/NOISE	EXPERIENCE / 99 BEST	PAGE / PAGE
Anytime / Diner	93 N. 6th St. (Wythe St.) / anytimeny.com	WM / $	718-218-7272	Original	113, 119
Artisanal / French	2 Park Ave. (32nd St.) / artisanalcheese.com	MH / $$	212-775-8585	Classic	144
Asia de Cuba* / Asian-Cuban	237 Madison Ave. (38th St.) / chinagrillmanagement.com	MH / $$$	212-726-7755	Cool	91
Aureole / New American (G)	34 E. 61st St. (Park Ave.) / charliepalmer.com	UE / $$$$	212-319-1660	Classic	138, 144
B Bar and Grill* / Seafood	40 E. 4th St. (Bowery) / bbarandgrill.com	GV / $	212-475-2220	Cool	91
B.E.D. NY* / New American	530 W. 27th St. (9th Ave.) / bedny.com	CH / $$$	212-594-4109	Hot / Of-the-Moment	52, 60 / 34
Babbo / Italian (G)	110 Waverly Pl. (MacDougal St.) / babbonyc.com	GV / $$	212-777-0303	Hot	60
Balthazar* / French	80 Spring St. (Crosby St.) / balthazarny.com	SH / $$	212-965-1785	Cool / Always-Trendy	84, 91 / 17
Barça 18 / Spanish	225 Park Ave. S. (18th St.) / brguestrestaurants.com	GR / $$	212-533-2500	Cool	91
Bette / New American	461 W. 23rd St. (10th Ave.)	CH / $$	212-366-0404	Hot	54, 60
BiCE Ristorante / Italian	7 E. 54th St. (5th Ave.) / bicenewyork.com	MT / $$$	212-688-1999	Hot	53, 60
The Biltmore Room* / Asian Fusion	290 8th Ave. (25th St.) / thebiltmoreroom.com	CH / $$$	212-807-0111	Cool / Informal Upscale	83, 92 / 31
BLT Fish / Seafood	21 W. 17th St. (6th Ave.) / bltfish.com	FL / $$$	212-691-8888	Cool	81, 92
BLT Steak / Steak House	106 E. 57th St. (Park Ave.) / bltsteak.com	MT / $$$	212-752-7470	Cool	92
Blue Fin* / Seafood	1567 Broadway (47th St.) / brguestrestaurants.com	MT / $$$	212-918-1400	Classic	137, 144
Blue Mill Tavern / American	50 Commerce St. (Barrow St.)	WV / $$	212-352-0009	Classic	144
Blue Ribbon Sushi / Sushi	119 Sullivan St. (Spring St.) / blueribbonrestaurants.com	SH / $$$	212-343-0404	Hot / Sushi	60 / 45
Blue Water Grill* / Seafood	31 Union Sq. W. (16th St.) / brguestrestaurants.com	FL / $$	212-675-9500	Cool	83, 92
BondSt* / Sushi	6 Bond St. (Broadway)	GV / $$	212-777-2500	Cool / Restaurant Lounges	82, 92 / 40
Boom / New American	152 Spring St. (Wooster St.)	SH / $$	212-431-3663	Cool	82, 93
Brasserie / Brasserie	100 East 53rd St. (Park Ave.) / rapatina.com/brasserie/	MT / $$	212-751-4840	Cool	93
Brasserie 8½ / French	9 W. 57th St. (6th Ave.) / rapatina.com/brasserie8/	MT / $$$	212-829-0812	Cool	93

Restaurants (cont.)

NAME / TYPE	ADDRESS (CROSS STREET) / WEBSITE	AREA PRICE	PHONE SINGLES/NOISE	EXPERIENCE 99 BEST	PAGE PAGE
Bread Bar @ Tabla* Indian Fusion	11 Madison Ave. (25th St.) tablanyc.com	GR $	212-889-0667 ⓨF ═	Hot Informal Upscale	61 31
Bridge Café Seafood	279 Water St. (Dover St.) eatgoodinny.com	WS $$	212-227-3344 F ▭	Classic	138, 145
Bryant Park Grill American	25 W. 40th St. (5th St.) arkrestaurants.com	MT $$	212-840-6500 B ═	Cool	81, 93
Café Boulud French	20 E. 76th St. (Madison Ave.) danielnyc.com/cafeboulud	UE $$$	212-772-2600 - ▭	Hot	61
Café Gray New American/French	10 Columbus Cir. (58th St.) cafegray.com	UW $$$	212-823-6338 - ▭	Classic	135, 145
Café St. Bart's New American	109 E. 50th St. (Park Ave. S.) cafestbarts.com	MT $$$	212-888-2664 ▭	Cool	82, 94
Cafe 2 (MoMA) Italian	11 W. 53rd St. (6th Ave.) moma.org/visit_moma/restaurants	MT $	212-708-9400 - ═	Hot	53, 61
Cafeteria New American	119 7th Ave. (17th St.)	CH $	212-414-1717 F ═	Cool All-Night	83, 94 16
Candela International	116 E. 16th St. (Irving Pl.) candelarestaurant.com	GR $$	212-254-1600 B ═	Cool	94
The Carlyle Restaurant French	35 E. 76th St. (Madison Ave.) thecarlyle.com	UE $$$	212-744-1600 - ▭	Classic	145
Carmine's Italian	200 W. 44th St. (Broadway) carminesnyc.com	MT $$	212-221-3800 - ═	Classic	137, 145
Carnegie Deli Deli	854 7th Ave. (55th St.) carnegiedeli.com	MT $$	212-757-2245 ◎ ═	Classic Delis	137, 145 25
Chow Bar* Asian	230 W. 4th St. (W. 10th St.)	WV $$	212-633-2212 ⓨF ═	Hot	61
Churrascaria Plataforma Brazilian	316 W. 49th St. (9th Ave.) churrascariaplataforma.com	MT $$	212-245-0505 - ═	Cool Steak Houses	84, 94 44
Ciao Bella Dessert	285 Mott St. (Prince St.) ciaobellagelato.com	SH $-	212-431-3591 - ▭	Hot	61
Cipriani Downtown* Italian	376 W. Broadway (Broome St.) cipriani.com	SH $$	212-343-0999 ⓨF ═	Cool Always-Trendy	83, 94 17
Corner Bistro* American	331 W. 4th St. (Jane St.) cornerbistro.citysearch.com	WV $-	212-242-9502 ⓨF ═	Classic	146
Craft New American (G)	43 E. 19th St. (Park Ave. S.) craftrestaurant.com	GR $$$	212-780-0880 B ═	Cool	95
Cru* Mediterranean	24 5th Ave. (9th St.) cru-nyc.com	GV $$$	212-529-1700 ⓨB◎ ▭	Classic	136, 146
Cupping Room Café* Café	359 W. Broadway (Broome St.) cuppingroomcafe.com	SH $$	212-925-2898 ⓨB ═	Hot	62
Daniel French (G)	60 E. 65th St. (Park Ave.) danielnyc.com	UE $$$$	212-288-0033 - ▭	Classic	146
davidburke & donatella New American	133 E. 61st St. (Park Ave.) dbdrestaurant.com	UE $$$$	212-813-2121 - ═	Hot	62

NAME TYPE	ADDRESS (CROSS STREET) WEBSITE	AREA PRICE	PHONE SINGLES/NOISE	EXPERIENCE 99 BEST	PAGE PAGE
DB Bistro Moderne French	55 W. 44th St. (6th Ave.) danielnyc.com	MT $$	212-391-2400 F⬭ ≡	Cool	95
Delmonico's Steak House	56 Beaver St. (Pearl St.) delmonicosny.com	WS $$$	212-509-1144 F ≡	Classic Power Lunches	146 39
Diner* Diner	85 Broadway (Berry St.) dinernyc.com	WM $	718-486-3077 ⬭F ≡	Original	114, 119
Diner 24 New American	102 8th Ave. (W. 15th St.)	CH $	212-242-7773 F ≡	Original All-Night	112, 119 16
Dos Caminos Soho Mexican	475 W. Broadway (Houston St.) brguestrestaurants.com	SH $$	212-277-4300 F ≡	Cool	83, 95
Dylan Prime* Steak House	62 Laight St. (Greenwich St.) dylanprime.com	TR $$$	212-334-4783 ⬭B ≡	Hot Steak Houses	62 44
E.A.T. Deli	1064 Madison (80th St.) elizabar.com	UE $	- ≡	Delis	62 25
El Parador Café Mexican	325 E. 34th St. (2nd Ave.) elparadorcafe.com	MH $$	212-679-6812 F ⬭	Classic	146
The Elephant French-Asian	58 E. 1st St. (1st Ave.) elephantrestaurant.com	EV $	212-505-7739 F ≡	Original	112, 119
Ess-a-Bagel Deli	359 1st Ave. (22nd St.) ess-a-bagel.com	GR $-	212-260-2252 - ≡	Cool Bagels	95 19
Estiatorio Milos Greek (G)	125 W. 55th St. (6th Ave.) milos.ca	MT $$$$	212-245-7400 B ≡	Cool	84, 95
Félix French Bistro	340 W. Broadway (Grand St.) felixnyc.com	SH $$	212-431-0021 B ≡	Cool French Bistros	96 27
Five Points Mediterranean	31 Great Jones St. (Lafayette St.) fivepointsrestaurant.com	GV $$	212-253-5700 F ≡	Original Informal Upscale	113, 119 31
Fornino Pizzeria	187 Bedford Ave. (N. 6th St.)	WM $	718-384-6004 - ≡	Original	120
The Four Seasons* New American (G)	99 E. 52nd St. (Park Ave.) fourseasonsrestaurant.com	MT $$$$	212-754-9494 ⬭B ≡	Classic Power Lunches	147 39
Fraunces Tavern* American	54 Pearl St. (Broad St.) fraunestavern.com	WS $$	212-968-1776 ⬭F ≡	Classic	147
Fred's at Barneys NY American	660 Madison Ave., 9th Fl. (60th St.) barneys.com	UE $$$	212-833-2200 - ≡	Hot	52, 62
Frederick's Madison French	768 Madison Ave. (66th St.) fredericksnyc.com	UE $$$	212-737-7300 - ≡	Hot	53, 63
French Roast French	78 W. 11th St. (6th Ave.) tourdefrancenyc.com	GV $$	212-533-2233 F ≡	Hot All-Night	53, 63 16
Gotham Bar and Grill New American (G)	12 E. 12th St. (5th Ave.) gothambarandgrill.com	GV $$$	212-620-4020 B ⬭	Hot	54, 63
Gramercy Tavern* New American (G)	42 E. 20th St. (Park Ave.) gramercytavern.com	GR $$$$	212-477-0777 ⬭F ≡	Hot	54, 63
Great Jones Café Cajun	54 Great Jones St. (Bowery) greatjones.com	EV $$	212-674-9304 F ≡	Original	113, 120

Restaurants (cont.)

NAME / TYPE	ADDRESS (CROSS STREET) / WEBSITE	AREA PRICE	PHONE SINGLES/NOISE	EXPERIENCE 99 BEST	PAGE PAGE
Grotta Azzurra Restaurant Italian	177 Mulberry St. (Broome St.) grottaazzurrany.com	SH $$	212-925-8775 F ⊟	Classic	147
H&H Bagels Deli	2239 Broadway (80th St.) handhbagel.com	VA $-	212-595-8003 - ≡	Bagels	19
Harry Cipriani Italian	781 5th Ave. (59th St.) cipriani.com	MT $$$$	212-753-5566 - ⊟	Cool Chic Restaurants	96 20
Horus Café* Mediterranean	93 Ave. B (6th St.) horuscafe.com	EV $	212-777-9199 ΥF ≡	Original	120
Hudson Cafeteria American	356 W. 58th St. (8th St.) hudsonhotel.com	MT $	212-554-6500 ⛾ ≡	Cool	96
Il Mulino Italian (G)	86 W. 3rd St. (Sullivan St.) ilmulinonewyork.com	GV $$$	212-673-3783 - ⊟	Classic	138, 147
Indochine* French-Asian	430 Lafayette St. (4th St.) indochinenyc.com	GV $$	212-505-5111 ΥF ≡	Cool Asian Dining	96 18
Jean-Georges French (G)	1 Central Park W. (60th St.) jean-georges.com	UW $$$$	212-299-3900 - ⊟	Classic	138, 147
Joe Allen New American	326 W. 46th St. (8th Ave.) joeallenrestaurant.com	MT $$	212-581-6464 - ≡	Classic	137, 148
John's of Bleecker Street Pizzeria	278 Bleecker St. (Jones St.) johnsofbleeckerstreet.com	WV $$	212-243-1680 - ≡	Original Pizza	120 38
Katz's Delicatessen Deli	205 E. Houston St. (Ludlow St.) katzdeli.com	LE $-	212-254-2246 ⛾ ≡	Original Delis	112, 121 25
Kittichai Thai	60 Thompson St. (Spring St.) kittichairestaurant.com	SH $$	212-219-2000 - ≡	Hot Asian Dining	54, 64 18
Koi Japanese	40 W. 40th St. (6th Ave.) koirestaurant.com	MT $$$	212-921-3330 B ≡	Hot	64
La Bottega Italian	363 W. 16th St. (9th St.) themaritimehotel.com/bottega.html	CH $	212-242-4300 - ≡	Cool	96
La Goulue French	746 Madison Ave. (E. 64th St.) lagouluerestaurant.com	UE $$$	212-988-8169 - ≡	Hot	51, 64
Le Bernardin Seafood (G)	155 W. 51st St. (6th Ave.) le-bernardin.com	UE $$$$	212-554-1515 - ⊟	Hot	64
Le Bilboquet French Bistro	25 E 63rd St. (Madison Ave.)	UE $$	212-751-3036 - ≡	Hot French Bistros	53, 64 27
Les Enfants Terribles French-African	37 Canal St. (Ludlow St.) lesenfantsterriblesnyc.com	TR $	212-777-7518 B ≡	Hot	65
Lever House New American	390 Park Ave. (53rd St.) leverhouse.com	MT $$$	212-888-2700 B ≡	Hot Chic Restaurants	54, 65 20
Lil' Frankie's Pizza* Pizzeria	19 1st Ave. (1st St.) lilfrankies.com	EV $	212-420-4900 ΥF ≡	Original	114, 121
Lombardi's Pizzeria	32 Spring St. (Mott St.) lombardispizza.com	SH $	212-941-7994 F ≡	Classic Pizza	148 38
Lucien French Bistro	14 1st Ave. (1st St.) luciennyc.com	EV $$	212-260-6481 FⅡ ≡	Original	114, 121

NAME TYPE	ADDRESS (CROSS STREET) WEBSITE	AREA PRICE	PHONE SINGLES/NOISE	EXPERIENCE 99 BEST	PAGE PAGE
Ludo* Middle Eastern	42 E. 1st St. (2nd Ave.) ludonyc.com	EV $$	212-777-5617	Original	112, 121
Lure Fishbar* Seafood	142 Mercer St. (Prince St.) lurefishbar.com	SH $$$	212-431-7676	Cool Of-The-Moment	82, 97 34
Magnolia Bakery Bakery	401 Bleecker St. (11th St.)	WV $	212-462-2572	Classic	148
March Restaurant New American (G)	405 E. 58th St. (1st Ave.) marchrestaurant.com	MT $$$	212-754-6272	Classic	148
Mas French	39 Downing St. (Bedford St.)	WV $$$	212-255-1790	Classic	148
Matsuri Japanese	363 W. 16th St. (9th St.) themaritimehotel.com/matsuri	CH $$	212-242-4300	Cool	97
Megu* Japanese	62 Thomas St. (Church St.) megunyc.com	TR $$$$	212-964-7777	Hot Asian Dining	65 18
Mercer Kitchen Mediterranean	99 Prince St. (Mercer St.) jean-georges.com	SH $$	212-966-5454	Cool	97
The Modern* New American/French	9 W. 53rd St. (5th Ave.) themodernnyc.com	MT $$$	212-333-1220	Hot	53, 65
Mr. Chow Chinese	324 E. 57th St. (2nd Ave.) mrchow.com	MT $$$	212-751-9030	Hot Chic Restaurants	53, 65 20
Murray's Bagels Deli	500 6th Ave. (13th St.) murraysbagels.com	GV $-	212-462-2830	Classic Bagels	149 19
Nobu Sushi (G)	105 Hudson St. (Franklin St.) myriadrestaurantgroup.com	TR $$$	212-219-0500	Classic Sushi	136, 149 45
North Square Restaurant New American	103 Waverly Pl. (W. 7th St.) northsquareny.com	GV $$	212-254-1200	Classic	149
Olives* Mediterranean	201 Park Ave. S. (17th St.) toddenglish.com	GR $$	212-353-8345	Cool	83, 97
One if by Land, Two if by Sea New American	17 Barrow St. (W. 4th St.) oneifbyland.com	WV $$$	212-255-8649	Classic	136, 149
Ono Asian Fusion	18 9th Ave. (13th St.) hotelgansevoort.com	MP $	212-660-6766	Hot	52, 66
Orsay Brasserie	1057 Lexington Ave. (E. 75th St.) orsayrestaurant.com	UE $$$	212-517-6400	Hot	54, 66
Otto* Pizzeria	1 5th Ave. (8th St.) ottopizzeria.com	GV $	212-995-9559	Cool Pizza	98 38
The Palm Steak House	837 2nd Ave. (45th St.) thepalm.com	MT $$$	212-687-2953	Classic Power Lunches	149 39
The Park* New American	118 10th Ave. (17th St.) theparknyc.com	CH $$	212-352-3313	Hot	54, 66
Pastis French Bistro	9 9th Ave. (Little W. 12th St.) pastisny.com	MP $$	212-929-4844	Hot French Bistros	53, 66 27
The Patio* American	47th St. (1st Ave.) thepationyc.com	MT $$$	917-446-0018	Classic	150

Restaurants (cont.)

NAME / TYPE	ADDRESS (CROSS STREET) / WEBSITE	AREA PRICE	PHONE SINGLES/NOISE	EXPERIENCE 99 BEST	PAGE PAGE
Peanut Butter & Co. / American	240 Sullivan St. (Bleecker St.) / ilovepeanutbutter.com	LE $-	212-677-3995 / - ▭	Original	121
Per Se / French (G)	10 Columbus Cir. (W. 59th St.) / frenchlaundry.com/perse/	UW $$$$	212-823-9335 / - ▭	Hot	66
Peter Luger Steak House / Steak House	178 Broadway (Driggs Ave.) / peterluger.com	WM $$$	718-387-7400 / - ▭	Original	122
Pink Pony* / Brasserie	178 Ludlow St. (Stanton St.)	LE $	212-253-1922 / ▯F ▭	Original	*112*, 122
Planet Thailand / Thai Fusion	133 N. 7th St. (Berry St.)	WM $	718-599-5758 / F ▭	Original	*114*, 122
Prune / New American/French	54 E. 1st St. (2nd Ave.)	EV $$	212-677-6221 / F ▭	Original	*114*, 122
Public* / Australian	210 Elizabeth St. (Prince St.) / public-nyc.com	SH $$	212-343-7011 / ▯B ▭	Cool / Always-Trendy	*82*, 98 / 17
Raga / Indian	433 E. 6th St. (Ave. A) / raganyc.com	EV $$	212-388-0957 / F ▭	Original	*113*, 122
Rainbow Room* / New American	30 Rockefeller Center Plz. (49th St.) / rainbowroom.com	MT $$$$	212-632-5100 / ▯F ▭	Classic	150
Relish / Diner	225 Wythe Ave. (N. 3rd St.) / relish.com	WM $	718-963-4546 / F ▭	Original	*113*, 123
Restaurant Above / New American	234 W. 42nd St., 21st Fl. (8th Ave.) / hilton.com	MT $$	212-642-2626 / B ▭	Classic	*137*, 150
Restaurant Florent / French	69 Gansevoort St. (Greenwich St.) / restaurantflorent.com	MP $$	212-989-5779 / F ▭	Hot	67
Sapa / French-Asian	43 W. 24th St. (Broadway) / sapanyc.com	FL $$	212-929-1800 / F ▭	Hot	67
Sarabeth's / American	40 Central Park S. (5th Ave.) / sarabethscps.com	MT $$	212-826-5959 / - ▭	Classic	*137*, 150
Schiller's Liquor Bar / French-American	131 Rivington St. (Norfolk St.) / schillersny.com	LE $	212-260-4555 / F ▭	Original	*112*, 123
Sidewalk Café* / Diner	94 Ave. A (6th St.)	EV $	212-473-7373 / ▯F ▭	Original	*112*, 123
Soup Kitchen International / International	259 W. 55th St. (Broadway) / therealsoupman.com	MT $	212-757-7730 / - ▭	Classic	150
Spice Market* / Asian Fusion	403 W. 13th St. (9th Ave.) / jean-georges.com	MP $$	212-675-2322 / ▯F ▭	Hot / Of-the-Moment	*52*, 67 / 34
The Spotted Pig* / British-American	314 W. 11th St. (Greenwich St.) / thespottedpig.com	WV $$	212-620-0393 / ▯F ▭	Hot	67
The Stanton Social* / New American (G)	99 Stanton St. (Orchard St.) / thestantonsocial.com	LE $$	212-995-0099 / ▯F ▭	Hot	67
Strip House / Steak House	13 E. 12th St. (5th Ave.) / theglaziergroup.com	GV $$$	212-328-0000 / B ▭	Hot / Steak Houses	*52*, 68 / 44
Sushi Samba 7* / Sushi	87 7th Ave. S. (Bleecker St.) / sushisamba.com	WV $$	212-691-7885 / ▯F ▭	Cool / Sushi	*84*, 98 / 45

NAME TYPE	ADDRESS (CROSS STREET) WEBSITE	AREA PRICE	PHONE SINGLES/NOISE	EXPERIENCE 99 BEST	PAGE PAGE
Sylvia's Restaurant Soul Food	328 Lenox Ave. (126th St.) sylviassoulfood.com	UE $	212-996-0660 B ≈	Classic	151
Tabla Indian Fusion (G)	11 Madison Ave. (25th St.) tablany.com	GR $$$	212-889-0667 F ≈	Cool	98
Tao* Asian Fusion	42 E. 58th St. (Madison Ave.) taorestaurant.com	MT $$$	212-888-2288 YF ≈	Cool	99
teany Vegetarian	90 Rivington St. (Orchard St.) teany.com	LE $-	212-475-9190 F ≈	Original	*111*, 123
Thor* New American (G)	107 Rivington St. (Ludlow St.) hotelrivington.com	LE $$	212-796-8040 YF ≈	Original	123
Town* New American	15 W. 56th St. (5th Ave.) townnyc.com	MT $$$	212-582-4445 YB ≈	Cool	*83*, 99
Tribeca Grill* New American	375 Greenwich St. (Franklin St.) myriadrestaurantgroup.com	TR $$$	212-941-3900 YF ≈	Cool	99
Turks and Frogs* Turkish	323 W. 11th St. (Washington St.)	WV $-	212-691-8875 YF ≈	Hot	68
212 Restaurant* New American	133 E. 65th St. (Park Ave.) 212restaurant.com	UE $$	212-249-6565 YF ≡	Hot	68
Umberto's Clam House Italian	178 Mulberry St. (Broome St.) umbertosclamhouse.com	SH $$	212-431-7545 B ≈	Classic	151
Union Square Cafe* New American (G)	21 E. 16th St. (Union Sq. W.) unionsquarecafe.com	FL $$$	212-243-4020 YF ≈	Classic	151
Vento Trattoria Italian	675 Hudson St. (14th St.) brguestrestaurants.com	MP $$	212-699-2400 ≈	Hot	68
Veritas American (G)	43 E. 20th St. (Broadway) veritas-nyc.com	GR $$$	212-353-3700 - ▭	Classic	151
Veselka Eastern European	144 2nd Ave. (9th St.) veselka.com	EV $	212-228-9682 F ≈	Original	*112*, 124
Wollensky Grill Steak House	201 E. 49th St. (3rd Ave.) smithandwollensky.com	MT $$	212-753-0444 F ≈	Classic	151
Yatagan Kebab House Middle Eastern	104 MacDougal St. (W. 3rd St.)	WV $	212-677-0952 - ≡	Original	124
Yonah Schimmel's Knishes Bakery	137 E. Houston St. (Eldridge St.) yonahschimmel.com	LE $	212-477-2858 - ≈	Original	124

Nightlife

NAME / TYPE	ADDRESS (CROSS STREET) / WEBSITE	AREA / COVER	PHONE / FOOD/NOISE	EXPERIENCE / 99 BEST	PAGE / PAGE
Aer Lounge / Nightclub	409 W. 13th St. (9th Ave.) / aerlounge.com	MP / C	212-989-0100 / - ≣	Hot	69
Angel's Share / Lounge	8 Stuyvesant St. (3rd Ave.) /	EV / -	212-777-5415 / B ⎯	Cool	100
The Apollo Theater / Performance	253 W. 125th St. (Amsterdam Ave.) / apollotheater.com	VA / C	212-531-5305 / - ≣	Classic	152
Arthur's Tavern / Club	57 Grove St. (7th Ave.) / arthurstavernnyc.com	WV / C	212-675-6879 / - ≣	Original	125
AVA Lounge / Ultra Lounge	210 W. 55th St. (Broadway) / avaloungenyc.com	MT / -	212-956-7020 / - ≣	Cool	83, 100
Bar Veloce / Wine Bar	175 2nd Ave. (11th St.) / barveloce.com	EV / -	212-260-3200 / B ≡	Cool / Wine Bars	84, 100 / 48
Barcade / Theme Bar	388 Union Ave. (Ainslie St.) / barcadebrooklyn.com	WM / -	718-302-6464 / - ≣	Original / Theme Bars	114, 125 / 46
Bemelmans Bar / Lounge	35 E. 76th St. (Madison Ave.) / thecarlyle.com	UE / -	212-744-1600 / B ⎯	Classic / Cocktail Mixologists	152 / 23
BiNY / Karaoke	8 Thompson St. 2nd Fl. (Canal St.) / biny.com	SH / -	212-334-5490 / B ≡	Original	112, 125
Black Betty* / Nightclub	366 Metropolitan Ave. (Havemeyer St.) / blackbetty.net	WM / C	718-599-0243 / F ≣	Original	114, 125
Blue Note / Jazz Club	131 W. 3rd St. (6th Ave.) / bluenotejazz.com	WV / C	212-475-8592 / F ≡	Classic / Jazz Clubs	136, 152 / 32
Bounce / Sports Bar	1403 2nd Ave. (73rd St.) / bouncenyc.com	UE / -	212-535-2183 / F ≣	Hot	69
Brandy's Piano Bar / Piano Bar	235 E. 84th St. (3rd Ave.) / brandyspianobarnyc.com	UE / -	212-744-4949 / - ≣	Classic / Piano Bars	152 / 37
brite bar / Bar	297 10th Ave. (W. 27th St) / britebar.com	CH / -	212-279-9706 / B ≡	Hot	69
Bungalow 8 / Nightclub	515 W. 27th St. (10th Ave.) /	CH / -	212-279-3215 / B ≡	Hot / Clubs for Celebrity	52, 69 / 22
Café Nicole Bar / Hotel Bar	226 W. 52nd St. (8th Ave.) / novotel.com	MT / -	212-315-0100 / F ≡	Classic	137, 152
Cain / Nightclub	544 W. 27th St. (11th Ave.) / cainnyc.com	CH / -	212-947-8000 / - ≣	Hot / Clubs for Celebrity	52, 70 / 22
The Campbell Apartment / Lounge	15 Vanderbilt Ave. (Grand Central) / hospitalityholdings.com	MT / -	212-953-0409 / - ≡	Classic	138, 153
Canal Room / Nightclub	285 W. Broadway (Canal St.) / canalroom.com	SH / C	212-941-8100 / - ≣	Cool	82, 100
Cherry Lane Theater / Performance	38 Commerce St. (Barrow St.) / cherrylanetheatre.org	WV / C	212-989-2020 / - ⎯	Classic / Off-Broadway	153 / 35
Chumley's / Bar	86 Bedford St. (Grove St.) /	WV / -	212-675-4449 / F	Classic / ≡	136, 153
Church Lounge / Ultra Lounge	2 6th Ave. (White St.) / tribecagrand.com	TR / -	212-519-6677 / B ≡	Cool	82, 101

NAME TYPE	ADDRESS (CROSS STREET) WEBSITE	AREA COVER	PHONE FOOD/NOISE	EXPERIENCE 99 BEST	PAGE PAGE
Cielo Nightclub	18 Little W. 12th St. (9th Ave.) cieloclub.com	MP C	212-645 5700 - ≈	Hot Dance Clubs	53, 70 24
Circa Tabac Cigar Bar	32 Watts St. (W. Broadway) circatabac.com	SH	212-941-1781 - - ≈	Classic	138, 153
City Hall* Restaurant Lounge	131 Duane St. (Church St.) cityhallnewyork.com	WS -	212-227-7777 B ≈	Classic	153
Comedy Cellar Comedy Club	117 MacDougal St. (Minetta Ln.) comedycellar.com	GV C	212-254-3480 F _	Classic	136, 154
Crobar Nightclub	530 W. 28th St. (10th Ave.) crobar.com	CH C	212-629-9000 - ≈	Hot	70
Cub Room* Restaurant Lounge	131 Sullivan St. (Prince St.) cubroom.com	SH -	212-677-4100 F ≈	Cool	101
The Daily Show Jon Stewart Performance	733 11th Ave. (51st St.) comedycentral.com	MT -	212-586-2477 - ≈	Hot Live Tapings	52, 70
Dick's Bar Bar	192 2nd Ave. (12th St.) 	EV -	212-475-2071 - ≈	Original Gay/Lesbian Bars	113, 126 29
Don't Tell Mama Piano Bar	343 W. 46th St. (8th Ave.) donttellmama.com	MT -	212-757-0788 - ≈	Classic Piano Bars	137, 154 37
The Dove Bar	228 Thompson St. (Bleecker St.) 	GV -	212-254-1435 - ≈	Cool Cocktail Mixologists	82, 101 23
Duplex Piano Bar	61 Christopher St. (7th Ave. S.) theduplex.com	WV -	212-255-5438 - ≈	Original Piano Bars	126 37
Duvet* Restaurant Lounge	45 W. 21st St. (6th Ave.) duvetny.com	FL -	212-989-2121 F ≈	Cool	84, 101
Earth NYC* Nightclub	116 10th Ave. (17th St.) earth-nyc.com	CH -	212-337-0016 F ≈	Cool	101
Embassy Nightclub	28 W. 20th St. (5th Ave.) 	FL C	212-741-3470 - ≈	Cool	82, 102
58* Ultra Lounge	41 E. 58th St. (Madison Ave.) 58newyork.com	MT -	212-308-9455 F ≈	Hot	53, 70
Fifty Seven Fifty Seven Lounge	57 E. 57th St. (Park Ave.) fourseasons.com	MT -	212-758-5757 - ≈	Hot	53, 71
Flatiron Lounge Lounge	37 W. 19th St. (5th Ave.) flatironlounge.com	FL -	212-727-7741 - ≈	Hot	54, 71
Flûte* Wine Bar	40 E. 20th St. (Park Ave. S.) flutebar.com	GR -	212-529-7870 F ≈	Cool	84, 102
40/40 Club Sports Bar	6 W. 25th St. (6th Ave.) the4040club.com	FL -	212-832-4040 B ≈	Hot	54, 71
44 Restaurant* Hotel Lounge	44 W. 44th St. (5th Ave.) royaltonhotel.com	MT -	212-944-8844 B ≈	Cool	84, 102
Frederick's* Ultra Lounge	8 W. 58th St. (5th Ave.) fredericksnyc.com	MT -	212-752-6200 F ≈	Hot	53, 71
G Spa & Lounge Lounge	18 9th Ave. (13th St.) hotelgansevoort.com	MP -	212-660-6733 - ≈	Hot	53, 71

Nightlife (cont.)

NAME TYPE	ADDRESS (CROSS STREET) WEBSITE	AREA COVER	PHONE FOOD/NOISE	EXPERIENCE 99 BEST	PAGE PAGE
The Garden of Ono* Ultra Lounge	18 9th Ave. (13th St.) hotelgansevoort.com	MP -	212-660-6766 B ⌐	Hot	*52*, 72
Gotham Comedy Club Comedy Club	208 W. 23rd St. (7th Ave.) gothamcomedyclub.com	CH C	212-367-9000 F ⌐	Hot	72
Grand Bar and Lounge* Hotel Lounge	310 W. Broadway, 2nd Fl. (Grand St.) sohogrand.com	SH -	212-519-6500 B ⌐	Hot Hotel Lounges	72 30
Gypsy Tea Nightclub	33 W. 24th St. (6th Ave.) gypsyanyc.com	FL C	212-645-0003 - ≡	Hot	*54*, 72
Happy Ending Theme Bar	302 Broome St. (Forsyth St.) happyendinglounge.com	SH -	212-334-9676 - ≡	Cool Theme Bars	102 46
Harbour Lights Lounge	Pier 17, Third Fl. (SSS) harbourlightsrestaurant.com	WS -	212-227-2800 F ⌐	Classic	*138*, 154
Heartland Brewery SS* Brewery	93 South St. (Fulton St.) heartlandbrewery.com	WS -	646-572-2337 F ≡	Classic	*138*, 154
Henrietta Hudson Dive Bar	438 Hudson St. (Morton St.) henriettahudsons.com	WV C	212-924-3347 - ≡	Cool Gay/Lesbian Bars	102 29
Hiro Lounge Nightclub	371 W. 16th St. (9th Ave.) themaritimehotel.com	CH -	212-727-0212 - ≡	Hot Rock Clubs	*54*, 72 41
Hudson Bar Hotel Lounge	356 W. 58th St. (8th Ave.) hudsonhotel.com	MT -	212-554-6500 - ⌐	Cool Hotel Lounges	*83*, 103 30
Hudson Library Hotel Lounge	356 W. 58th St. (8th Ave.) hudsonhotel.com	MT -	212-554-6317 - ⌐	Cool	*83*, 103
Iridium Jazz Club Jazz Club	1650 Broadway (51st St.) iridiumjazzclub.com	MT C	212-582-2121 F ≡	Cool Jazz Clubs	*83*, 103 32
Late Night Conan O'Brien Performance	30 Rockefeller Plz. (49th St.) nbc.com	MT -	212-664-3056 - ≡	Cool	*83*, 103
The Late Show w/Letterman Performance	1697 Broadway (W. 53rd St.) cbs.com	MT -	212-975-6644 - ⌐	Classic Live Tapings	*136*, 154 33
Level V Nightclub	675 Hudson St. (14th St.) brguestrestaurants.com	WV -	212-699-2410 B ≡	Hot Singles Scene	*53*, 73 42
Libation* Lounge	137 Ludlow St. (Stanton St.) libationnyc.com	LE -	212-529-2153 F ≡	Original Singles Scene	126 42
Lincoln Center Performance	62nd St. (Columbus Ave.) lincolncenter.org	UE C	212-875-5456 - ⌐	Classic	155
Living Room Nightclub	154 Ludlow St. (Stanton St.) livingroomny.com	LE -	212-533-7235 - ≡	Original Easy Local Vibe	126 26
Lotus* Ultra Lounge	409 W. 14th St. (10th Ave.) lotusnewyork.com	MP C	212-243-4420 F ≡	Cool Restaurant Lounges	103 40
Lucky Cheng's Cabaret	24 1st Ave. (2nd St.) planetluckychengs.com	EV C	212-995-5500 F ≡	Original	*113*, 126
Lucky Strike* Restaurant Lounge	59 Grand St. (W. Broadway) luckystrikeny.com	SH -	212-941-0772 F ≡	Cool	104
Mannahatta* Lounge	316 Bowery (Bleecker St.) mannahatta.us/index_flash.html	GV -	212-253-8644 YB ≡	Original	*113*, 127

NAME	ADDRESS (CROSS STREET)	AREA	PHONE	EXPERIENCE	PAGE
TYPE	WEBSITE	COVER	FOOD/NOISE	99 BEST	PAGE
Marion's Continental*	354 Bowery (4th St.)	GV	212-475-7621	Original	_113_, 127
Lounge	marionsnyc.com	-	F ≡		
Marquee	289 10th Ave. (26th St.)	CH	646-473-0202	Hot	_52_, 73
Nightclub	marqueeny.com	C	- ≡	Clubs for Celebrity	22
Max Fish	178 Ludlow St. (Stanton St.)	LE	212-529-3959	Original	127
Dive Bar	maxfish.com	-	- ≡		
MercBar	151 Mercer S. (Houston St.)	SH	212-966-2727	Cool	_82_, 104
Ultra Lounge	mercbar.com	-	≡		
MObar	80 Columbus Cir. (60th St.)	UW	212-805-8826	Hot	_54_, 73
Hotel Lounge	mandarinoriental.com	-	- ≡		
Morrell Wine Bar & Café*	1 Rockefeller Plz. (49th St.)	MT	212-262-7700	Classic	_138_, 155
Wine Bar	morrellwinebar.com	-	F —	Wine Bars	48
Oak Room	59 W. 44th St. (5th Ave.)	MT	212-840-6800	Classic	155
Hotel Lounge	algonquinhotel.com	-	F —	Hotel Lounges	30
Odea*	389 Broome St. (Mulberry St.)	SH	212-941-9222	Cool	_82_, 104
Lounge	odeany.com	-	F ≡	Restaurant Lounges	40
One	1 Little W. 12th St. (9th Ave.)	MP	212-255-9717	Hot	73
Lounge	onelw12.com	-	F ≡		
Onieal's Grand Street*	174 Grand St. (Lafayette St.)	SH	212-941-9119	Classic	_138_, 155
Lounge	onieals.com	-	F ≡		
Pen-Top Bar & Terrace	700 5th Ave. (55th St.)	MT	212-956-2888	Classic	_138_, 155
Hotel Lounge	newyork.peninsula.com	-	B ≡		
Pete's Candy Store	709 Lorimer St. (Frost St.)	WM	718-302-3770	Original	_114_, 127
Bar	petescandystore.com	-	B ≡		
Pete's Tavern	129 E. 18th St. (Irving Pl.)	GR	212-473-7676	Classic	156
Pub/Tavern	petestavern.com	-	F ≡		
Pianos	158 Ludlow St. (Stanton St.)	LE	212-505-3733	Original	127
Club	pianosnyc.com	C	F ≡	Easy Local Vibe	26
Pink Elephant	527 W. 27th St. (10th Ave.)	CH	212-463-0000	Hot	73
Nightclub	pinkelephantclub.com	C	- ≡	Dance Clubs	24
PJ Clarke's	915 3rd Ave. (55th St.)	MT	212-317-1616	Classic	156
Pub/Tavern	pjclarkes.com	-	F —		
Playwrights Horizon	416 W. 42nd St. (9th Ave.)	MT	212-564-1235		
Performance	playwrightshorizons.org	C	- —	Off-Broadway	35
Plunge	18 9th Ave. (13th St.)	MP	212-206-6700	Hot	_52_, 74
Ultra Lounge	hotelgansevoort.com	-	≡		
PM	50 Gansevoort St. (Greenwich St.)	MP	212-255-6676	Hot	74
Nightclub	pmlounge.com	-	B ≡		
Pravda	281 Lafayette St. (Prince St.)	SH	212-226-4944	Cool	_82_, 104
Lounge	pravdany.com	-	- ≡		
The Public Theater	425 Lafayette St. (Astor Pl.)	GV	212-539-8500		
Performance	publictheater.org	C	- ≡	Off-Broadway	35
Quo	511 W. 28th St. (10th Ave.)	CH	212-268-5105	Hot	_52_, 74
Nightclub	quonyc.com	C	- ≡	Dance Clubs	24

Nightlife (cont.)

NAME TYPE	ADDRESS (CROSS STREET) WEBSITE	AREA COVER	PHONE FOOD/NOISE	EXPERIENCE 99 BEST	PAGE PAGE
Radio City Music Hall Performance	1260 6th Ave. (W. 50th St.) radiocity.com	MT C	212-307-7171 - ⌐	Classic	156
Red Rock West Theme Bar	457 W. 17th St. (10th Ave.) redrockwestsaloon.com	CH -	212-366-5359 - ≡	Original Theme Bars	128 46
Rhone Wine Bar	63 Gansevoort St. (Greenwich St.) rhonenyc.com	MP -	212-367-8440 B ≡	Hot Wine Bars	74 48
Rififi Club	332 E. 11th St. (1st Ave.) rififinyc.com	EV C	212-677-1027 - ≡	Original	113, 128
Sardi's Restaurant Bar	234 W. 44th St. (Broadway) sardis.com	MT -	212-221-8440 F ⌐	Classic	137, 156
Saturday Night Live Performance	30 Rockefeller Plz. (49th St.) nbc.com	MT -	212-664-3056 - ≡	Original Live Tapings	114, 128 33
Session 73 Bar	1359 1st Ave. (73rd St.) session73.com	UE -	212-517-4445 F ≡	Cool Easy Local Vibe	104 26
6's & 8's Nightclub	205 Chrystie St. (Stanton St.) 6sand8s.com	LE -	212-477-6688 - ≡	Original Rock Clubs	113, 128 41
Slipper Room Cabaret	167 Orchard St. (Stanton St.) slipperroom.com	LE C	212-253-7246 - ≡	Original	112, 128
Snitch Nightclub	59 W. 21st St. (6th Ave.) snitchbar.com	FL C	212-727-7775 B ≡	Hot Rock Clubs	54, 74 41
Stonewall Pub/Tavern	53 Christopher St. (7th Ave. S.) stonewall-place.com	WV -	212-463-0950 - ≡	Classic Gay / Lesbian Bars	136, 156 29
Tavern on the Green* Restaurant Lounge	Central Park W.est (W. 67th St.) tavernonthegreen.com	UW -	212-873-3200 F ≡	Classic	157
Tenement* Restaurant Lounge	157 Ludlow St. (Stanton St.) tenementlounge.com	LE -	212-766-1270 F ≡	Original	112, 129
Three of Cups* Dive Bar	83 1st Ave. (5th St.) threeofcupsnyc.com	EV -	212-388-0059 F ≡	Original	112, 129
21 Club* Restaurant Lounge	21 W. 52nd St. (5th Ave.) 21club.com	MT -	212-582-7200 F ≡	Classic	157
Union Pool Dive Bar	484 Union Ave. (Meeker Ave.) myspace.com/unionpool	WM -	718-609-0484 - ≡	Original	114, 129
Upright Citizens Brigade Comedy Club	307 W. 26th St. (7th Ave.) ucbtheatre.com	CH C	212-366-9176 - ⌐	Cool	84, 105
Verlaine Lounge	110 Rivington St. (Essex St.)	LE -	212-614-2494 B ≡	Original Cocktail Mixologists	112, 129 23
Village Vanguard Jazz Club	178 7th Ave S. (Greenwich Ave.) villagevanguard.com	WV C	212-255-4037 - ≡	Classic Jazz Clubs	138, 157 32
Whiskey Blue Hotel Lounge	541 Lexington Ave. (49th St.) midnightoilbars.com	MT -	212-407-2947 - ≡	Cool Singles Scene	83, 105 42
White Horse Tavern* Pub/Tavern	567 Hudson St. (11th St.)	WV -	212-243-9260 ⓎF ≡	Classic	136, 157

Attractions

NAME TYPE	ADDRESS (CROSS STREET) WEBSITE	AREA PRICE	PHONE	EXPERIENCE 99 BEST	PAGE PAGE
American Folk Art Museum Museum	45 W. 53rd St. (5th Ave.) folkartmuseum.org	MT $-	212-265-1040	Cool	84, 106
Am. Museum Nat. Hist. Museum	175 Central Park W. (61st St.) amnh.org	UW $	212-769-5000	Classic	135, 158
Angelika Film Center Cinema	18 W. Houston St. (Mercer St.) angelikafilmcenter.com	GV $	212-995-2000	Original	130
Anthology Film Archives Cinema	32 2nd Ave. (2nd St.) anthologyfilmarchives.org	EV $-	212-505-5181	Original	114, 130
Apple Store Shop	103 Prince St. (Greene St.) apple.com	SH -	212-226-3126	Cool	82, 106
Babeland Shop	94 Rivington St. (Ludlow St.) babeland.com	LE -	212-375-1701	Original	130
Bethpage State Park Golf Course	99 Qkr. Mtg. House Rd. (Puritan Ln.) nysparks.state.ny.us/	VA $$$$	516-249-0700	Hot	53, 76
Big Onion Walking Tours Tour	476 13th St. (8th Ave.) bigonion.com	VA $	212-439-1090	Hot	76
Bite of the Big Apple Tour Tour	2 Columbus Cir. (59th St.) centralparkbiketour.com	MT $$$	212-541-8759	Classic	158
Bliss Soho Spa	568 Brdwy, 2nd Fl. (Houston St.) blissworld.com	SH $$$$	212-219-8970	Hot Spas	53, 76 43
Brooklyn Brewery Site	79 N. 11th St. (Kent Ave.) brooklynbrewery.com	WM -	718-486-7422	Original	130
Brooklyn Bridge Site	South St. Seaport	VA -		Classic	138, 158
Bryant Park Park	500 5th Ave. (42nd St.) bryantpark.org	MT -	212-768-4242	Cool Outdoor People	82, 106 36
Central Park Park	58th & 110th Sts., 5th & 8th Aves. centralparknyc.org	VA -		Classic Outdoor People	135, 158 36
Central Park Cons. Gardens Gardens	5th Ave. (104th & 106th Sts.) centralparknyc.org	UE -		Classic	158
Chelsea Market Shop	75 9th Ave. (W. 17th St.) chelseamarket.com	CH -	212-243-6005	Cool	81, 106
Chelsea Piers Health Club	W. 23rd St. (Hudson River) chelseapiers.com	CH -	212-336-6666	Cool	83, 106
Christine Chin Spa Spa	79 Rivington St. (Allen St.) christinechin.com	LE $$$	212-353-0503	Original	112, 130
Chrysler Building Site	405 Lexington Ave. (42nd St.)	MT	212-682-3070	Cool	107
Circle Line Cruise Tour	Pier 83, W. 42nd St. (12th Ave.) circleline.com	MT $$	212-563-3200	Classic City Tours	137, 159 21
Cooper-Hewitt, NDM Museum	2 E. 91st St. (5th Ave.) cooperhewitt.org	UE $	212-849-8400	Hot	76
Dyker Beach Golf Course Golf Course	86th St. (7th Ave.) americangolf.com/foresight.cfm	VA $$$$	718-836-9722	Original	131

Attractions (cont.)

NAME TYPE	ADDRESS (CROSS STREET) WEBSITE	AREA PRICE	PHONE	EXPERIENCE 99 BEST	PAGE PAGE
Empire State Building Site	350 5th Ave. (Broadway) esbnyc.com	GR $	212-736-3100	Classic	*137*, 159
Exit Art Art Gallery	475 10th Ave. (36th St.) exitart.com	MT $-	212-966-7745	Cool	107
Gabay's Shop	225 1st Ave. (13th St.) gabaysoutlet.com	EV -	212-254-3180	Original	*113*, 131
Grand Central Terminal Site	42nd St. (Park Ave.) grandcentralterminal.com	MT -	212-532-4900	Classic	*138*, 159
Ground Zero Site	Broadway and Liberty Sts. groundzero.nyc.ny-us	TR -		Classic	*136*, 159
Hudson River Greenway Park	West Side Hwy. (Hudson Rvr.) hudsongreenway.state.ny.us	CH		Original	131
Integral Yoga Health Club	227 W. 13th St. (7th Ave.) iyiny.org	WV $$	212-929-0586	Cool	*83*, 107
Int'l Center of Photography Museum	1133 Ave. of Americas (43rd St.) icp.org	MT $	212-857-0000	Cool	*84*, 107
Intrepid SAS Museum Museum	Pier 86 (12th Ave. & 46th St.) intrepidmuseum.org	MT $	212-245-0072	Classic	160
Jeffrey New York Shop	449 W. 14th St. (Washington St.) -	MP	212-206-1272	Hot	*54*, 77
Liberty Helicopter Tours Tour	W. 30th St. (12th Ave.) libertyhelicopters.com	CH $$$$	212-967-6464	Hot	77
The LimoTour Tour	1623 3rd Ave. (E. 90th St.) limotours.com	UE $$$$	212-423-0101	City Tours	21
Madison Square Garden Site	4 Pennsylvania Plz. (W. 31 St.) thegarden.com	CH $	212-465-6741	Cool	*84*, 107
Manhattan Carriage Co. Tour	59th St. (7th Ave.) ajnfineart.com/mcc.html	MT $$$$	914-374-3893	Classic	160
Manhattan Rickshaw Co. Tour	Central Park & Greenwich Village manhattanrickshaw.com	GV $$	212-604-4729	Original	131
Marc Jacobs Shop	163 Mercer St. (W. Houston St.) marcjacobs.com	SH -	212-343-1490	Cool	108
Marcoart Art Gallery	181 Orchard St. (Stanton St.) marcoart.com	LE -	646-479-2263	Cool Galleries	108 28
Metamorphosis Day Spa Spa	127 E. 56th St., 5th Fl. (Park Ave.) metspa.com	MT $$$$	212-751-6051	Cool Spas	*83*, 108 43
The Metropolitan Museum Art Museum	1000 5th Ave. (82nd St.) metmuseum.org	UE $	212-535-7710	Classic	*135*, 160
Michelle Nevius Tour	 walknyc.com	VA $$$$	877-572-9719	Cool	108
Momenta Art Art Gallery	72 Berry St. (N. 9th St.) momentaart.org	WM -	718-218-8058	Original Galleries	*114*, 132 28
Morrison Hotel Gallery Art Gallery	124 Prince St. (Wooster St.) morrisonhotelgallery.com	SH -	212-941-8770	Cool	*82*, 108

NAME TYPE	ADDRESS (CROSS STREET) WEBSITE	AREA PRICE	PHONE	EXPERIENCE 99 BEST	PAGE PAGE
Museum of Chinese Museum	70 Mulberry St., 2nd Fl. (Bayard St.) moca-nyc.org	LE $-	212-619-4785	Original	*112*, 132
The Museum of Fashion Institute Museum	7th Ave. (27th St.) fitnyc.edu	CH -	212-217-5970	Cool	*83*, 109
Museum Jewish Heritage Museum	36 Battery Pl. (West St.) mjhnyc.org	TR $	646-437-4200	Classic	160
Museum of Modern Art Art Museum	11 W. 53rd St. (6th Ave.) moma.org	MT $$	212-708-9400	Hot	*52*, 77
Museum of Sex Museum	233 5th Ave. (27th St.) museumofsex.org	FL $	212-689-6337	Cool Unusual Museums	*83*, 109 47
Museum of TV & Radio Museum	25 W. 52nd St. (5th Ave.) mtr.org	MT $	212-621-6800	Hot Unusual Museums	*52*, 77 47
New York Stock Exchange Site	11 Wall St. (New St.) nyse.com	WS -	212-656-3000	Classic	*136*, 160
northside JUNK Shop	578 Driggs Ave. (N. 6th St.)	WM -	718-302-1045	Original	*114*, 132
Oasis Day Spa Spa	108 E. 16th St. (Irving Pl.) oasisdayspanyc.com	GR $$$$	212-254-7722	Classic Spas	*137*, 161 43
Oscar Wilde Mem. Bkshp. Shop	15 Christopher St. (W. 9th St.) oscarwildebooks.com	WV -	212-255-8097	Classic	161
Paul Kasmin Gallery Art Gallery	293 10th Ave. (W. 27th St.) paulkasmingallery.com	CH -	212-563-4474	Cool	*81*, 109
Paul Morris Gallery Art Gallery	530 W. 25th St., 5th Fl. (10th Ave.) paulmorrisgallery.com	CH -	212-727-2752	Cool	*81*, 109
Realform Girdle Building Shop	218 Bedford Ave. (N. 5th St.) billbury.com/girdlebuilding	WM -	718-302-3007	Original	*113*, 132
The Rink Rockefeller Ctr. Activity	601 5th Ave. (50th St.) therinkatrockcenter.com	MT $	212-332-7654	Classic	*138*, 161
Rock Junket NYC Tour	Bowery & Bleecker St. rockjunket.com	EV $$	212-696-6578	Original	*113*, 132
Sex and the City Tours Tour	5th Ave. (E. 58th St.) sceneontv.com	MT $$$	212-209-3370	Cool City Tours	*82*, 109 21
Solomon R. Guggenheim Museum Art Museum	1071 5th Ave. (89th St.) guggenheim.org	UE $	212-423-3500	Hot	78
South Street Seaport Museum	19 Fulton St. (Water St.) southstreetseaport.com	WS -	212-732-8257	Classic	*138*, 161
The Spa at Mandarin Or. Spa	80 Columbus Cir. (60th St.) mandarinoriental.com	UW -	212-805-8880	Hot	*53*, 78
St. Mark's Place Site	St. Mark's Pl. (Bowery & 2nd Ave.)	EV -		Original	*112*, 133
St. Patrick's Cathedral Religious Site	14 E. 51st St. (5th Ave.) saintpatrickscathedral.org	MT -	212-753-2261	Classic	*138*, 161
Statue of Liberty Site	Battery Park Ferry nps.gov/stli	TR $	212-269-5755	Original	*111*, 133

Attractions (cont.)

NAME TYPE	ADDRESS (CROSS STREET) WEBSITE	AREA PRICE	PHONE	EXPERIENCE 99 BEST	PAGE PAGE
Stella McCartney Shop	429 14th St. (10th Ave.) stellamccartney.com	MP -	212-255-1556	Hot	*54*, 78
The Strand Shop	828 Broadway (12th St.) strandbooks.com	GV -	212-473-1452	Classic	*136*, 162
Tenement Museum Museum	108 Orchard St. (Delancey St.) tenement.org	LE $	212-431-0233	Original Unusual Museums	*111*, 133 47
Trapeze School New York Activity	Hudson River Park (Piers 34 & 26) trapezeschool.com	UW $$$$	917-797-1872	Hot	78
Trinity Church Religious Site	Broadway (Wall St.) trinitywallstreet.org	TR -	212-602-0800	Classic	162
United Nations Site	1st Ave. (46th St.) un.org/tours	MT $	212-963-8687	Hot	*54*, 78
Van Cortlandt Park Golf Golf Course	Van Cortlandt Park S. (Bailey Ave.) nycgovparks.org	VA $$$$	718-543-4595	Classic	162
Washington Square Park Park	5th Ave. (Thompson St.) nycgovparks.org	GV -		Classic Outdoor People	*136*, 162 36
Whitney Museum Am. Art Art Museum	945 Madison Ave. (75th St.) whitney.org	UE $	212-570-3676	Hot	*51*, 79
Williamsburg Art Center Museum	135 Broadway (Bedford St.) wahcenter.net	WM -	718-486-7372	Original	*114*, 133
Zito Studio Gallery Art Gallery	122 Ludlow St. (Delancey St.) zitogallery.com	LE -	646-602-2338	Original Galleries	*111*, 133 28

Notes

New York Unique Shopping Index

NAME	(212) PHONE	AREA	PRODUCTS	PAGE
A.P.C.	966-9685	SH	Unisex French fashions for hipsters	86
Aedes de Venustas	206-8674	WV	Rare and hard-to-find fragrances	87
Albertine	924-8515	WV	Cool fashions from up-and-comers	87
An Earnest Cut & Sew	242-3414	MP	Trendy denim and custom cuts	56
Apple Store	226-3126	SH	Mother lode of Apple gizmos	86, 106
Babeland	375-1701	LE	Ultimate adult kink shop	116, 130
Barneys New York	826-8900	UE	Clothes for uptown old guard/fashion elite	56
Bergdorf Goodman	753-7300	MT	High status clothes and shoes galore	140
Chelsea Market	243-6005	CH	Cluster of gourmet food boutiques	106
Clyde's on Madison	744-5050	UE	Upscale Euro beauty products	56
Edith and Daha	979-9992	LE	Modernized vintage pieces/accessories	116
Eva	925-3208	SH	Women's clothing with rock 'n' roll edge	87
F.A.O. Schwartz	644-9400	MT	Toy central for the inner child	140
Flying A	965-9090	SH	Cutesy-kitschy and funky fashions	86
Gabay's	254-3180	EV	Designer goods for up to 70% off	116, 131
Henri Bendel	247-1100	MT	Super-trendy pop star fashions	140
I Heart	219-9265	SH	Art, music, and hard-to-find fashions	87
Ito En	988-7111	UE	Vast selection of tea in a Zen setting	56
Jeffrey New York	206-1272	MP	Upscale mini-dept store	56, 77
Kirna Zabete	941-9656	SH	Avant-garde, indie designer clothing	86
Louis Vuitton	758-8877	MT	International flagship of all things LV	140
Marc Jacobs	343-1490	SH	3 stores of ready-to-wear/accessories	86, 108
Museum of Modern Art (Store)	708-9400	MT	MOMA-inspired posters and books	77, 140
Moss	204-7100	SH	Quirky, imaginative housewares	86
northside JUNK	302-1045ᵂ	WM	Vintage/retro furniture, accessories	132
Oscar Wilde Memorial Bookshop	255-8097	WV	Extensive collection of gay literature	161
Prada	327-4200	UE	Of-the-moment designer clothing	56
Ralph Lauren	606-2100	UE	All-American clothes and housewares	56
Realform Girdle Bldg.	302-3007ᵂ	WM	Mini-mall of boutiques, cafes, spa	132
Resurrection	625-1374	SH	Pricey, vintage designer clothing	87
Saks Fifth Avenue	753-4000	MT	Designer threads for men and women	140
Saved Gallery of Art & Craft	388-5990ᵂ	WM	Museum of hip peculiarities	116
Scoop	691-1905	MP	Trendy unisex clothing	56
Sigerson Morrison	941-5404	SH	Handbags for the modern woman	87
Sigerson Morrison	219-3893	SH	Shoes for the modern woman	87
Sleep	384-3211ᵂ	WM	Linens and lingerie in flapper-era boudoir	116
Some Odd Rubies	353-1736	LE	Vintage pieces by celeb designers	116
St. Mark's Bookshop	260-7853	EV	Indie bookstore with art books, photos	116

ᵂ items = Williamsburg area code (718)
For Neighborhood (Area) Key, see p.219.

BLACK BOOK

New York Unique Shopping Index (cont.)

NAME	(212) PHONE	AREA	PRODUCTS	PAGE
Stella McCartney	255-1556	MP	Designer shop for fashionistas	56, 78
The Strand	473-1452	GV	18 miles of new and used books	162
Sunrise Mart	219-0033	SH	Japanese food, ceramics, videos	86
TG-170	995-8660	LE	Shop of quirky fashion labels	116
Tiffany & Co.	755-8000	MT	Renowned jewelry store	140
Tokio 7	353-8443	EV	Second hand designer clothing	116
Trash and Vaudeville	982-3590	EV	Homage to punk threads	116
Via Bus Stop	343-8810	SH	Quirky, Japanese designer wear	86
Vivienne Tam	966-2398	SH	Asian-influenced women's fashion	86
Zachary's Smile	924-0604	WV	Reworked vintage for men, women	87

Notes

For Neighborhood (Area) Key, see p.219.

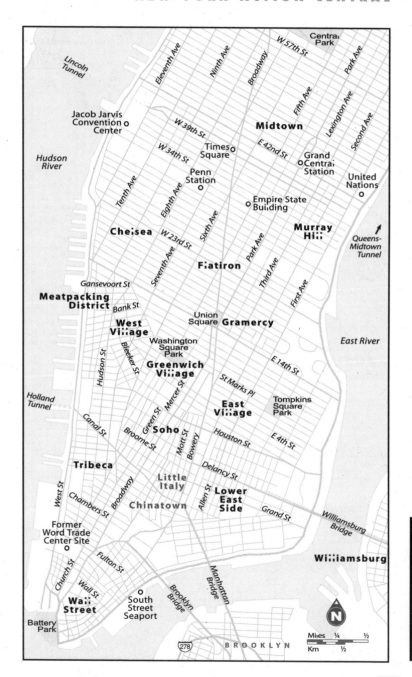

Lincoln Tunnel

Jacob Jarvis Convention Center

Hudson River

Central Park

W 57th St

Eleventh Ave

Ninth Ave

Broadway

Fifth Ave

Park Ave

Lexington Ave

Second Ave

W 39th St

Midtown

Times Square

E 42nd St

W 34th St

Penn Station

Grand Central Station

United Nations

Tenth Ave

Eighth Ave

Sixth Ave

Empire State Building

Chelsea

W 23rd St

Murray Hill

Seventh Ave

Park Ave

Third Ave

Flatiron

Queens-Midtown Tunnel

First Ave

Gansevoort St

Meatpacking District

Bank St

West Village

Union Square

Gramercy

East River

Washington Square Park

Bleeker St

Greenwich Village

Hudson St

E 14th St

St Marks Pl

Holland Tunnel

Canal St

Green St

Mercer St

East Village

Tompkins Square Park

Soho

Mott St

Bowery

Houston St

E 4th St

Broome St

Tribeca

West St

Broadway

Little Italy

Delancy St

Chambers St

Chinatown

Allen St

Lower East Side

Grand St

Williamsburg Bridge

Former Word Trade Center Site

Church St

Fulton St

Williamsburg

Wall St

Wall Street

South Street Seaport

Brooklyn Bridge

Manhattan Bridge

Battery Park

278

BROOKLYN

N

Miles   ¼   ½
Km   ½

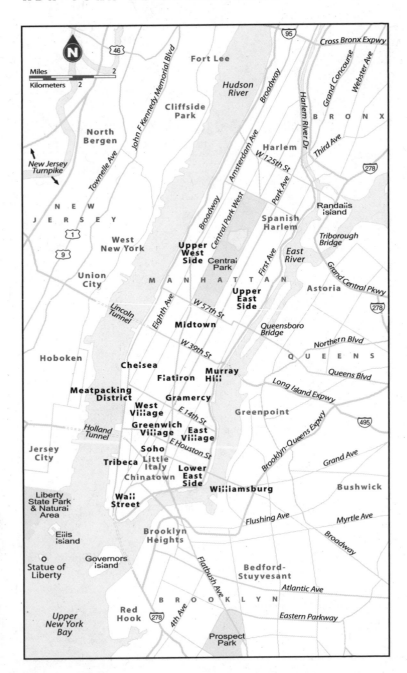